H. G. WELLS

Lovat Dickson was born in Australia and brought up in Central Africa and Canada, and began his working life at the age of nineteen as the editor (and founder) of a weekly newspaper in a mining town in western Canada. In London he was editor of the *Fortnightly Review* and then founded his own publishing firm. Subsequently he became first an editor and then a director of Macmillan & Co., who had been H. G. Wells's publishers as he came to world-wide popularity. Lovat Dickson's previous books include an account of his own career, told in *The Ante-Room* (1960) and *The House of Words* (1963). He now lives in Toronto.

LOVAT DICKSON

H. G. Wells

His Turbulent Life
and Times

PENGUIN BOOKS

Penguin Books Ltd, Harmondsworth, Middlesex, England
Penguin Books Australia Ltd, Ringwood, Victoria, Australia

—

First published by Macmillan & Co. 1969
Published in Pelican Books 1972
Copyright © Lovat Dickson, 1969

—

Made and printed in Great Britain
by Hazell Watson & Viney Ltd
Aylesbury, Bucks
Set in Linotype Georgian

H. G. WELLS TO G. K. CHESTERTON
[1933]

'If after all my Atheology turns out wrong and your Theology right, I feel I shall always be able to pass into Heaven (if I want to) as a friend of G. K. C.'s. Bless you.'

G. K. CHESTERTON TO H. G. WELLS
[IN REPLY]

'As to the fine point of theology you mention. If I turn out to be right, you will triumph, not by being a friend of mine but a friend of Man, for having done a thousand things for men like me in every way, from imagination to criticism. The thought of the vast variety of that work, and how it ranges from towering visions to tiny pricks of humour, overwhelmed me suddenly...'

Contents

Apology – with Acknowledgements

WHAT follows is not a full-scale life of H. G. Wells, nor a critical examination of his works. All the Wells letters and papers lie in the archives of the University of Illinois, providing a mine of rich ore of which only a few veins have so far been tapped. The full Life and Letters based on these papers is in preparation by Professor Gordon Ray.

There have been several attempts at sketching a portrait. Of these the best is Geoffrey West's *H. G. Wells*, published in 1930, a work of perception and acute observation of character, but written in consultation with Wells, and bearing the marks of his supervision. *H. G. Wells and His Critics*, by Ingvald Raknem, is a most enlightening account of Wells's relations with contemporary critics and the reading public of his time. Its scholarship is meticulous, the industry that went into its vast composition almost oppressive. In its harvesting of every fact and implication in the life and writings of one of the busiest authors of this century, it fills in many gaps noticeable in Wells's own account, *Experiment in Autobiography*. Listed in its bibliography are over five hundred articles about Wells written in his lifetime.

Since his death in 1946, aspects of Wells's genius, of his relationship and correspondence with other writers of his time, notably Arnold Bennett and Henry James, have been revealed from the Illinois source in admirable works of scholarship. Bernard Bergonzi's *The Early H. G. Wells*, the most accomplished of the critical books that have so far appeared, established the view of Wells first put forward by his son Anthony West,* as a mythopoet whose work after

* *Encounter*, February 1957.

the age of thirty-six – he lived until he was eighty – was in contradiction to the essential quality of his vision, which was one of despair. Wells's *Experiment in Autobiography*, written when he was sixty-eight, unconsciously sustains this view. Four-fifths of it, the story of his climb to fame, has the quality of Rousseau's *Confessions*. The last one-fifth, covering his life from 1901 on, is a justification of the passion that came to consume his life and, of course, his art – the Utopian ideal of the World State.

All this might be thought enough until we have the final judgement of Mr Gordon Ray's book. But all that has so far appeared leaves the picture of the kind of man Wells was rather blurred; every account, even H.G.'s own self-portrait, is tinctured by the prejudice of the observer. I was interested, while there was still time, in catching the memories of a few witnesses who had been closely associated with his life. As a publisher, I had been indirectly connected with most of his published work, and had access to the correspondence that arose, particularly that covering the most dramatic years of his climb to fame – 1905–15. That which happened to him in this period imposed different and definite contours on Wells's life, and awoke in me a publisher's appetite to know more, which the confidences later given me by his friends sharpened very considerably.

I must emphasize the publisher's attitude. I was curious to know why a professional writer, which Wells was to his very bones, whose early books had brought the world to his feet, should have spurned the success which he had valued so extremely when he began to write. Was it resolution to reach a higher goal? One distrusted that notion. Did he really care all that much about humanity? Beneath the stirring visions for the betterment of the race one glimpses from time to time something like contempt for the helpless and the uneducated, the 'people of the abyss'. Was his own disordered life the result of a lack of moral muscle, or – as he represented it – a search for the ideal?

The biographer of Wells soon comes up against such

contradictions in the *persona* he is putting together. Wells was primarily a novelist, an imaginative tale-spinner, who could not stop in the headlong rush of creation to disguise that what he was writing about – often very frankly – was his own experience; what drove him on was his burning desire to tidy up the mess we had made of life, and push forward to a future free from the oppressions of war and want and from that dominance maintained by what today we would call the Establishment. The sharp mind of a clever boy, brought up in impoverished circumstances, had had burnt into it an undying resentment against the conditions from which he had been lucky enough to escape. In his first marvellous books – those unforgettable masterpieces of scientific fantasy – he imagines only distantly the alteration of the status quo. Science promises that one day things will be better. He is concerned only with whether mankind, blind and ignorant and fated always to be so, will not be taken in by wicked men; whether this new power which has freed man from the blind superstitions of organized religion will not be used to put him in chains again in a world enslaved by perverted science. Success fed in Wells the illusion that he could lead mankind to the promised land. Hence the growing seriousness with which he took himself and his purpose.

My study is mainly of Wells in those years when he was turning away from the certain prospect of a successful career as a highly popular novelist to become a prophet and teacher, when in the wider social world to which his growing fame was introducing him he was throwing off the constraints of his narrow upbringing and seeking satisfaction among a more interesting, better-educated and opulent class for another dominant instinct in his nature, sex. Yet he was never really at home in the society to which his genius had lifted him; and he had never really been happy in the one from which his gifts had extricated him. He could be the best company in the world, and he could be mean, spiteful and quarrelsome, defects of most natures but ones that seem somehow incompatible with the role of seer and prophet pointing the way to salvation.

But this disability was not widely noticed. In the world of the Twenties and Thirties when he had this role on a world-wide scale thrust upon him, he was admired for his wisdom the more because mankind itself was so uncertain where it was going. A figure like Swift or Voltaire but of the mould of the twentieth century, a genius of near-Cockney origin who commanded the world's attention at a time when the Age of Reason was passing into the Age of Violence, here was a man whose life took the shape of a dramatic tragedy. We begin with the emerging picture of the deprived and struggling youth who seized upon 'science' as a cornered man might seize on any weapon however little he understood its nature, becoming the mythopoetic novelist, suddenly set free by a vision that was essentially one of despair; then rising to heights of fame on the wings of prophecy. Essentially a false vocation this, but seized on, as science had been, as a road to power. Then followed disillusionment when humanity refused to be what he so desperately wanted it to become; and at the end we see a despairing and in part disregarded sage, crying out against the cosmic Antagonist whose patience with the species was exhausted, whom the dying Wells saw as turning now to destroy the human formicary in which men had once dreamed of building Utopias. The near coincidence of his death and the apocalyptic flash over Hiroshima lent a lurid dramatic light to this curtaindrop on a life. It was this aspect of a fascinating career that led me on to what follows.

I wish to thank the following for their kindness in giving permission for the use of copyright material: Professor G. P. Wells and the Wells Estate, for extracts from the works and letters of H. G. Wells; Macmillan and Co. Ltd, for the extracts from Sir Frederick Macmillan's letters; Mrs Cheston Bennett, Rupert Hart-Davis Ltd and the University of Illinois Press, for extracts from the letter of 16 October 1901 from *Arnold Bennett and H. G. Wells: A Record of Their Personal and Literary Friendship,* edited by Harris Wilson; Miss D. E. Collins, for the extract from the letter from G. K. Chesterton to H. G. Wells; John Farquharson Ltd, for extracts from Henry James's letters; the London School of Economics and Political Science and David McKay Company Inc., for extracts from *Our Partnership,* by Beatrice Webb; Lady Gregory, for access to the papers of Sir Richard Gregory; Mrs Margaret Cole, for the extract from Professor G. D. H. Cole's memorial tribute to H. G. Wells; and *New Statesman,* for the substance of the Wells–Stalin talk quoted in Chapter 18. I should also like to acknowledge the benefit derived from the vigorous talks I had with Christopher Derrick in planning this book, and the generous assistance of so may friendly hands in the English Library at Urbana.

L.D.

Toronto, 1969

[1]

Digression with
a View

I

I saw H. G. Wells for the first time one evening in London in 1931. The P.E.N. Club was holding one of its dinners at the Café Royal. John Galsworthy, as President, was receiving the guests, and Wells was one among a number of well-known writers present. But he was the one nearly everyone was eyeing in this pre-dinner interval in which the majority of us who were not celebrities stared at the few who were. This was not only because he was so instantly recognizable, so unmistakably the reflection of the energetic, thrusting, cerebral little figure the cartoonists had made familiar to us. In 1931 his fame was still immense. Fifteen years before his death, and thirty-six years after he had burst upon an astonished London with his first books, he was still busy prophesying, proclaiming, analysing, fictionalizing, journalizing. Hardly a week passed when he was not in the news. In all this long writing and public life he had been turning out never less than two books a year, sometimes three or even four.

His novels no longer made the same impression that *Kipps* and *Tono-Bungay, The History of Mr Polly* and *Ann Veronica* and *The New Machiavelli* had done. For that matter, no novel in 1931 could have created the same kind of stir as these, appearing in the first decade of this century, had done. They were annals of a social revolution written while it was happening, and now the revolution was over; people were distracted in the Twenties and Thirties with what seemed weightier problems, and not at all hopeful about the future.

Wells had become more than a novelist. He had become a great teacher, a prophet who deserved the name since the greater number of his prophecies had come true. He was a positivist in a world becoming increasingly negative in its attitude towards the growing complexity of modern life. Yet no one living in the twentieth century but had had his life touched at some point by this phenomenal figure. And that is why we stared at him.

Face to face with such an intensely autobiographical writer as this, one searched instinctively at a first encounter for a hint in his own face and figure of the lineaments of one of his characters plainly based on himself, say, Artie Kipps, or Lewisham, Mr Polly, Mr Britling, or William Clissold. For over the thirty years in which he had been writing these novels the central figure had been nearly always the same, varying only in age and circumstance, and there was a clear line from the simple innocence of Artie Kipps, through the knowingness and the longing for faith of a prosperous Mr Britling, to William Clissold, convinced that only by means of a world republic could the great herd of mankind, wandering in difficult and dangerous places, be led upwards to the light.

And yes, the likeness was there, in this fine head suggesting the visionary, bulging shirt front suggesting confidence, dwindling away to those short legs which in the cartoons always looked as though they were skipping off somewhere, the dreamer and the man of action compounded in one body. With hair plastered flat across his head, old-fashioned toothbrush moustache, jewellery in his shirt front, the polish of prosperity glowing in him, he might have seemed a comic figure, more like Mr Polly, say, than Clissold. He wasn't. The general effect, on the contrary, was of a good-looking man. He had really beautiful eyes, deep blue and well set, and his other features were small and even, and his skin was healthy and clear. Age had thickened him but had not coarsened him. One could understand why he was said to have such success with women. The face had nothing like the carved handsomeness of Galsworthy's, but it glowed with life and intelligence and humour. The whole comic rotundity of figure and flash of jewellery invited warmth, but the blue eyes challenged one's seriousness and the face was magisterial; one sensed the fierce intelligence that might quickly laugh at you for a fool if you made one false step.

Hermann Ould, the Secretary of P.E.N., who was in a group talking to Wells, called me over and introduced me as newly come to London from Canada to edit the *Fortnightly Review*. From my greater height I looked down nervously about four or five inches below me. Some years before this a Canadian schoolmistress, Miss Deeks, had submitted a manuscript called *The Web* to the Macmillan Company of Canada; it had been sent to London Macmillans for consideration, and it had been declined. Miss Deeks had got it into her head that H. G. Wells, whom she had never met, had stolen her idea for a history of the world, and ever since she had kept up a lawsuit against him for alleged plagiarism in *The Outline of History*. She had taken the case through the Ontario Court, the Court of Appeal there, and had finally brought it to the Privy Council in London. Wells had only recently won the final appeal, but had not been able to recover the costs. The case must have cost him many thousands of pounds. The activities of this lady, more reported at home than here, suddenly obtruded between me and the great man. Had this turned him against all Canadians? But he only smiled in an encouraging, friendly way and said, in a voice that came unexpectedly high-pitched from that barrel chest, that the *Fortnightly* under Frank Harris's editorship had published the first essay he had written. 'We must talk about it sometime,' he said, and drew me into the circle of friends gathered round him.

He had not then written his autobiography. But even with my recently acquired knowledge of literary London, I knew some of the gossip that attached to him. His life had got into his books, so that he had become the most talked-about writer in London.

He had started life by being apprenticed to the drapery trade. He had hated it, and had managed to extricate himself from his apprenticeship and at the age of sixteen had become an assistant usher, really a pupil-teacher, little older than the boys he taught, in a school where by dint of fierce and unrelenting study in his spare time he had got a scholarship to the Royal College of Science at South Kensington.

He had failed at first to take his degree and, like Lewisham, he had been subsequently trapped by matrimony. Returning to teaching, he had fallen ill with consumption, and had chosen that moment to leave his wife and run off with one of his pupils. Too ill to continue teaching, he had been literally forced into becoming a writer. Before this, he had put out two books in a desperate attempt to make enough to marry on. The first had been a cram-book, *Honours Physiography,* in which he and his equally hard-up friend Richard Gregory had collaborated. It had netted them twenty pounds, which they had divided. The other was a *Text-Book of Biology* which he had put together for the correspondence college for which he was working part-time as a tutor. His upbringing had been narrow and dull, and life, first as a drapery apprentice and then as an un-qualified teacher, had not provided experience from which to gather material for stories. But the few years he had spent as a student at the Royal College of Science had had one profound result. Suddenly at South Kensington science had been revealed to him as the great force that had created the modern world. His imagination was captivated by its promise and its threat; he saw it all in terms of a drama, not in terms of its essence. Unconsciously a mythmaker he turned, when necessity forced him to write for money desperately needed, when with his health broken down he could no longer go on teaching, to the only imaginative experience he could draw on, his visions of the great power that science now held over the world of men.

At first in stories, then in novels, he drew on this exciting new field, and found an immediate, excited response from a new public hugely augmented just at this time by the beneficiaries of the Education Act of 1870, and very much alive to the 'wonders of science' which promised such miraculous changes in their lives. 1895, the year in which he published his first books, was the year in which X-rays were discovered, the year of Oscar Wilde's trial, the year that saw the end of the aesthetic movement. The Victorian world was dying; the new one we know, a world of urban tumult, was being born. In 1895 Wells was a consumptive supporting two households on what he was beginning to earn as a writer. His life was cramped and painful, and it promised to be brutally brief. The scientific fantasies with which he made his name, from *The Time Machine* to *The War of the Worlds*, were all written in these harsh circumstances.

The revolt against the oppressive religious discipline of Victorian England was bound to come anyhow, and the longing to loosen old restraints, to give free play to passion, to make companionship between men and women a natural, pleasurable thing, was in the hearts of all who were young. Religion seemed to Wells the false doctrine which blighted life, the Victorian conventions and restrictions about sex something which his ardent nature longed to expose, and science the new illumination which would lead twentieth-century man to a better world and a better relationship between men and women. The three myths of science, sex and religion which dominated his own imagination found an echo in some degree in the minds of everyone young and old. When he turned from the scientific fantasies after 1900 to write novels of character, he delighted everyone with *Kipps* and *Tono-Bungay* and *Mr Polly*, but he began to arouse considerable agitation in the minds of parents, concerned over the effect on their children of the liberalizing tendencies of the time, when in *Ann Veronica* and *The*

New Machiavelli he wrote with unprecedented and shocking frankness about the sexual relationship between men and women.

But amongst younger people one can see that he gave the gleam of hope and the bright qualities of leadership as vibrant, relentless, energetic, outspoken, uncompromising, he pressed against old prohibitions and conventions, those grab-hooks by which the past keeps its hold upon the present. With a steady persistence he urged men's minds to the future, reminding them that it was in this direction that they were going. When I first saw him that night at the Café Royal he was sixty-five, but he was as active as ever on platforms, with pamphlets, articles and books, and always advocating the idea of the New Republic which should replace the ramshackle sovereign states of the past; pressing for the Open Conspiracy in which mankind would have to engage to bring this about. It was to be the New Jerusalem, and the way that led to it was science, and the practices that would be kept there would be bold and exciting.

2

It really required an effort of the imagination to recall, seeing him so plump and glossy now, so finely dressed and well-fed looking, that he had been born the child of domestic servants who had ventured timidly out of the great rambling kitchen basement of a Victorian country mansion and invested their all in a little shop in the High Street of Bromley. The fourth and youngest child, he had been christened Herbert George, shortened to Bertie for common use. All Wells's early years up to the age of fourteen had the background of the dusty little china shop, always on the edge of bankruptcy, with its basement kitchen and scullery where the family had their being all day in a sort of half-light drawn from the pavement-grating in the front and the scullery door at the back which led on to a little paved yard, odorous with its brick dustbin and bricked outdoor privy and rainwater rank. At night they moved to bedrooms above the shop.

Mrs Wells, who had been a lady's maid, had the timid confused manner of a Victorian domestic servant. Joe Wells was a jovial outdoor sort of man. He hated the shop and kept out of it as much as possible. He was a natural-born cricketer and had the excuse that the few pounds he picked up bowling to the gentlemen or playing in country matches, which often took him away all day in the summer, kept the derelict little home together. There were two brothers older than little Bertie; a sister who came between died in childhood. Each child as it was born was greatly loved, none more so than Bertie, who, the last to arrive, inherited the full force of his mother's love and desperate planning for his career.

The many letters still preserved between both parents and their younger son give a good idea of their individual characters. They were 'Pater' and 'Mater' to him, and he 'Buss' or 'Bussy' to them, a diminutive which seems to have come from Bushwhacker, perhaps an echo of a projected move at one time to Australia. In spite of her manner, Mrs Wells was the dominant character who bullied them in a fretful, worrying way. From Joe Wells, it is plain from his letters to Buss, came the individual ironic style, the imagination, the tendency to dream, that were to mark the son. It was Joe Wells who brought home books borrowed from the Literary Institute, and who talked to his son about the stars, and worlds that might lie beyond this one. Mrs Wells, nervous, never at ease away from the safe community of the servants' hall, finding herself shipwrecked in a bankrupt shop in Bromley, devoted herself to getting her sons started in respectable occupations, and tried to induce in them a sense of respect for the gentry, and a sense of awe towards the greatest gentleman of them all, God the Father, whom she petitioned constantly for favours which were very rarely and grudgingly granted.

The early part of *Experiment in Autobiography*, published

in 1934, a few years after my first glimpse of him, vividly pictures this little family struggling for survival in the late Victorian world of the 1870s. You get from it the picture of this pale under-sized little boy, with bold eyes, very blue in colour, which dreamed or were alight with mischief, playing by himself in the small yard at the back of the shop, or chattering incessantly in the kitchen, or, his body twisted in a chair, reading in that dim light books borrowed from the local library. He was the clever one. Some genetic chance had produced in this youngest son of almost uneducated parents a child with an extraordinary mind, possessed of amazing powers of memorization and a brilliant imagination that dreamed and quickened alone. His early years were almost completely solitary. His elder brothers were away at school when he was playing alone in the basement kitchen or in the little yard; they were already out in the world, fettered to their trade, when he himself ventured forth to school. The exaggerated fear of the working class, not uncommon to those brought up in domestic service who unconsciously parodied the manners and attitudes of 'upstairs', would not allow Mrs Wells to let her youngest play with other boys in the neighbourhood for fear of the infection of 'commonness'.

3

He was to be torn abruptly from the dark kitchen that was home, and from the little school he attended, for at fourteen life began in earnest for boys like Buss. He was approaching his fourteenth birthday when at five o'clock one evening in the year 1880 he and his portmanteau were dropped at the side door of Messrs Rodgers & Denyer, drapers, in Windsor, opposite the Castle, for his start in life. He first letter home gave an account of his routine, written 'sitting in my bedroom after the fatigues of the day. Cough slightly better'. 'I don't like the place much,' he wrote. 'It is not at all like home.'

He got to like it no better as the weeks went by. The 'living-in' – he shared a bedroom over the shop with two other apprentices and an assistant, and they ate in a gloomy basement room lit by a naked gas flame – the deadly monotony, the servility, the feeling that he was imprisoned for life in a great machine from which escape was impossible: all this made him seriously contemplate the extremes of running away or suicide. He was saved the trouble of deciding; the feeling of distaste was mutual. At the end of two months, Messrs Rodgers & Denyer wrote to Mrs Wells that her boy was inattentive, uncivil, dreamy, didn't seem interested, and was singularly inept at giving the right change, and they requested his removal.

His start in life had been a failure, a terrible blow in Victorian times. He had been gone only two months, and in that time Mrs Wells, having got her youngest off her hands, had left her husband in charge of the derelict shop and had thankfully returned to domestic service, to the same mistress to whom she had been lady's maid before her marriage to Joe. In the interval since she had left her, her young mistress had inherited the great house of Up Park in Sussex. Miss Fetherstonhaugh rashly promoted her former lady's maid to the position of housekeeper, an upper servant with a parlour of her own and keys to all the stores, a person of some consequence below stairs, a position for which Mrs Wells had neither the aptitude nor the training. So it was not to the basement of the gas-lit little shop in Bromley but to the grandeur of the upper servants' quarters of a country mansion that Bertie returned while fresh plans were made for his disposal. This brief interval of respite in a great country house, to a sharp boy who had known till then only the world of shops, was to leave a mark on him always.

There was, to begin with, the great library in the house. The housekeeper's son was given permission to borrow books from it. Lying amid the bracken on summer days, or in his little attic bedroom in the winter (for he was to return there frequently as each attempt to get him started in life ended in failure), looking down on the most beautiful part of England, his mind opened to the discovery that England was not just one great Bromley; that there were other existences than that to which he seemed doomed. Amongst other fascinating books from the library he took Plato's *Republic*. Without doubt, there was a better world than the hateful one of commerce with which he was finding it so difficult to come to terms. The evidence of beauty he suddenly discovered everywhere about him. It had been a sensuous imagining before, but here were paintings and wonderful furniture, and silks and stuffs in the great house which rose out of the landscape, a thing of beauty in itself, against the English sky, so unlike the Bromley High Street dwelling.

One day in 1966 when Wells was beginning to absorb my thoughts and I was thinking of this book, I went to visit Up Park. My aim was to re-create in my own mind what it must have been like to be the child of one of the upper servants, returned in disgrace from the employment to which he had been put. I was trying to imagine the effect on the sharp mind of the boy. Disapproval would have been the dominant note in the housekeeper's parlour, where by custom every afternoon the butler and the head housemaid, the housekeeper and cook, and occasionally the personal servants of very distinguished visitors to the house, met to take tea. Glimpses of that sacred hour are unforgettably caught in *Tono-Bungay*:

Tea lasted for nearly three quarters of an hour, and I sat it out perforce; and day after day the talk was exactly the same.

'Sugar, Mrs Mackridge,' my mother used to ask. 'Sugar, Mrs Latude-Fernay?'

The word *sugar* would stir the mind of Mrs Mackridge. 'They say,' she would begin, issuing her proclamation – at least half her sentences began 'they say' – 'sugar is fatt-an-ing, now-adays. Many of the best people do not take it now at all.'

'Not with their tea, ma'am,' said Rabbits (the butler) intelligently.

'Not with anything,' said Mrs Mackridge, with an air of crushing repartee, and drank.

'What won't they say next?' said Miss Fison.

'They do say such things!' said Mrs Booch.

'They say,' said Mrs Mackridge inflexibly, 'the doctors are not recomm-an-ding it now.'

My mother: 'No ma'am?'

Then to the table at large: 'Poor Sir Roderick, before he died, consumed great quan-ta-ties of sugar. I sometimes fancy it may have hastened his end.'

This ended the first skirmish. A certain gloom of manner and a pause was considered due to the sacred memory of Sir Roderick.

'George,' said my mother, 'don't kick the chair.'

When I made arrangements for the visit, Lady Mead-Fetherstonhaugh had invited me to take tea with her after I had viewed the house and grounds. I was especially interested in the rooms below the stairs, and particularly the housekeeper's room, where so many little dramas in the life that was beginning to fascinate me had been enacted.

On the afternoon of my visit the B.B.C. had taken possession of the house and grounds and were engaged in making a film record of Wells's early years to honour his centenary. The Corporation's activities were responsible for the consternation of scores of black-faced sheep, disturbed in their grazing on the Downs by the mechanical equipment and the earnest young men dashing about in preparation of scenes to be shot. Lady Mead-Fetherstonhaugh had dared where the sheep were hesitant and bleating; she had taken flight and abandoned me to the housekeeper. The green vans and electric cables cluttered the broad drive to the front door. From the tall windows at the back of the great house, looking out on the Downs, cameras protruded. Three young men formed a knot of anxious consultation below the library windows, and in a paved garden at the side of the house, sitting on a bench together, I found – Mrs Wells and Bert! The cast! She was in black bombazine, bonneted, with brolly and shawl, he in cap and knickerbockers, his

portmanteau by his side. They were awaiting their cue. It
was a curious experience in the next half-hour to stand there
and see enacted a scene which I had already pictured in my
imagination.

I had imagined him coming for the first time to Up Park
from his failure at Windsor, disinclined temperamentally to
play the penitent, a bouncy little boy used to shrilly justifying himself, but at this moment a little subdued by his
mother's anger and, in spite of himself, overawed by the
grandeur of his surroundings; glad to have escaped the hell
of Messrs Rodgers & Denyer, at the same time resentful at
what he had been made to bear. When the young men were
ready to shoot, the replicas of mother and son hand-in-
hand came marching up the path that led from the village
of South Harting towards the south aspect of the beautiful
great house. One of the bearded young men drove the sheep
galloping across their path to lend an air of naturalness
and isolation to the scene; and mother and son, with the
expressions they might so easily have worn, his mutinous
but curious, hers grim but loving, advanced on the great
house, while from the window of the library where with his
telescope Sir Harry Fetherstonhaugh, who had built this
house, had speculated in the admirable manner of his time,
the camera recorded the scene.

4

Wells's autobiography, appearing in 1934, explained much
about his earlier years that could only be guessed at from
his novels. But its silences about his later years tantalized a
curiosity that the earlier part aroused. For the very frank
self-revelation ceases in 1900, his thirty-fourth year, when
he built Spade House at Sandgate and attained the high
plateau of success as a novelist. The last two hundred pages
deal almost wholly with his aim of a World State, and the
essential Wells, the unique figure, is lost. It is like a badly
constructed novel in which the main character dies before

the story reaches its climax. Odette Keun, who had shared his life for some years, and who had been a stabilizing factor in it at a time when he had badly needed that kind of support, wrote for *Time and Tide*, when the autobiography appeared, a series of articles analysing him and his work in a merciless way. My admiration for him, affection even, had grown as I got to know him, re-read his books, and read about his activities in the paper. I was forever hearing him speak or reading his speeches, attending him at the P.E.N. Club, talking to his friends, especially his lady friends, and building up unconsciously in my mind a picture of him as a great man, even if I did not believe much in the New Republic. These biting articles implied that he was merely an actor putting on a stunt, that he was hardhearted and not really high-minded. He did not seem to mind nearly as much as I did, but chuckled at them, and took his revenge in a biting, witty little novel, *Apropos of Dolores*.

5

In 1936 Wells became seventy, and a dinner was arranged at the Savoy by P.E.N. to honour the great man. Hundreds were gathered there that evening, for Bernard Shaw, then aged eighty, was to propose the toast to which Wells would reply. They were old friends and adversaries, the two great sages of the time, and their debates, quarrels and argument had provided public entertainment for nearly forty years.

In every way they formed a complete contrast, except in brain power, and even there a subtle distinction of creativity made a contrast. Shaw had all the physical advantages: a melodious voice, graced with a Dublin lilt, a tall figure, an extremely handsome head, marred slightly by an overlarge nose, and, of course, a profusion of whiskers that set him apart from other men. He had the clearest possible mind and a gift for lucid exposition that made him an effective public speaker, a practice in which he had trained himself arduously. In fact, every quality of his was the outcome of a relentless discipline of mind and spirit, even his vegetarianism. He was, it seems, immune from the demands of the sexual appetite, and lived in great amity with his wife, Charlotte Shaw, whose wealth had rescued him from starvation and had supported him during a long and unrewarding apprenticeship as a writer.

Different in every respect from my lusty, whoring meat-eating, tubby hero, torn by this temperamental storm and that, who had absolutely no vanity but immense seriousness of purpose, whose life had been one long seething trouble interspersed with radiant sensual experiences which Shaw could never know, and who was altogether and fiercely devoted to saving the human species from self-destruction. Wells had what was withheld from Shaw, an original and rich creative imagination. Shaw could create characters, but first there must be provided the ground-plan of a problem, a human dilemma, and then, scornfully deriding all previous attempts to solve it, the sagacious Shaw, mixing fun and criticism and the doctor's order into one heady brew, showed with a flick of his pen how it could be, should be, solved.

Such consuming vanity, such self-confidence, such an untortured mind revolving as in a bath of oil, plainly maddened little Wells, whose tendency was to get very worked up over any problem to which he addressed himself; and just as plainly Shaw was green with envy, though always hiding it, of Wells's superior intellect. What is the good of having panache – Rebecca West says that there was a pride in his mental movements that reminded one of the bull-ring, of the walk of the matador into the centre of the arena when he is going to fight the bull to the finish – what avails the splendid pride if the bull is not impressed?

Shaw rose to speak. How he revelled in what most men hate, public speaking. There he stood, having eaten little and drunk nothing on this festive night, twinkling with vitality, teasing his old adversary for his mistaken enthusiasms, his heavy weight of years. Wells was ten years his junior, but the phrase that tolled through Shaw's sparkling denigration was 'Poor old Wells, poor old Wells!' as he went on to explain how close and intimate his association with Wells had been through the years, and how misguided Wells had been in some of his enthusiasms, but what a good chap he really was at heart: all delivered without a note, in that Irish voice that seemed always to chuckle at its own superiority. Detestable man, wonderful man, who had given us all such exciting notions and intellectual ambitions; who spoke with such ease and wit.

It was light amusing stuff, and we all laughed to show that we knew he was teasing. Only the guest of honour seemed unamused.* Perhaps it was the onus of making a speech. Unlike Shaw, he was never at ease in public speaking, and extemporaneity was not for him. My sympathies were all with the humped figure who sat scowling down at his papers. Two large bulges, his head and his shirt front, looking more than ever like Low's familiar caricature of him. A life's work being headed like a football in a soccer match. What must he be thinking on this night of his seventieth birthday? 'Fools,' one could imagine him thinking, 'detestable fools. Will the human race never learn? Why don't they do what I tell them? Bracketing me with this comic Irishman, Shaw. I have given all my life and thought to trying to save these contemptible slaves from their native mess. They've spurned my advice, now they titter at Shaw. Won't they ever learn? My God, I'll make them pay! No, I won't. I'm licked!'

The room fell silent while the little figure gathered his notes together and began, in his querulous, high-pitched

* One is reminded here of a letter H.G. wrote to Shaw about *John Bull's Other Island* in which, perhaps jokingly, he sees himself caricatured as Broadbent: 'You are a great swell, Shaw, really – with something in your blood that ever and again breaks out in little blemishes of perversity. You have every element of greatness except a certain independence of your own intellectual excitability. You can't control your own wit and love of larking. You ought to dull yourself with meat and then you'd be vast' (February 1905).

voice, to read his talk. ' "Now, Master Bertie, it's time to put your toys away. Come along." But I don't want to go,' he said rather piteously. 'I *hate* being seventy.' He looked a little like Edward Ponderevo, and one felt like George Ponderevo comforting his dying uncle.

He wanted, he said, to go on playing. His work on *The Outline of History*, *The Science of Life*, and *The Work, Wealth and Happiness of Mankind* had taught him the need and the possibility of an encyclopaedia of human knowledge, and he wanted time for that. He wanted time to work with this new medium of communication, the films, and to try to make the 'talkies' *say* something. Then there were novels. Every age of man has the novel best suited to the writer's stage of development. If we write short stories when we are young, it is because we delight to play with possibility. As we grow up we become more and more interested in character, our own and other people's, and we write about personal reactions. Few of us have any original political sense until we are round about forty, and then we incline to the novel of affairs. Perhaps after seventy one should attempt the novel of experience. 'I should like to, if only Nurse will let me.'

He not only found life too short, he found it too narrow. Instead of seeing life broadly as a whole, one was compelled to see it as if looking through a chink.

Mankind is still adjusting itself painfully and confusedly to an unprecedented change of scale and pace and scope. Many things have to break, many things have to grind. The world will become worse before it is better. Political life is more and more a succession of stampedes. The rational life becomes a struggle against hysteria. New generations press upon us and find us unprepared. This is not the fault of the old. The old know no better. It is the stress of change. There has not been time enough to meet our new needs. We are all explorers together, but the young suffer most. Seven-eighths of the hideous killing going on in the world is being done by young people under thirty, youngsters fed mentally on stale old dogmas, or

not fed at all. Only a great *free* intellectual and moral drive –
an educated encyclopaedism – can restore the shattered morals
of our race, and give a definite direction to its disordered will.

Man must age and man must pass, but the life of which our
work is a part need have no end. And that is a very consoling
thought for an elderly gentleman of seventy, more or less under
notice to go.

6

The years had indeed rolled by since Wells first came on the
scene, lifting up our fathers' hearts with hopes, exciting them
with the feeling that a new world was at the point of being
born and they were to inherit it. Millions had died; millions more had the mark of death upon them, for the future
in 1936 was threatening, to say the least. The universal
tragedy seemed pointed in the fate of this man who in
1936 was still striving to make humanity see the way to
universal peace in a united world, the prophet crying to the
heavens of the wrath to come while the audience turned
indifferently aside and melted away.

The image haunted me from time to time. It was like a
ghost creeping along that panelled corridor of Macmillan's
old building where I worked, along which Wells had hurried so may times on his way to have it out with Frederick
Macmillan. 1943 marked Macmillan's centenary, and for
Charles Morgan, who was to write a short history, we turned
out from the archives the correspondence of the many
great authors of the past and the equally great old partners.
In that queer time of war, these old letters were like voices
heard from another room, indistinct, muffled, the tone at-
testing to the importance of the conversation but the matter
nearly nothing. It was a treasure-trove of literary history,
but the unceasing whine of war shrilled over these thousands of old-dated pages in the handwriting of Bernard
Shaw, Wells, Kipling, Henry James, Matthew Arnold,
Lewis Carroll, Mr Gladstone, Charles Kingsley; one turned
them over with wonder that such a world had once existed.

But that which held me was a great bundle of letters from H. G. Wells. The small neat handwriting made them very easy to read. What interested me chiefly was that they began where the autobiography had left off, just as he was beginning to be world-famous as a writer, successful, self-assured, at the very height of his powers. In Frederick Macmillan he collided with a publisher who was not content just to issue his books but insisted that they should conform to certain standards that the firm upheld. The struggle between the two men coincided with Wells's most productive and most privately troubled period, and the books that caused the trouble reflected events in his life. Here were some, at least, of the unwritten chapters missing from the autobiography. They offered a footnote to the history of publishing, too, because here were one of the most successful authors of the day and one of the most successful publishers, and out of their joint enterprise there was, surprisingly, little profit.

As I was reading these letters, the first signs of his last fatal illness might have been apparent in him. It was young men whose deaths dramatized themselves to us at that time; old men slipped silently down like leaves from the trees. This death, when it came finally in 1946, seemed the end of an age, an age that somehow had not fulfilled its splendid promise. Fumbling, I set about trying to re-create this life which interested me so much, and at the beginning I went back to that moment when in disgrace, but excited by his new surroundings, he had come tramping up the hill from South Harting to Up Park, a defiant small boy in cap and knickerbockers carrying his portmanteau, with his future unmade.

Beginnings, and the
Breaking-Out

MRS WELLS held the home together. Without her the family might have sunk below the line, finely drawn and observed, between the independence of a home and business however threatened by bankruptcy, and the slums. She was determined to get her family on in the world. Grandiloquently named Atlas House, the building had been run up in a hurry, was dark, airless and inconveniently planned. Joe Wells had bought the business from his uncle for fifty pounds. The disordered shop with its dusty, unwanted stock did not yield a living, but with Joe Wells's sporting gear added to the china and the oil for lamps, and with Joe's connections with professional cricket producing a little cash with which to buy the weekly joint, it just managed to survive. A slavey was needed to keep it clean, to serve the occasional customers, to wash and cook and darn. Mrs Wells was the slavey. Through those difficult years when the boys were growing up, she kept them respectable, tried to instil in them a respect for God and their betters, and as her boys reached the age of thirteen, she settled them as apprentices in a trade where they might hope to wear stiff collars, striped trousers and tail coats, and attain the ultimate satisfaction of serving the gentry.

None of the family rebelled against her plan of life; they protested, but their protests were overborne, and off the boys had gone, one after another. Bertie made the loudest protest of all, but he too eventually had to submit.

Evoking those early years in his autobiography fifty years later, H.G. was plainly impatient with the mental confusion and the dumb acceptance of the order of things that held them all in that disordered home and sent him out when the time came into a way of life that could mean for himself only a continuation of these oppressive conditions. He had a talent for drawing, he had a passion for reading, and in his school examinations he had come first, tied with another pupil, for all England in book-keeping. He was already aware that he had brains, and that, given a chance where he could use his cleverness, he might rise out of this world of shops on which his mother's ambition, in spite of the lack of success of their own establishment, was firmly fixed. But his mother was in command, and no one in the family stood out against her very long, especially as she had a powerful ally in God the Father, to whom she always turned tearfully when there was any difficulty in making her decisions prevail.

So H.G. obeyed, as his brothers had done, but obstinately and reluctantly. He loved and feared his mother, and before he could bring himself, as he was eventually to do, to rebel against her plan for his life, he was going to deny God.

Turned out of Rodgers & Denyer, he hoped for a reprieve, but his mother was adept at seeking practical help from relatives and acquaintances. With Bertie back on her hands, she appealed to a second cousin by marriage, known to all the family in Victorian fashion as 'Uncle' Williams, who had just returned to England from the West Indies and had been appointed headmaster of a little National School in Wookey in Somerset. Perhaps there was a future for her clever boy in teaching.

What she did not know was that Uncle Williams did not have the qualifications necessary for the headmastership of a National School, subject to inspection. He had forged the necessary references and documents to obtain the position, knowing quite well that sooner or later the truth would be discovered. He was a smooth, fast-talking rogue of great ingenuity and charm, As we get to know Uncle Williams better, we see that the anticipated eventuality of being discovered merely added spice to the situation, confirming his sardonic view of the oppressive nature of all authority, which would not leave men alone. He readily agreed to make a place for Sarah Wells's boy in the school as an 'improver', a title given to a pupil-teacher, not much older than the boys he taught, who could pass on to them what he himself had just learned, while at the same time studying for still higher certificates.

Although he was with Uncle Williams only three months before the Department of Education caught up with the facts and summarily ejected both headmaster and his improver, this period left an indelible mark on young H.G.'s character. He was still only fourteen, undersized, indistinct in voice and shuffling in manner – all the result of his upbringing – but he was highly intelligent, imaginative and observant. He was also at that stage of adolescence when sexual tides were beginning to sweep through him, adding to the confusion of his manner, but making him more sharp and cheeky than ever. It was sheer chance that just at this time he should be thrown into the close company of someone quite different in character and morals from anyone he had ever met before. Uncle Williams's talk was copious; his continuous flow of anecdote and comment merged into the openly derisive and blasphemous when he found it necessary to touch upon the clergy or organized religion. In fact, he was an impatient critic of life's muddled progress, and he saw himself only as trying to help to straighten it. He might have replied to any charge of duplicity – for instance, about forging a headmaster's certificate – not with denials or evasions but with those laughing, urgent persuasions with which, in *Love and Mr Lewisham*, Chaffery was later momentarily to confuse the honest Lewisham:

Honesty is essentially an anarchistic and disintegrating force in society, communities are held together and progress made possible only by vigorous and sometimes even violent lying; the social contract is nothing more or less than a vast conspiracy of human beings to lie to and humbug themselves and one another for the general Good. Lies are the mortar that binds the savage individual man into the social masonry ...

He must have been an entertaining talker, and he adopted towards young Bertie the same air of confidence between understanding equals that marked Mr Micawber's relations with Copperfield.

In that little house in Wookey that went with the headmastership, Bertie lived for these exciting three months with Uncle Williams and the daughter who kept house for him, a girl who was a few years older than Bertie. With her he had his first experience of sex. It left him curious rather than satisfied. At least it made him feel a man, and this revelation, together with Uncle Williams's precepts and table talk, and the experience of getting up in front of other boys and teaching them something, made him on his second unheralded return to Up Park, a very different boy from the one who only a few months before had been marched up the hill from South Harting on his return home from Windsor.

Mrs Wells could not understand what had happened to Uncle Williams, and why Bertie was back on her hands. Confused enough about a great houseful of guests at the holiday season, for it was just on Christmas, she was in no state at that moment to set about finding a fresh place for this troublesome boy. The snow came unexpectedly but picturesquely to seal him and his mother and the whole little world of Up Park from the outside. What joy! To have his mother temporarily powerless to arrange his future, to have the season of festivity making a good excuse for parties in the servants' hall. That side of his nature that loved revels and games, the 'bouncy' side so at variance with the deep, dark, pessimistic strain as yet unsuspected that ran through him, flowered for a brief spell. In this few weeks' interval he produced for the enjoyment of the staff a daily paper of a facetious character, written and illustrated by himself, *The Up Park Alarmist*, which had them all agog with excitement and laughter.

Word spread to the drawing-room upstairs of the cleverness of this son of the housekeeper, and Miss Fetherstonhaugh graciously allowed him again to borrow books from the library. He met for the first time Voltaire and Tom Paine, and books like *Gulliver's Travels* and Dr Johnson's *Rasselas*. The effect of these great works with their ice-cold clear prose, on a mind which was as yet bare as the walls of an unfurnished house was tremendous. He had none of that background of general knowledge that drifts into most children's minds unconsciously and sticks there. He had heard no conversation except the exchanges of persiflage and grumble that had passed for talk in the dormitory at Windsor or the servants' hall below stairs. All that was resentful and envious in his nature rose to protest against the dull life of servitude into which he was being driven; in these books he could hear voices proclaim that men were their own masters; they ordained their own fates.

Throughout the day, when the great house was busy with its domestic tasks, he sat in his cold little bedroom at the top of the house reading, enthralled, until it was too dark to make out the print and he would be forced to join the company and the light and chatter of the world below, putting aside reluctantly the books in which these amazing and heartening revelations were made to him. But it was not something to talk about in the housekeeper's room or the servants' hall. In either place, at any moment, the problem of the 'housekeeper's boy' and the worry he caused his Ma might emerge as a subject of lugubrious conversation.

Then the snow melted, the roads were open again, the pony-trap could negotiate the short drive to Midhurst, and suddenly he was face to face with the next attempt to find a place in life for him. Mr Cowap, chemist, of Midhurst, young and enthusiastic and in love with his pretty young wife, was seeking an apprentice to look after the shop while he and Mrs Cowap went out and about.

The scene of Bertie's installation at Mr Cowap's is faithfully mirrored in *Tono-Bungay* when young George

Ponderevo is taken over from Bladesover, which is Up Park, to the sleepy little town of Wimblehurst, which is Midhurst, and put in the charge of his energetic uncle, Edward Ponderevo. A chemist's shop was an infinitely more exciting place than a draper's, especially as Mr Cowap, like Edward Ponderevo, made up pills of his own design and had invented his own cough linctus. But it was a shock to find himself in servitude again, bound by articles as firmly as a convict is restrained by prison. The sole ray of light was that it was necessary for him to learn a little Latin to handle prescriptions, and arrangements were proposed for him to do this with the headmaster of the local grammar school at night. George Ponderevo is recalling in *Tono-Bungay*.

> 'What, me learn Latin,' I cried with emotion.
> 'A little,' he said.
> 'I've always wanted –' I said, and 'Latin.'

For some reason, again it did not work. In spite of the joy of learning Latin and the greater interest the little drawers in the chemist's shop with their Latin names had for him compared with the counters of the drapery and the shapeless bundles of stuffs, again it did not work. In his autobiography H.G. says that he discovered early on that the cost of taking the necessary examinations to become a licensed chemist was more than he felt his mother could afford, and he asked leave to break his articles. Whatever the cause, the end was as sudden as the beginning, and Mr Cowap was urgent to have him removed to make way for another apprentice; and as he could not so soon be taken back to Up Park – the third time in less than a year – his distracted mother arranged for him to stay on as a boarder at the local grammar school where he had been learning his Latin until she could make fresh arrangements for his disposal.

This break lasted only for about six weeks, but they were six of the happiest weeks he had ever known. He was learning; he had not duties other than to learn, and, like someone famished, he gulped down everything. Mr Byatt, the headmaster, was impressed with his capacity for mastering a subject and looked at him in a calculating way; there was a method by which Byatt could turn such enterprise to his own advantage, but Mrs Wells spoilt his plan. The agent for the estate of Up Park, Sir William King, whose interest and patronage had been besought by Mrs Wells, got the boy a place with a friend of his, the leading draper of South-sea, and Bertie was torn away from this paradise of books and solemnly articled again with the Southsea Drapery Emporium.

Fifteen now, and bound again in an apprenticeship, this time for five years. There seemed no hope of escape. He wanted to please his mother, and he wanted to get on in life. But he had had a taste of other things, of what books could mean and a little learning do to liberate one from this thralldom. He felt now that he had lost the world of books and learning for ever; that fate had decreed for him a way of life that would effectually prevent him for ever from pushing back the door beyond which lay further miraculous truths and discoveries, where the universe had a meaning other than this simple and convenient arrangement by which the better-off and the better-born were served by those less well favoured by circumstance and origin and the whole system was kept in being by organized religion.

A shrill young voice, endlessly arguing and disputing and protesting, saying dangerous things, reaches up to us out of that gas-lit world of shops in the 1880s, protesting against the chains that bound its owner inexorably to the frame of life he had inherited. He fought against everything; he must have been a tiresome boy for the manager of the shop to handle. Protesting against confirmation, denying the sacraments, arguing with his fellow drapers; dreaming in his dormitory and on lonely walks on his only free day, Sunday, about women and love; reading every moment he could get, and lots of moments that he stole from work, finding out about socialism and its proposals for a new establishment of justice on earth, and talking dangerously about that as he did about God, first to the uneasy derision and then to the mounting apprehension of his fellow workers, fearful of attracting thunderbolts.

Until suddenly, after two years, when he was sixteen he made up his mind that he could stand it not a moment longer and that he must escape, whether by drowning himself in Portsmouth harbour or by running away. Of the two alternatives, the second seemed worth trying first. He had never forgotten Midhurst Grammar School and the few idyllic weeks he had known after Mr Cowap had dispensed with him. Nor, as it turned out, had Mr Byatt, the headmaster, forgotten the vigour and aggressive appetite he had shown for acquiring Latin. On an impulse Wells wrote and asked if he might work for the school as an under-master. To his surprise, he got a prompt answer, and it was in the affirmative.

He now had only to persuade his mother to let him break his articles, doubly difficult this time because Sir William King had arranged the introduction. After this there could be no turning back, no fresh starts made. This was the parting of the ways, and with a sense of the drama involved, Bertie, instead of writing, got up at five o'clock one Sunday morning and walked the seventeen miles from the shop at Southsea to Up Park to break the news to his mother. He reached the open parkland that surrounds the house on all sides just as he knew the household would be returning from church in the village.

George Ponderevo is describing the scene in *Tono-Bungay:*

I took a short cut through the Warren across the corner of the main park to intercept the people coming from church. I wanted to avoid meeting anyone before I met my mother, and so I went to a place where the path passed between banks . . .

Presently, down the hill, the servants appeared, straggling by twos and threes, first some of the garden people and the butler's wife with them, then the two laundry maids, odd inseparable old

creatures, then the first footman talking to the butler's little
girl, and at last, walking grave and breathless beside old Ann
and Miss Fison, the black figure of my mother.

My boyish mind suggested the adoption of a playful form of
appearance. 'Coo-ee, Mother!' said I, coming out against the
sky, 'Coo-ee!'

My mother looked up, went very white, and put her hand to
her bosom . . .

The bad penny had turned up again! One sees the small
distraught figure in black and the lumpish son drawing
away from the curiosity of the others, the son beseeching,
the mother tearfully remonstrating as they disappear from
view, and one knows from the account H.G. gives in his
autobiography the course of the debate that continued tearfully in the housekeeper's room. It lasted all through the
middle of the day. In the end Mrs Wells promised to think
the matter over on condition that Bertie returned immediately to the shop. He agreed, but only on condition
that his indentures should be cancelled. The alternative was
suicide. He kept repeating this threat. He knew that this
time he had to stand out against his mother's remonstrances
and tears.

So he was released and became an under-master at the
age of seventeen in the little two-roomed grammar school
that stood opposite the great gates of Cowdray Park in
Sussex. The earnest youth in the cheap, ready-made clothes,
wearing in his rambles around the countryside as well as in
the town and at school the mortarboard which signified his
association with the profession of teaching, suddenly found
himself happier than he had ever dreamed would be possible. The years of intellectual starvation had left him with
such an appetite for learning that he felt he could never
read enough. In order to make up for lost time, he vowed
not to read any novels or to play any games. He and the
other assistant master, Harris, shared rooms over a little
confectionery shop in the High Street, rooms hung with

encouraging slogans and schema, very much like the room with its slanting ceiling, its lead-framed, diamond-paned dormer window, its bulging walls and its view of the vicarage garden, described in *Love and Mr Lewisham*.

Byatt, the headmaster, an M.A. of Dublin University, was anxious to supplement his very modest salary in any possible way. Among the ways that offered was a scheme authorized by the Department of Education whereby head-masters with university degrees were encouraged to organize evening classes with a view to training teachers to specialize in the teaching of the new subject of science. The Education Department scheme offered up to thirty subjects, and payment for the headmaster was by results. Four pounds for a first-class pass, three pounds for a second, and so on down the scale to zero for a failure. Byatt let his young assistant master loose among nearly the whole range of subjects, provided him with text-books, and sat back at his desk in the schoolroom attending to his own correspondence and thoughts while below him, fiercely concentrating, Wells submerged himself in uncharted seas of human and vegetable physiology, elementary inorganic chemistry, physics, mathematics, and the rest.

In May came the examinations, and when the results were announced Byatt found himself the richer by a considerable cheque, while a whole shower of 'A' certificates descended on the head of Wells. An official letter from the Department of Education followed, offering him a studentship at the Normal School of Science in South Kensington with a bursary of a guinea a week, leading on possibly to a degree as Bachelor of Science. To give oneself to learning, and to be paid for it! To sit under such famous men as Professor Huxley, Darwin's friend and defender, and Norman Lockyer, the astronomer, who taught at the Great Gallery of Iron on Exhibition Road. He had to thank for this the miracle and mystery of science, the beginnings of which he fancied he had mastered in those evenings of concentration in the schoolroom. He knew that he was crammed with indigestible fact, that he had seen nothing illustrated or demonstrated, and he could only imagine what a laboratory was like. But he was full of self-confidence. Science held out to nearly everyone at that time the promise of a new dawn; how much more vividly to this highly imaginative youth whom it had plucked from obscurity and servitude, proposing to set him down in London under great teachers to carve a career for himself as a pure scientist. He was never to lose the rapture of that first vision.

He was just eighteen when he registered at South Kensington in September 1884. There had been a certain degree of confusion in getting a start in life, but even among the company in the housekeeper's parlour at Up Park the tendency to criticize and the agreeable expectancy of imminent disaster were stilled, though the renowned godlessness of Professor Huxley, who was a declared atheist, left room for some doleful anticipations that the worst might yet befall.

3

Science Student – and
Failure

LONDON in 1884 held nearly one seventh of the population of the kingdom. Coming into it from any direction, the train ran along above miles of crowded poor brick dwellings crowned with a forest of smoking chimney-pots. The Industrial Revolution had brought the poor in from the country to these dingy brick burrows where they lived in circumstances of savage poverty unequalled in any other European city, and knew a standard of eating which was lower than at any time since the Middle Ages. At the other extreme, in the West End, sheltered like a pearl in the shell of an oyster, another part of the population lived in a degree of luxury unknown in earlier times even by the very wealthy. In between these two extremes the great body of London lay spread; this huge complex of brick and mortar, warehouse and factory, crowded river and narrow back streets, with suburban villas rising on either side of the Thames valley, a surging flood spreading out year by year to engulf in its lapping tide little villages like Bromley on the high road to Dover, where the young man in the train, riding in triumph to the College of Science, had spent his early years.

Science was responsible for the smoke and haze and the hideousness of this wilderness of brick and chimney-pot, for turning London from an eighteenth-century capital of remarkable beauty into an ugly factory town. It had created wealth, and wealth bred this residue. But when Wells came to London, science seemed momentarily to have paused in its advance. The scientists themselves were in a questioning phase. You cannot suddenly wrench out a supporting column of life like traditional religious faith and not replace it with something. Biology gave the explanation of the origin of life, but what of its conduct? Ethics were now demanding consideration. Huxley, who was to become Wells's god, said: 'I deem it an essential condition of the hope (i.e., that the evil of the world may be abated) that we should cast aside the notion that the escape from sorrow and pain is the proper object of life.' There was a nobler purpose, and in this short interval before in 1895, with the discovery of the electron, science began its second and more destructive phase, there was an urgent search for an understanding of the universe in which man had to make his life.

He came extravagantly greedy for learning, and with a very good opinion of himself. He meant to carve out a scientific career, and he was particularly pleased to discover that he was to be in Professor Huxley's class in the first year. Huxley was a magnetic and noble figure, a friend of Darwin and perhaps Darwin's most eloquent and ardent defender, and a born teacher. Huxley's subject was biology, the beginnings, the meaning and the purpose of life. In the lecture room, with perhaps fifty or sixty students silent before him, explaining clearly and steadily how life came into being, turning now and then to illustrate a point on the blackboard behind, turning to face them again, fastidiously dusting the chalk from his fingers, coming up silently behind them as they made in the laboratory the dissections which he had illustrated for them in his lectures, he overshadowed their lives. To them he was the very spirit of learning, and its champion. He was renowned as a controversialist. His famous retort from the platform at a meeting of the British Association for the Advancement of Science seemed to them to be the very mark of his championship. The Bishop of Oxford had inquired with a sarcastic smile whether it was through his grandfather or grandmother that Huxley claimed descent from a venerable ape, and Huxley had replied: 'If I am asked whether I would choose to be

descended from the poor animal of low intelligence and stoop-
ing gait, who grins and chatters as we pass, or from a man,
endowed with great ability and a splendid position, who
should use these gifts to discredit and crush humble seekers
after truth, I hesitate what answer to make.' He had even
disputed with Gladstone in the pages of the *Quarterly* on
the subject of the Gadarene swine.

Wells was one of three in Huxley's class to get a first-class
pass at the end of the year, and he returned in triumph to
spend the summer at Up Park and at Bromley with his
father. After a year under Huxley, he was only too conscious
of the sketchy nature of his general education, and, inspired
by this great teacher, and burning with ambition, he meant
to use the vacation to read up the general background of
the course in zoology which he was to take in his second
year.

Mrs Wells, secretly proud of her clever boy, would have
noticed some alterations in his character not altogether
pleasing. His cleverness made him very quick, and she had
always to be crushing him when he was likely to offend
other people. He weighed nothing at all, he was a bag of
bones, and his suit hung upon him. Very little could be got
out of him about his life in London. The conversation in
the housekeeper's room at Up Park must have seemed intolerably dim when he returned. In fact, he was struggling
out of his class, and the elderly band of retainers sitting
round the housekeeper's table were not such fools as not to
see it and resent it.

He was indeed a different character. If Professor Huxley
had enlarged his mental horizon and lit it with a fascinating glow, his conscious relationship with the world had
equally largely and rapidly expanded. When he came to
London he had had very little contact with life. Just as Up
Park with its wide drawing-room windows opening on to the
Downs that fell away to Portsmouth and the English Channel had first enlarged the scope of his imagination that had
sprouted in the back-yard of the shop at Bromley, so South

Kensington took him on at this next stage in his life and poured into his receptive mind a whole load of new ideas and new contacts with the world. So far, except for books, he had been kept rigidly within the narrow class in which he had been born; even at Up Park he had seen the world from below stairs. At South Kensington there were no social differences; the orderly army of science, marching steadily towards progress, took everyone into its ranks on equal terms.

In the old Gallery of Iron in South Kensington, he soon acquired the reputation of being a wit, and he and a number of other students in his year were drawn together in a little group, lent each other books, took coffee and their four-penny vegetarian lunches together, debated life and its meaning, socialism and the future of man, religion, sex and every other subject that sprang to their quick and lively young minds.

A dramatic contrast existed between the high atmosphere of Huxley's lecture room during the day, and that which obtained on the other side of the park, in Westbourne Grove, where Wells lodged in a house extensively let off in rooms. There was no bathroom, no slavey to carry coals and empty slops, and there was only an outside privy. The smell of unwashed bodies, unemptied slops and heterogeneous cooking, the din of raucous voices raised in quarrel or drunken singing and laughter, the sounds of lovemaking and domestic dispute that came in under the ill-fitting doors, were very different from the atmosphere of lecture rooms or the intelligent ragging of his fellow students. There was the difficulty of studying at night against the background of these suggestive noises in the crowded quarters of Westbourne Grove. The yearnings of adolescence, excited by these clamorous novelties, shook his young frame, but he did not have the money to do anything about them. Prostitutes were beyond his means. He went out with the household on their Saturday-afternoon shopping expeditions and played on the edge of making love to the women, but nobody was much interested in the approaches of an undersized youth too poor even to stand anyone a drink.

A niece of his father, working in the 'costumes' at Dickins & Jones, seeing how he was settled, was appalled, and took him off to 181 Euston Road, where two aunts – one the widow (she had been the abandoned wife) of Uncle Williams, who had since 'passed on', the other her sister – lived by letting rooms. In contrast to the house in West-bourne Grove, this one was enormously and heavily respect-able. It was arranged that Bertie should have a room there, and this is where he lived for the rest of the time he was a student at South Kensington. It was while he was talking to his Aunt Mary on this first visit that a pretty girl entered the room whom Aunt Mary introduced as her daughter, Isabel. She was to become, in a few years' time, his first wife. All his passionate yearnings were to centre upon her in the next two years, but he never introduced her to his fellow students. She was to become by an act of imagination the vessel for all the physical ardour that he carried trembling in his undersized body, but the side that was his brain would not allow him to expose her simple innocence to the teasing fun of his friends.

He had no difficulty at the end of his first year, following his first-class pass under Huxley, in getting his scholarship renewed for a second year. But he came back to South Ken-sington in September a very different character from the earnest youth inspired with the drive to succeed who had looked through the microscopes and handled the dissecting tools in the laboratory in a spirit of dedication on his way to a great scientific career.

He was no scientist-in-the-making, in spite of his first-class pass. He had established a reputation as a wit who was given to daring blasphemy, a literary desperado quick at turning a phrase. In his second year, with the help of one or two others, he started a journal, grandiloquently named *The Science Schools Journal*, which to this larger audience was

what the *Up Park Alarmist* had been to the servants' hall.
It lasted longer than he did, and five years after he had left
the science schools he wrote a retrospective article for it,
recalling its beginnings.

But he was not a natural student, and he was heading for
disaster. He had the vision, but not the capacity for detailed
work; his imagination was creative, not analytical; he had
within him unique powers which he did not even suspect,
but they were not of the kind that would stand him in good
stead in examinations. The guinea-a-week investment the
state was making in this teacher-in-training was being
wasted, but neither he nor the Department of Education
suspected it at this stage. Wells blamed the comparative
failure of his second year on Professor Judd, who did not
illuminate physics and astronomy for him as Professor Huxley had done biology. A change was coming over him
physically and mentally; he was fully aware of it, recognized
the perils into which it might lead him, but was helpless to
withstand it. It seemed to his teachers as though there were
a slackening of concentration, a dispersion of interests – 'not
applying himself', as the report says. But he could not control the play of his imagination, which, with an onslaught
as fierce and irresistible as that with which puberty assails
the growing body, seized and fed on all the circumstances
of his new life. He had just enough of science to imagine its
potentialities; he had just enough of intimacy with his
pretty cousin, stealing kisses, pouring into her ear all his
theories about life, caressing her with his tumultuous
thoughts put into words, to imagine what it would be like to
possess her completely.

And for the first time in his life he had friends just as
clever and witty as himself. At last, after years of dominating the conversation, others could shout him down. The ex-
hilaration of it!

Half a dozen names stand out among the number of his
friends at South Kensington. He had a genius for friendship.
His undernourished body in the well-worn cheap suit and

the celluloid collar and billycock hat of the day, the cockney accent which still marked his speech, combined to
make him a caricature of what a normal healthy young man
should be. He was climbing out of the backyard of Atlas
House and generations of dark, deprived life. He made his
friends laugh, but they loved him too. They were not all
as poor as he was. The one he shared a work-bench with in
the laboratory, A. V. Jennings, was the son of a doctor.
Jennings worried because on Tuesdays (pay-day for the
scholars was Wednesday) his friend would sometimes go
lunchless, so Jennings would sometimes take him out on a
Tuesday, fill him up with steak and beer, and return him
replenished to the laboratory. A. T. Simmons and William
Burton, Elizabeth Healey (to whom he wrote much the best
letters of the next few years, when he was making his effortful rise and moving towards his marriage with Isabel) and
Richard Gregory (the son of a boot-repairer to Clifton College, who had come to the science schools on the same sort
of scholarship) – these were his chief friends.

In due course Sir Richard Gregory was to become editor of
Nature, the great journal of the scientific world, of which
Sir Norman Lockyer, then one of their teachers, was the
first editor. Simmons was to become editor of the *Times
Educational Supplement*. They were all to succeed in some
degree. It was Wells, the most promising one, who failed.

When from such companions he drew applause and
laughter and affection for his wit and the intelligent slant of
his caricatures and clowning, he began to display this side
of his nature, to affect to be the literary dilettante rather
contemptuous of mechanical science. His vanity was to be
his undoing. He ceased to concentrate and, in order to hide
his failure, made himself more active in other matters, the
Debating Society, socialism, literature. He spent days when
he should only have spared hours preparing papers and in-
terventions in the Debating Society. He declared himself an
out-and-out socialist after a number of them had trailed out
to a meeting in the gardens of William Morris's house in

Hammersmith, and had there listened to a thin, pale, tall young Irishman called Bernard Shaw speaking eloquently with a Dublin accent about Fabianism.

One guesses that he listened with a half-attentive ear while his imagination roved over the speaker and the scene. And yet he was sharply attracted at this first encounter by the lucid exposition of Fabianism which fell from the lips of the young Irishman, ten years his senior, the message losing none of its ring of conviction by the fact that it was dispensed with an air of aristocratic hauteur. Five-feet-seven himself, skinny, shabbily dressed, he could glimpse the contrast between himself and this wraith-like creature with the aristocratic face, and could recognize painfully that the contrast was not to his advantage. They had gone to the meeting as a lark, but they announced themselves on their return converted to socialism, and bought red ties and wore them to signify the fact. But it was not a passionate conviction. It was one of those things to which the mind opened in this second year when the need for concentration was greater than ever.

The scholarship was, though not very enthusiastically on the part of the College, renewed for the third year, at the end of which he could expect to take his degree. But it was too late. Literature and love and socialism had captured his interest. There is a touching passage in his autobiography describing the quite valiant effort he made in the last stretch before his finals to make up for lost time. He would go to the Dyce Reading Room intending to work hard for a couple of hours at his notes and texts, and then, as a little treat, allow himself fifteen minutes of looking at the prophetic works of William Blake, or read a chapter or two of Carlyle's *French Revolution*. The books that were the promised diversion lay side by side on the table before him. But long before the two hours were up, granite and gabbro and gneiss became all one to him, and there was little sense in their being different; their twinning capacities when treated with potassium left him cold. There on the table within reach was a folder, say of Blake's tinted designs, and Blake seemed to him to have everything to say and Professor Judd nothing.

The bright hopes with which he had started were coming to nothing, and he was quite conscious of it but helpless to do anything about it. His mind was alive and glowing, all right, but not with the facts necessary to pass his examination. Reading the works of the great English writers was of no use there, and when he left the examination hall he knew that he had failed, and that he was ending the three long hungry years he had spent at the Royal College of Science without a degree.

Suddenly he was aware of the practical considerations of this failure. He had no qualifications, no resources, no self-discipline, no physique, and no longer even a guinea a week. For a moment panic overcame him. Alone in his room in Euston Road, he looked at himself in the glass and cried: 'What is to become of me now?'

In the weeks that followed, Wells must have come as near to despair as he ever did afterwards in his life. Facing, after all his high talk, his bold ideas, his plans for reforming the world, the simple people in Euston Road who knew nothing of his student life except what he told them, and who could not have guessed that failure was on the cards, must have been a bitter enough experience. Even harsher must it have been to send the news to Up Park. Luckily, he did not have to face them. His career as a scientist lay in ruins about him; he could lose no time in finding a job.

His characteristic bounce soon allowed him to recover his spirits. He had made up his mind to become a writer, and what he hoped for was a living-in job as a schoolteacher in some remote country school where his spare time might be devoted to the business of writing books.

He got the job all right, but it was a rude awakening from dreams of sylvan peace and long hours with his thoughts and pen. The school, on the borders of Wales, might have come from the pages of a Victorian novel. The headmaster and his wife both drank, the pupils slept several in a bed, discipline was non-existent, some of the loutish pupils were bigger than Wells and their menacing attitude towards this undersized new master was all too apparent. One Saturday afternoon while refereeing a football match he fell on the muddy field, and one of the bigger boys took advantage of the opportunity to kick him in the back. The result was a ruptured kidney, a chamber-pot full of blood, and he spent his twenty-first birthday, his coming-of-age, in bed in this appalling house.

He was no sooner up than he had a haemorrhage of the lungs, and again he had to take to his bed. Not only his hopes of a scientific career but his health also was now lost, and the little that he was able to write seemed to him turgid and imitative.

He told none of his friends of his illness; it was too much like a further confession of failure. But he could not keep it from his mother, and she petitioned Miss Fetherstonhaugh once again. Thus it was that he was enabled to exchange the dirty bedroom he had to share with two others at the school for a chintz-curtained attic room at Up Park, with a coal fire and the excellent meals that the cook provided for the below-stairs members. He was there for three months, and one can only marvel at the kindness of Miss Fetherston-haugh, who by now was disillusioned about her former maid's capacity to be housekeeper of a great house and had every reason to be disenchanted with the housekeeper's family who were continually in evidence. She probably saved H. G. Wells's life.

When he was better in the spring, he went to stay with his old college friend William Burton, who was now married and living in the Potteries. He was with the Burtons for some months, doing nothing but reading and trying to finish the novel on which he had been labouring for some time, 'Burton victualling manfully', as he wrote to a friend. But he was getting nowhere with his writing.

He said to himself one day, lying in the woods above Burslem, 'I have been dying long enough. I mean to live.' He walked home to the Burtons' and told them that he was leaving for London next day to look for work. He had a five-pound note torn in half which his mother had given him against an emergency, and with that he meant to make his way back into the world. It was midsummer in 1888, and the effortful rise was about to begin.

[4]

Second Assault
on London

WELLS was not yet twenty-two when he made this second descent on London. After the winter of recurring haemorrhages, he was paler and thinner than ever, but he was on fire with the resolve to write and publish something at last, and justify the faith of his friends before death snatched him away. He set about the business of making his five-pound note last while he accomplished his intended masterpiece. He took a room in Theobald's Road in Bloomsbury at four shillings a week, aiming to sustain himself on one meal a day, generally a piece of fish or a few sausages fried over an open gas jet in a little shop opposite, which catered for the homeless and the nearly penniless. Such a repast, taken standing, with a slice of bread and 'scrape' and a cup of tea could be had for tenpence. Thus immured against the loving attentions of his friends, a roof over his head, and the inner man provided for, he set out his writing things and sat down to his task.

But it was too soon. Like all imaginative people, he had plenty of ideas, but these, while good enough for the amusing sketches he had contributed to the *Science Schools Journal,* seemed too youthful in spirit and mocking and ironical in tone to be the right material for the readers of romantic fiction to whom he now wanted to address himself. The moment he became self-conscious, his style stiffened, and although what the story of *Lady Frankland's Companion* * was about we shall never know, the title suggests

* This was the novel, 35,000 words in length, which he had been writing while he was staying with the Burtons in the Potteries, and which he now devoted himself to completing and revising.

that its milieu was polite society. A letter from Wells to Dr Collins, the physician who had been called in to attend him at Up Park, shows the sort of language he felt constrained to use when writing to someone in a class above him. He is reminding the Doctor that 'when you did me the favour of last examining my chest', the Doctor had mentioned the need he would have of a personal introduction to find light part-time work that would give him time to try out his own writing. He had already confided in the Doctor his literary ambitions.

You are acquainted [writes Wells] with men like Harrison [a noted late Victorian editor], Bernard Shaw and the Huxley's who must from the active and extensive nature of their engagements of necessity employ fags to assist in the more onerous and less responsible portion of their duties.

And he ends with a flourish:

I would rather do what I felt is right to be done, and retire soon with some irradiation of human dignity and self-applause than survive for a long period to my own detriment and general impoverishment.

We see from this portentous phraseology what a handicap it was for one who hoped to be a writer to be born into the lower classes in Victorian times. He was perfectly capable of writing natural, flowing English. A letter written to Elizabeth Healey at the same time, in answer to one from her making some gentle criticisms of a poem he had sent her, has none of this stifled, pompous phrasing:

You say my lines are lacking in metre – metres are used for gas, not the outpourings of the human heart. You say my poem has no feet! The humming bird has no feet, the cherubim around the Mater Dolorosa have no feet. The ancients figured the poetic afflatus as a horse *winged* to signify the poet was sparing of his feet.

It was this kind of swift response, the unaccustomed striking imagery he used, and always so ironically, that delighted his friends and convinced them that a literary future lay before him. But it vanished when he sat down to compose something saleable. He was unaware yet of where his true genius lay. It was exposed in the files of the *Science Schools Journal* in such sketches as 'A Tale of the Twentieth Century', written in 1887, only a year earlier, in which his inventive power summons up the idea of a perpetual-motion machine applied to the new London underground railways, and the disaster that eventuates; 'A Vision of the Past', written in the same year, which satirically presents humanity's complacent view of itself as the end and triumph of evolution; and 'The Lay of the Sausage Machine', displaying in nonsense verse the triumph of the Man of Science over the Poet. It was also strikingly evident in the serial story, *The Chronic Argonauts*, which he had contributed to the *Journal*, which is the story of *The Time Machine*, his first great public success, in primitive form.

Wells did not know his power, and the public in 1888 were not ready for this dark quality of despair about the future of the human race. Intelligent young students could joke along these lines – this was their private language with each other – but no paper for the public was ready to publish such daring predictions about the future, and such ironical doubts about the efficacy of all that science had done. He was ahead of his time, but time was catching up with him. The nineties were to show a new questioning moods. Wells had to wait. By then he would have passed through 'a cleansing course of Swift and Sterne', and his personally desperate situation, the need for money if he was not to starve, would force him to write naturally and simply, and his triumph would be immediate. Meanwhile, living on his five-pound note, he endeavoured to imitate the popular novelists of the day, and the result was thirty-five thousand words of *Lady Frankland's Companion*, finally to be consigned to the flames.

Meanwhile, he came near to starvation. It was no life for a man threatened with death from damaged lungs. But par-

ticularly it was no life for one who loved his friends, ached
for human companionship, and thought too much about sex,
the hunger for which was much harder to bear than the
want of stomach-filling food. Only a thin partition divided
his attic room from one shared by a young newly-married
couple, and their physical intimacies drove him nearly distracted. If he had had a friend to talk to, he could have
found relief in laughing at his own deprivation in this regard. With a little more money he could have spent more
time out of his confined quarters. But the five pounds was
vanishing shilling by shilling. He could not ask his mother
for further help. She knew that he was here. She thought he
was looking for work as a teacher, and in an aimless and unfruitful way he was. His adventures with scholastic agencies
are amusingly reflected in Lewisham's search for employment in *Love and Mr Lewisham*. Mrs Wells would have
been shocked if she had known the way he had to live, but
she was distracted with troubles of her own. Joe Wells, who
had fallen and broken his thigh, was no longer able to pick
up the extra needful by playing cricket, and the little shop
of which he had been left in charge when Mrs Wells returned to service had finally collapsed into the bankruptcy
on the edge of which it had teetered for so many years.
Joe and one of the boys, Frank, had moved to a cottage
near Up Park, from where they turned up very frequently at
Up Park for meals. There were unmistakeable indications
that Miss Fetherstonhaugh's indulgence of her housekeeper's hapless family was wearing thin. Knowing all this,
H.G. could not possibly ask her for help. The outlook was
gloomy.

Overcome by loneliness, his resolution not to get in touch
with his friends weakened, and he squandered a precious
halfpenny despatching a card to Jennings, the old friend
of South Kensington days who had occasionally stood him
a blow-out lunch. His quick caricatures, once made only for
the amusement of his family, had delighted the band of

brothers at the Royal College. He adorned this card with one, a sketch of himself wearing a laurel wreath, a manuscript under his arm and sucking a pen, turning away from a sandwich-board which bears the notice: 'Wanted 1,000 men to carry advertisement boards.' Above and below this drawing is the heartfelt cry:

> I am in London seeking work
> But at present finding none.
> I am not in for the Intermediate,
> or any such games.
> > Yours in God
> > H. G. Wells

Jennings, who was lecturing on biology at the Birkbeck Institute in Chancery Lane, was quick to respond helpfully. Perhaps Wells guessed that he would. Jennings confided that he aimed at setting up a coaching establishment of his own and required a collection of wall diagrams. He insisted on commissioning Wells to make them for him. They were to be copied from existing textbooks and high-priced diagrams at the British Museum Reading Room, with a fine disregard of the law of copyright.

Jennings's intervention and kindness came just in time, literally when Wells was down to his last penny. The advance Jennings obliged him with allowed him to satisfy for a little while the protesting gurgles of his stomach, but insufficient diet, shoes that let in the wet, and the feeling that he was getting nowhere and must sooner or later sink back into the world of shops, if only to survive, all combined to reduce his spirits to a low ebb. The strongly sensuous side to his nature loved human contact and affection, and his dedication to being a writer was not proof against his loneliness. He felt it particularly on Sundays, when the Reading Room at the British Museum was closed and he had nothing to do but wander the streets and parks.

His thoughts strayed from time to time to his pretty cousin Isabel, and one Sunday, spruced up for the occasion, he presented himself where she and her aunt now lived on Primrose Hill. His resolution about making his own way weakened, and when Aunt Mary suggested that they join forces, he moved in with them, and lived there until he and Isabel were married in October 1891, when they set up an establishment of their own.

From his arrival in London with the five-pound note to the day of his marriage three years later, existence was a long hard haul, with scarcely an hour to spare from the concentrated task of breadwinning. He managed to get a 'living-out' job at a school in Kilburn, the headmaster of which was an understanding man, J. V. Milne, the father of A. A. Milne, who was a boy in the school at the time.

Living in such close contact with his pretty young cousin, he came to spend nearly all his spare time in her company. Isabel must have been an attractive young girl; her photographs show a beautiful and thoughtful face and a slender graceful body. Throughout their troubled and passionate life together, she is always the passive, uncomplaining one. We see her only through Well's eyes. He makes no secret of his obsession with her, and portrays her as often in ardent as in exasperated terms. We know that this obsession lasted well into his second marriage. There are close friends of Wells who believe that she was the only woman he ever really loved. His own account denies this. He presents her as a simple, naïve girl, frigid or shy in love-making, and totally unaware and unappreciative of the intense struggles a creative artist goes through in producing his work. Perhaps the truth is that Isabel was a calm and happy girl who had no ambition to rise out of her own class. Wells was an urgent, restless man, ambitious as well as being an artist, determined to get on in the world but quite unable to do so without the company of a woman. When she failed to keep up with him, he ran ahead, and – his mother's passion for respectability being strongly marked in him still – he had to justify his questionable conduct by presenting as silly and inadequate someone who was merely placid and contented with her own lot.

In the beginning at any rate she listened gravely to the torrent of talk he always poured out, uncomprehending but uncomplaining, until he himself lost the thread of his discourse in contemplation of her pretty profile and they ended in kisses and struggles and protests about 'going too far'. Unless he won this prize, life would have nothing to offer him. But, persuadable in most matters, Isabel was firm enough about this: that he must be making a certain assured income before she would marry him.

To add to his income, he took on some additional cramming work with a tutorial establishment called the University Tutorial College. This was the London branch of a highly successful correspondence college which had been founded at Cambridge some years before by a gifted man, William Briggs, M.A. The London branch offered lectures and laboratory work to candidates working externally for scientific degrees. As Wells was still teaching at Milne's school, he could do no more for Briggs than mark papers in his spare time, which also had to be given over to working for his own external B.Sc. from London University. With all this he found time somehow to build up a little connection as a reviewer. Richard Gregory was by now assistant to the editor of *Nature* and could turn things his way, and the *Educational Times* was being edited by his friend Walter Low. The cramming establishment ran a journal called *The University Correspondent*, and he became an active contributor to this. The *Science Schools Journal*, which he had founded while still a student, was going strong, and he continued to write for it in these years. All this was giving him practice as a writer, and was even producing a few guineas in the way of income.

Mr Briggs had undertaken to increase Wells's pay according to the class of degree he took extramurally in his finals. In the event he got a first class in zoology, and came first in the second class honours in geology. Mr Briggs was able to add the name of Wells as a tutor (First Class Hons.) to his notepaper, and Wells was remunerated according to promise. He thereupon left Milne's school, and with this additional increment he had cleared the final hurdle set by Isabel; on 31 October 1891 they were married. With his bride, as well as his Aunt Mary, he moved to a little house of his own in Wandsworth. He was climbing steadily up.

But at what a cost, and in a few hours on his wedding night he knew that the effort had not been worth it. He had wanted so ardently to be a writer, and all those dreams of glory had ended in a few reviews and articles, most of them anonymous. He had wanted to be a great lover; he had dreamt for so long of what it would be like to hold in his arms the delicate body of his cousin Isabel, no barrier between them any longer of clothes or chaperoning aunt or fear of the consequences; and all his passionate longing and waiting ended with a crying girl, frightened by his ardour, who lay trembling in his arms. This was not a momentary difficulty. Their temperaments were utterly unsuited to one another, physically as well as mentally.

Lewisham, so faithful a copy of the Wells of these years, looks back regretfully to a scientific career abandoned for love:

Why [Lewisham mused] had he felt that irresistible impulse to seek her out? Why had his imagination spun such a strange web of possibilities about her? He was involved now, foolishly involved. ... All his future was a sacrifice to this transitory ghost of lovemaking in the streets.

He had to put a brave face on this crushing disappointment, but the hard streak that is in every domineering character, and was certainly in his, would not let him stay crushed. He had waited so long for this joy, and it had evaded him. What was the use of being faithful! He took his revenge on his timid wife by entering almost immediately on a secret and enterprising promiscuity which did much to restore his vanity. But it is typical of the narrowness of his upbringing that it does not seem to have occurred to him to leave an intolerable situation. At that stage in his development he would have been shocked at the idea.

Chiefly with Walter Low, whose portrait appears as Ewart in *Tono-Bungay*, and Richard Gregory, who had married a girl who turned out to be a confirmed invalid, he shared the confidences of his unhappy married life. Walking the streets of London, discussing, arguing, building myths, a slight insignificant-looking young man with a wispy moustache, representative of his time and class, he waited for his cue to walk to the front of the stage.

He was literally bursting with ideas. They poured from him in a profusion of talk, half wild and boasting, half urgent and passionate because of the frustration of his marriage. 'We had hardly a judgment in common,' he wrote of Isabel later. 'Throughout our married life, with no sense of personal antagonism, unconsciously, she became the gently firm champion of all that I felt was suppressing me. Conversation between us died away as topic after topic ceased to be a neutral topic.'

He talked all the more copiously outside because he could not talk at home. Aunt Mary was there, looking reproving, or Isabel looking piteous and injured or, what was worse, absent-mindedly indifferent, simply unable to understand why he laboured so long with increasing fury and impatience to get some little bit of written work right; why he had to walk the streets with his friends instead of bringing them home. He knew that she would not understand their private language, their quickness of thought, their teasing fun. He lived in two different worlds, one with his friends on the streets, the other a seething little bundle of energy in his own home, where he corrected papers, prepared tutorials, worked at his manuscripts.

His efforts 'to get some little bit of work to come right' succeeded unexpectedly just at this time. The *Fortnightly Review*, then under Frank Harris's lively editorship, took an essay from him called 'The Rediscovery of the Unique', and gave it a leading place in the July 1891 issue. This was success indeed. Cards went to all his old friends calling upon them to rejoice. To Simmons he wrote: 'Is this the dove with the sprig of bay? Is it poor Pilgrim's first glimpse of the white and shining city? Or a mirage?'

The essay is remarkable not only because it marks Wells's first public appearance as an author, and in a famous journal, but because it clearly shows what was absorbing his attentions all these years before he published his first book. When this piece was published in July 1891 – Harris had accepted it in February – Wells had not even taken his degree, though he was on the point of doing so. He was working immensely hard at his tutorials, and he had only an hour or two at the end of a long day to keep up his correspondence with the small circle of friends he had made at the Royal College, and to walk on a Saturday afternoon or Sunday with Walter Low or Gregory or one of the others, talking, talking. The letters which they exchanged and kept, some of the best of which are quoted by Wells's first biographer, Geoffrey West, show not only the matter of their continuing discourse – immensely serious, constructive, trying to get a grasp of the universe and of their place in it – but the humour and brotherliness with which these poor young men egged each other on. To Simmons, for example:

There are two deadly sins. Vanity and meanness – shun these more than adultery, murder or parricide. Make your brain and body a cunning instrument in the hand of your will, and dissociate your mind from sympathy with the weapon. Disabuse your mind of the illusion of identity, associate yourself with the great humanity of making, teaching, conquering the dead world. Be an enthusiast devoid of sentiment, a dumb prophet like Moses, a materialist in earnest.
This is

> the true gospel of
> faithfully your friend
> H. G. Wells

To Davies:

I am exceedingly glad to hear of your vigorous Atheism. It behoves us, who deny, to make it as clear to the world as we can for the good of ourselves and the world, that we think in this way. I am toiling now to attain the day when it will be possible for me to shake off the last vestiges of convention, and I still hope to see it before I die.

It was in the mood of these letters, sometimes echoing their very phraseology, that 'The Rediscovery of the Unique' was composed. The 'cleansing course' of Swift and Sterne had done much for his literary style – this is recognizably Wellsian – but it is the theme of the essay that catches the eye immediately. The theme is the assertion of the uniqueness of all being, something that was inclined to be lost sight of in the triumph of scientific advance, and with science's tendency towards classification. It is the cry of the artist who believes in the unique mystery of life, and who reminds his readers that it was Darwin's clear assertion of the uniqueness of living things that had changed the whole conception of life. Science is the illuminant that can help us to comprehend the mystery, but science too is limited, for Nature, like individuals, has 'character'; it is at once true to itself and subtly unexpected. Every time it startles us by breaking away from the assumptions we have made about it, we discover in the long run that our assumptions have been premature, and that harmony is still there. Beyond and beyond there is mystery still.

It was a strange mood for a young teacher to express, not yet twenty-five, struggling to take his degree externally, possessed of a very sketchy general education and living in a narrow dull home: that all might *not* be well for us in this wider universe to which science has led us; that surrounding us still there is infinite darkness, where the great tides of the unknown race in a mighty harmony and order, in relation to which man on his earth is as the squirrel in a swinging cage responsive to mightier laws than he can comprehend. In place of that ordered Nature, wound up as by clockwork when time began and ticking steadily on, which had been heaven's first law for our grandfathers, we now have to accept the symbol Goethe, the intellectual father of the nineteenth century, had first put forward, the figure of the universe as a roaring loom with unique threads flying and interweaving, working out a pattern beyond all human interpretations.

The mood of doubt about whither science was leading man was, of course, not peculiar to this band of intelligent young pushful men, with little money to spend on pleasures and diversions, who tramped the streets of London talking about these things. It was customary to accept science as wonder-working; and that its discoveries had improved man's lot was not to be questioned. Looking back from the end of the nineteenth century to its beginnings, everything that science had done appeared beneficent. The contribution to art and letters in that century had been not substantially greater than in previous centuries. But in less than a century science had altered out of all recognition the condition of man, and still this was only a beginning.

They were all young scientists, but the great teacher Huxley had left his imprint on them all, on none more than this one who had failed because his imagination had blazed at the prospect. This inclination to believe that the margins of man's world having been pushed back, the laws of the universe dimly apprehended, old superstitions and faded creeds laid aside, all would now be well, that man was at the threshold of his glory, was something that this article questioned.

For Nature, like man, was unique. No two things are ever identically alike. Classification, science's inescapable method of reaching its conclusions, is subject to marginal error; there is a quiver of idiosyncrasy in every sequence, though this idiosyncrasy may dissolve into a larger symmetry over a longer view. Meanwhile,

Science is a match that man has just got alight. He thought he was in a room – in moments of devotion, a temple – and that his light would be reflected from and display walls inscribed with wonderful secrets and pillars carved with philosophical systems wrought into harmony. It is a curious sensation, now that the preliminary splutter is over and the flame burns up clear, to see his hands lit and just a glimpse of himself and the patch he stands on visible, and around him, in place of all that human comfort and beauty he had anticipated – darkness still.

Here, in this concluding paragraph, was the first flash of the true genius that was in Wells. Four years were to pass before circumstances and necessity combined to produce his first novels, but this was their theme. The quiver of idiosyncrasy in every sequence offered the mythmaker what he wanted, and to connect the Sussex countryside, an inn in Kent, a house in Richmond Park with the wide and windy spaces of the universe, to put man in space, or man from there in our familiar houses and fields, was an enlargement of scope which no writer in English had been able to seize on before. The mythmaker was born. The butterfly was beginning to emerge from the Bromley caterpillar.

But the successful article seemed for a time to have been only the mirage he had feared in writing to Simmons. A second attempt at an article for the *Fortnightly* called 'The Universe Rigid' fell very flat. 'Good Gahd,' said Harris, summoning the young author to an interview, 'what's it all about?' And Wells was unable to explain.

Among his new students at the beginning of the autumn term of 1892–3 at Briggs's London headquarters were two girls. The one that particularly appealed to him was the less handsome of the two, but he found himself very much taken by her steady purposeful gaze and immense seriousness which contrasted so charmingly with her slight delicate body dressed in the heavy mourning clothes worn at that time for the loss of a relative. This was Catherine Amy Robbins, who had lost her father in a railway accident shortly before and who lived with her widowed mother in Putney. She had come to Briggs's for coaching in the

London University B.Sc. degree with the idea of taking up
teaching.

She was a complete contrast to Isabel, both physically and
mentally. There was something fragile and delicate about
her which made a strong appeal to his masculine sexuality.
He himself was slight and undersized. But he was a male;
he was teacher and leader here, he was fiercely dominant in
character, and she was young and shy. He was to discover
that she was not half so fragile as she looked.

The attraction between them developed quickly. In a
class as small as this, shut in the laboratory in those short
winter days in London, the barriers that should have
existed between teacher and young girl student soon broke
down. He got to know her first amongst the whole group.
It was the custom in the late afternoon for the students to
make tea in the laboratory, and to spend a relaxing hour at
the end of a hard day gossiping and fooling. Wells often
joined these parties, unable to resist the chance of exchanging talk and ideas. The discussions would begin seriously
enough with socialism, or the rights of women, or Darwin,
or religion; but, as at South Kensington, the impish mood
that sometimes possessed him would prompt him to lead
them on to wild fancies and speculations, and what had begun seriously would end in laughter and farce. He began to
draw Miss Robbins out at these sessions, and he found that
she had a sense of fun very like his own. The contrast here
with Isabel struck him painfully. He saw that she was intelligent and witty enough to take her full part in the discussions that filled in this pleasant hour. He found himself
watching her with closer and closer attention, moved by the
contrast between her fair hair and her dark brown eyes, the
slenderness of her body, the liveliness of her expression. It
was not long before, in so small a class, he would find himself drawing up a stool beside her in the laboratory as she
worked at an experiment, in order to comment on what
she was doing. Soon his predatory and amatory instincts
were fully aroused and Miss Robbins was responding. Soon

they were meeting outside the laboratory on the pretext of exchanging books, or in tea-shops where they halted for more talk as he accompanied her part of the way home. Soon he was in love with her, and she with him.

This could not be one of those swift illicit passions in which he had been indulging whenever he had the chance. Miss Robbins was just as serious about love as about her work. There was an immense amount of talking that they had to get through. What Wells had to state was his desire for her, and he had to make speeches to her about his reluctance to accept the responsibilities that would flow from translating this desire into action. Words, words, words! What a quantity he had poured out in his lifetime. And so often prompted by sex.

He was twenty-six and married and he thought of himself as a man of the world, but he knew very little about human nature. His range of experience had been shallow, and his masterful instinct to dominate any situation tended to prevent him from understanding what the great tide of humanity flowing round him in this city was really like. He had talked and theorized a lot, but beneath his clever knowingness this fair-haired young man with the wispy moustache as soft as down had a simple heart and an unsophisticated, inexperienced mind. He was no match at all for a determined young woman six years his junior, just emerged from a small middle-class suburban home. Having fallen in love with her teacher, Miss Robbins, with no experience of life but with all the firm directness Ann Veronica was to show, broke through his voluble defence. At first there was no sign of the breach that had been made, but he was pushing himself – or was he being pushed? – towards the brink of matrimonial disaster. How does one know this? By admissions in his autobiography and by placing over it the pattern of *Ann Veronica*, so clearly drawn from this experience. Then by adding to this all that we know of Catherine Amy Robbins, whom after a succession of facetious endearing pet names he was to call Jane, the very

name – purposive, plain, direct, an admission of something –
a little governessy? Jane was to become the moral background of his chequered love-life. But at the time we are now
coming to, she represented adventure, romance, the warm
response to his ardent nature, starved, so he believed, of
what it craved.

But his mother's influence worked strongly on this young
man. 'Keeping up appearances' was implicit in all that he
had learnt at Atlas House and below stairs at Up Park, and,
re-creating the situation in *Ann Veronica*, he recalled in
the self-portrait of Capes, the tutor, facing his Ann Veronica, what must have been his own emotions in meeting the
gentle but persistent onslaught of the determined Miss Robbins. 'I thought we were going to be friends,' Capes was to
say resentfully, charging Ann Veronica with the ruin of
their situation when her confession of love and desire for
him had been wrung from her. And later: 'There's something – something adult about you. I think you are hard.'
Capes had imagined Ann Veronica as fragile, but she had
revealed herself capable of an inflexibility that, aimed at
capturing him, was, whatever else might be said about it,
sensually exciting.

The account H.G. gives, in his introduction to *The Book
of Catherine Wells* and in his autobiography, of his running
off with Miss Robbins is admirably direct and honest. *Ann
Veronica*, when it was written in 1908, was centred on the
love-affair he was then having with Amber Reeves, an
attractive young Cambridge blue-stocking and a member of
the Fabian 'nursery'; and its sequel, *The New Machiavelli*,
was sparked off by his quarrel with the Old Guard in the
Fabian Society, especially Bernard Shaw and the Webbs,
and by the sense of guilt he must have felt at behaviour that
he knew was outrageous but was quite powerless to prevent.
It was his method of defence to shout down the opposition,
and these two novels were very strident shouts at his
opponents. But they were also mercilessly self-revealing, not
only of H.G. but of those who shared his private life. To

the story of Ann Veronica's bid for freedom and the man she wanted in 1908, H.G. attached for all to see the story of Catherine Robbins and himself in 1893.

'I want you as a friend,' Capes persists, almost as if he were disputing something. And: 'What do you want?' he asks bluntly. Ann Veronica replies: 'You!' – that single bold assertion which, coming from a young girl and addressed to a married man, was to send such shock tremors through Edwardian society.

These desperate dialogues, concentrated in a few weeks' time in *Ann Veronica*, occupied in Wells's personal life nearly the whole of the winter of 1892–3. Then the crisis towards which he and Miss Robbins were heading was precipitated by yet another breakdown in his health.

One evening in May 1893 he left the school in Red Lion Square, hurrying for his train at Charing Cross Station. As he ran down the steps to the platform, he coughed sharply, and there came the familiar gush of blood to his mouth and he knew that once again he had started a haemorrhage. In the night a second and much greater haemorrhage occurred. There was no question of a stained handkerchief now; this looked like death itself. He seemed to be finished with life before he had really begun.

It was a night when, fevered and coughing up blood, his spirits should have been at their lowest ebb. But instead of feeling depressed, he confesses that he felt a subdued state of excitement. He believed this to be so because he knew that if he survived this attack he would not be able to go on teaching and that now he would have to depend on his pen for a living. But it is possible that he saw this illness as a solution to his unhappy marriage. He had been afraid to abandon Isabel, but now, with death staring him in the face, he thought only of not letting it cheat him of Catherine.

Miss Robbins – she was still this to him in correspondence – was among the first to whom he wrote when he could sit up in bed.

Your unworthy teacher of biology is still – poor fellow – keeping recumbent, though he knows his ceiling pretty well by this time, but no doubt he is a-healing, and by Saturday he will be, he hopes, put out in the front parlour in the afternoon. But he will be an ill thing to see, lank and unshaven, and with the cares of this world growing up to choke him as he sprouts out of his bed.

Isabel added a postscript which shows that she knew about Miss Robbins as one of his pupils, perhaps had even met her: 'I think he will not be fit to see you before Sunday, but I will write you before then. I.M.W.'

It was June when he got out of bed. On the doctor's advice, though the question of their survival economically was as urgent as his hanging on to life had been for two months before, he drew a cheque for £30, and he and Isabel, taking Aunt Mary with them, went off to rooms in Eastbourne, where, as he wrote to Miss Robbins, he was 'led out daily to an extremely stony beach and there spread out in the sun for three, four or five hours as it might be . . .'

It was while he was lying on the beach here, idly watching an English family settling itself for the morning, that the talents which he had been nursing all these years, which had so entertained his friends and had had free run in the *Up Park Alarmist*, suddenly flowered into an article that he sketched out on the back of some old envelopes he had in his pocket. 'On Staying at the Seaside' was a mere imitation of something similar he was reading at the moment, J. M. Barrie's *When a Man's Single*, but it was like the facetious light things that he had continued to contribute from time to time to the *Science Schools Journal*. He had it typed, and on an impulse sent it to the *Pall Mall Gazette*. Within twenty-four hours the *Pall Mall Gazette* had sent him proofs and begged him to submit more. He had struck gold.

The *Pall Mall Gazette*, which then had a circulation of only about 12,500, had just undergone a change of proprietorship, W. W. Astor, the American millionaire, having bought it and installed as editor Harry Cust, the son of Lord Brownlow, a young man of fashion who knew nothing about editing but had useful connections and very definite tastes. Astor had given Cust unlimited financial backing, and Cust had set out to transform the *Pall Mall Gazette* from a political organ heavy with solemnity into something much more lively and entertaining, something like the *New Statesman* and *Spectator* of our day.

Astor and Cust had shrewdly estimated the instincts and appetites of the middle class emerging out of Victorian respectability and stuffiness, and very conscious of matters like taste, wit, fashion, literary and dramatic entertainment. This new class wanted to be sure of themselves about these things; the *Pall Mall Gazette* gave them the assurance they were seeking. At one end of the social scale at Harmsworths, Newnes and Pearson were offering something to those whose parents had scarcely been able to read. At the other, for the new middle class with more money than their parents had had, with liberal, broader views, here was the *Pall Mall Gazette*, an evening newspaper – few read morning papers in those days – quite different from its rivals, the literary pages of which were especially to become famous.

'On Staying at the Seaside' was exactly what Harry Cust was looking for, and returning to London from his brief convalescence at Eastbourne, Wells lost no time in accepting Cust's invitation to call on him to discuss further work. He had already told Briggs that he would continue to mark papers for him at home, but he had resigned as lecturer and demonstrator, and this invitation set ablaze his hopes.

Cust introduced him to Lewis Hind, who was editing the *Pall Mall Budget*, an offshoot of the *Pall Mall Gazette* which published chiefly fiction. It was Hind who suggested to Wells that he should use his scientific training to provide subjects, and commissioned from him as many 'single-sitting' stories – they were to be published under that name – as he could write at five guineas a time.

It was really like a miracle. He had been trying so long to get started as a writer, and nothing – except the accident of 'The Rediscovery of the Unique' – had worked. And suddenly it did. Suddenly everything that he wrote was not only publishable, but eagerly snapped up by editors. He was smart enough to see why this was. He had aimed too high with articles like 'The Universe Rigid', and had been too slavishly imitative of the romantic writers in *Lady Frankland's Companion*. What everyone apparently wanted was his natural humour and high spirits threaded into sketches and short stories of everyday life. People wanted to read about themselves, and Cust and Hind, with Mr Astor's ample money-bags to support them, were clever enough to recognize that someone who could write wittily, and on occasion frighteningly, about science, in terms which the ordinary man could understand, a Darwinian young man, fluent and highly productive, was just the thing.

The flow of good fortune, having started, continued to augment. Cust gave him some book-reviewing to do for moments when invention might slacken. He proved to have real gifts as a critic, a clear incisive approach, an ability to make a constructive evaluation of a book that was illuminating, stimulating, and as helpful to the author as to the reader.

Cust also introduced him to W. E. Henley, the famous poet and an experienced editor himself, who was then editing the *National Observer*. Henley was also fascinated by the young man's scientific background, and was interested when Wells told him of *The Chronic Argonauts*, which he had written for the *Science Schools Journal*. Henley read it, saw its possibilities, and invited him to rewrite it as a serial in six parts for the *National Observer*; he suggested the title of *The Time Traveller*, and promised to try to find a publisher for it. Thus began Wells's career as an author of books. To Cust, Hind and Henley he owed his start, but sooner or later he would have hit on the secret that was to bring him unique success. The serious haemorrhage had hastened the start. What had looked like the threat of death had in fact been the signal for the start of a new life.

In August, two months after this first lucky encounter, he was writing from 'the melancholy oven' of London to Miss Robbins, who was on holiday, congratulating her on the results of her examinations, advising her about her future studies, and saying that he would like 'to deal with this matter of the future at a greater length than is possible in a letter'. He sent his wife's sincerest congratulations on her success, and added: 'They have let me sign an article in *The Pall Mall Gazette* [his first contributions, like the majority, had been printed without author's name] and signed articles in dailies is a distinct advance for a poor wretch like me.'

What happened between then and the end of the year? Now that he had given up teaching, he was no longer seeing Miss Robbins daily; he was alone writing at home all day in Sutton, for Isabel went to work at a photographer's shop in Regent Street to augment their income, and his mind must have dwelt a lot on the attractive young student. They must have met from time to time, and not always surreptitiously, for, writing to his mother on 1 December to send a little cheque, he included as news the fact that:

I and Isabel are going off this afternoon to stop with Mrs Robbins at Putney until Monday – you will remember Miss Robbins who came to tea one Sunday, and we are going to a concert tonight with them.

It was a curious visit to make. Week-ending was not a fashion in the circle in which the Wellses and the Robbinses moved, and a visit of such duration from houses only a few miles apart was certainly unusual. It was something that neither Isabel nor Mrs Robbins would have arranged, and it suggests that H.G. and Jane were taking risks to be together that were bound eventually to lead to disaster. Something must have happened on this occasion to arouse Isabel's

jealousy, for they returned to Sutton on Monday with H.G.
determined to leave his wife and run off with the girl who had
been his student. A confidant in these plans was Richard
Gregory. Together, H.G. and 'Rags' walked over the Ban-
stead Downs, where Rags was then living in acute unhappiness with his invalid wife, while H.G. unfolded his plans.
They had come up the same way from equally humble back-
grounds, vigorously fought for survival, and each had begun to make his mark. Each of them had burdened himself
with an unsatisfactory wife, and they were lusty ambitious
young men, thirsting for all that life could offer them.
Gregory must have longed for the same chance of riddance
his ruthless young friend was taking, but that was not in
his nature.

A day came early in January when the trunk stood roped
in the hall of the small house, waiting for the station fly.
How often had he set off on new changes of life with his
luggage. Here he was going again. Isabel, after the one outburst, had been silent, perhaps even a little relieved. He
must have been a difficult husband for such a placid-natured
girl. She simply did not understand what he was up to with
his writing, and, like H.G.'s mother, thought that steadiness
was all.

He had taken rooms in Mornington Road for himself and
Catherine Robbins, and in the Robbins home in Putney, as
in the Wells one in Sutton, the moment of departure had
almost come. Isabel was grim and silent, but Mrs Robbins
was loud and tearful in grief, and it must have taken extreme resolution for this young girl to abandon her mother.
But resolution was a quality in which she was never lacking
then or till the end was reached thirty-three years later,
when there was wrung from him the uttermost tribute:
'She stuck to me so well that in the end I stuck to myself.'

First Fame

THE neighbourhood in which they started their life together, Mornington Place, and the Terrace, Crescent and Road of the same name which adjoin it, lies in a narrow quadrilateral north of Euston Road and eastwards of Regent's Park, like a flower head on the long stalk of Tottenham Court Road. Today the houses in this area have a neglected air, the paint is flaking on their narrow stone fronts, their windows and steps are unwashed, and the railings enclosing the small paved gardens in front are rusty with neglect. The railway lines from Euston run parallel with the Morningtons, and the inhabitants, railway workers mostly, are foreign. The social revolution has swept the Londoners of Wells's time further afield.

But when H.G. and Jane came there in January 1894, the district was typical of lower-middle-class London: bright, crowded, noisy, gas-lit at night, hazy with smoke by day, and with its inhabitants spending a lot of their time on the streets. The houses were well kept, most of them being divided into lodgings. The one in which the young lovers finally settled was at 12 Mornington Road and was run by a retired housemaid from the household of the Duke of Fife. It was a lively, stimulating place for runaway young lovers from the outer suburbs, and it was the very heart of London. A good idea of its atmosphere at that time can be got from *Tono-Bungay*, for it was in Tottenham Court Road that Edward Ponderevo managed his pharmacy, and in such a street as one of the Morningtons that he kept his home.

Wells was enormously busy. Cust, Hind and Henley saw to that. Quite apart from the gratification of being a writer whose work was in constant demand, there was desperate

need at this time for the guineas he could earn from journalism. He still had Isabel to support. He also had to be the
main support of his parents, for Mrs Wells had been dismissed suddenly from Up Park in the high-handed Victorian
fashion. The parents were now entirely dependent on their
three sons, the eldest of whom slaved away as a draper's
clerk, while the second was an itinerant vendor whose income was uncertain.

Yet in this desperate situation Wells was blissfully happy,
and from early morning until late at night fiercely at work.
Articles, short stories, sketches and book reviews poured
from him in a constant stream and found a ready market
in the capacious *Pall Mall Gazette* and its sister paper, the
Pall Mall Budget, in the *Saturday Review*, now being edited
by Frank Harris, and in *Nature;* even in the *Yellow Book
Magazine.* He had no trouble thinking of plots for the short
stories. He had at hand a green file-box full of sketches he
had written for the *Science Schools Journal*, or had attempted over the last few years and had laid aside unsatisfied.
Now that he had found the recipe, they needed only to be
polished and shaped.

If invention failed momentarily, then, emerging from the
pair of rooms, he and Jane could comb London for article
material. The great city in all its infinite variety was spread
around them; the green glades of Regent's Park a minute or
two away in one direction; running northwards, Hampstead
Road, then very much a place of character, winding its long
way uphill to the Highgate Heights; southwards, Tottenham Court Road merging into Charing Cross Road, which
then fell away towards the river. There it was, this great
furnace of human life, with all its bustle, noise, excitement,
its ancient buildings, its teeming, pushing, shouting crowds
– all of it brought under his observant eye, just as the
microscope at South Kensington had first brought specimens
into his view. All this happened to him at the very moment
when he had acquired the skill to render it in the form of
art. The creative excitement he was experiencing gave him

increasing confidence in his writing powers, and the feeling of elation at having escaped from an unsatisfying marriage buoyed him up with hope in spite of his financial burdens.

On those walks in search of material, Jane was the ideal companion. Her intelligent and amusing comments, in such delightful contrast to Isabel's placid receptiveness, stimulated his own powers of observation, his natural humour and feeling for character. Everything was proving nearly perfect. But these little Victorian figures from Putney and Wandsworth who had felt themselves to be doing what Shelley and Mary had done, defied the world and fled together to happiness, found in their Mornington Road eyrie a check to the high passion that should go along with such a desperate runaway match. For H.G. it was a second disappointment. Isabel had been silly, and her unresponsiveness had been largely due, he felt, to lack of intelligence. With his new love it was no question of that. Few women could have met his expectations. Sex had for so long dominated his imagination while he dreamt of what the perfection of bodily response could mean between two people whose minds were attuned to one another, that when the experience fell short of his dreams it was a blow to him.

All this he does not hesitate to reveal in the dissection he makes of himself and of their relationship in his autobiography. Venus Urania, that goddess of whom he had dreamt ever since his first sight as a boy of the semi-draped marbled statues of goddesses in museums, the smooth contours of whose bodies had excited his sensual imaginings at the same time that their serene faces promised him understanding and wisdom – this vision of perfect intellectual companionship with perfect physical response for which he was always searching evaded him still in the fragile, earnest, affectionate little figure who had given up everything to fly with him, was timidly anxious to join his transports – not shocked by them as Isabel had been. Yet did not have – who could have done? – his inbuilt energy, his fiery imagination, his temperament to sustain the flight. Who had instead a frailty, and a trust in his greater strength and wisdom which called forth a protective instinct in him. He was the father-figure who had been missing from her life. She gave him her adoration, unaware to begin with that she was not giving him the passionate response his ardour demanded.

Then there was her family, who were enough to drive a chap mad. Large male cousins, of whose existence he had been unaware, manifested themselves noisily and aggressively at the pair of rooms in Mornington Place. They came to demand restitution. They found themselves met by a young man who showed not the slightest sense of shame, who was volubly argumentative and rudely dismissive, and who, when it was suggested that at least he should wait until his divorce was through and could marry her, responded with the curt announcement that they had no intention of ever marrying as they did not believe in the institution.

These flaws apart, there was much else to be prized – an intimate companionship he had never known before with a woman, and all the day and night free to write. Night after night, enclosed in their little apartment, they worked, H.G., like Lewisham, drawn up to his table under the light, while Jane with her textbooks spread about on the floor went on with her studies for her B.Sc., the finals of which she hoped to take that summer.

Something of what London was like in those days comes back as one reads his description of the second-floor pair of rooms, separated by a folding door. The bedroom had a double bed, a chest of drawers, and a tin bath, for which water had to be brought up from below, and here they accomplished their morning ablutions. Then, he in trousers over his nightshirt, she in a wrapper, they would go through the folding doors to the front room already warmed by a blazing coal fire, which had been lit by a slavey in the dawn, and to the morning post, which had been brought up with the coals. After breakfast they would each settle to work. The afternoon was given over to walks; then back through the winter dusk to Mornington Road and tea before the fire, to more work until supper was brought up, then still more work until they retired to the back room, where, with the house shaking from trains roaring by, they fell asleep in that large double bed.

Of course it was not all unadulterated bliss. As Lewisham was to say, 'a chap can't always be making love'. His mother was shocked at the irregularity of the situation and wrote to say so, though she was inclined to blame Isabel for not 'holding' him. Then he was made edgy by the very hours he was working.

What he wanted was to write books, not articles, and much of the time not devoted to his journalistic work he spent calling on publishers or writing to them. He sent collections of his articles or stories to one and then another, sometimes to several simultaneously. Two publishers took the very slight risk involved in investing in such a highly productive journalist, Methuen agreeing to pay £10 for *The Stolen Bacillus*, a selection of his stories, and John Lane agreeing to issue *Select Conversations with an Uncle*, chosen from the sketches he had been contributing to the *Pall Mall Gazette* based on the character of the wicked and now deceased Uncle Williams. Mr Dent, a third publisher, renowned neither for his generosity nor for his gambling instincts, on being offered the first sixty pages of *The Wonderful Visit* and an outline of the rest, agreed to pay an advance of £75 for the book when completed. But from others he got only grudging expressions of the 'would be interested to see anything substantial that Mr Wells might write' variety.

It was from W. E. Henley, who had published in the *National Observer* the 'Time Traveller' articles built up from *The Chronic Argonauts* originally written for the *Science Schools Journal* in three parts, that he got in the early summer the first really sizeable commission which would make him into a novelist. Henley was to take over the

editorship of a new paper, the *New Review*, in the coming
January, and he was looking about for material. He suggested to Wells that he should rewrite these articles yet
again, turning them this time into a novel. He offered Wells
100 guineas for the serial rights, and he undertook to try to
get him book publication. On Henley's advice, Heinemann
made a contract, with an advance of £50. This was something more substantial than the insignificant sums offered
for the reprinted articles and stories, and there was less
work involved than in finishing *The Wonderful Visit*. His
doctor had been recommending a holiday. Mrs Robbins
had let her house in Putney, having accepted the appalling
situation that her daughter had a lover and would not be
returning, and now rather tearfully adhered to them. In
August all three of them departed from Charing Cross
station by train for Tusculum Villa, Sevenoaks, where they
had taken rooms for a fortnight.

In those two weeks Wells rewrote the 'Time Traveller'
articles as *The Time Machine*, an amazing feat for a man,
physically far from strong, who was supposed to be on holiday. There was more to it than revision, for though *The
Time Machine* was still basically the old *Chronic Argonauts*, it was almost completely rewritten, and this time
extensively enlarged.* In the last version the story had
stopped short at the Professor's escape from the Morlocks,
but on Henley's suggestion, Wells made the Professor 'cycle
on' in time instead of returning to his own. Working under
pressure, working in emotional circumstances that were dis-
tracting, he wrote this – the most memorable part of a
brilliant book – in those two weeks.

Besides containing some of Wells's finest writing – the

* Geoffrey West, Wells's first biographer, provides in a fascinating
appendix to *H. G. Wells: A Sketch for a Portrait* an account of the
growth of *The Time Machine* from its first appearance as *The Chronic
Argonauts* in three parts in the *Science Schools Journal* in 1888 to its
final appearance in 1895. Altogether it was rewritten six times and
printed in various forms four times, undergoing quite extreme revision each time.

picture of the dying world, for example – the end of *The Time Machine* is important because it provides evidence of the kind of writer he was to become. Allegorically presented as yet, but pointed and emphatic, is the message that the future may not be as hopeful as late Victorian complacency assumed. The pleasant little humans, the Eloi, our distant posterity, whom the Professor discovers on alighting in time in the year 802701, the whole of whose days seem to be spent in amorous love-play, and who live communally, appear to do no work of any sort. With typical nineteenth-century anxiety to get at the economic facts, the Professor finds the Eloi are served by an underground race, the Morlocks, of whom – with good reason, as it ultimately appears – the Eloi move in fear.

'Gradually [the Professor tells his listeners in Richmond on his return] the truth dawned on me: that Man had not remained one Species, but had differentiated into two distinct animals: that my graceful children of the Upper-world were not the sole descendant of our generation, but that this bleached, obscene, nocturnal Thing which had flashed before me, was also heir to all the ages.'

The Professor's escape with his machine, after a battle with the Morlocks, lifts the narrative to a high pitch of suspense and excitement. Plunging forward into futurity, he comes down at last thirty million years hence, when the sun is dying and the life of the old earth is ebbing away. The picture is unforgettable. Even today one feels a sense of shock which comes from a conviction of its probability. In the epilogue, the Professor having again disappeared on his machine, the narrator is left wondering where he may be now, wandering perhaps by the lonely saline lakes of the Triassic Age, or gone into some nearer age of the future, 'in which, maybe, the riddles of our time have been answered, and its wearisome problems solved'. The characteristic note of pessimism which was to mark all Wells's finest imaginative writing is plainly seen in this epilogue.

He, I know [the narrator recalls], – for the question had been discussed among us long before the Time machine was made – thought but cheerlessly of the Advancement of Mankind, and saw in the growing pile of civilization only a foolish heaping that must inevitably fall back upon and destroy its makers in the end. If that is so, it remains for us to live as though it were not so.

The determination to live as though it were not so was to animate Wells's whole career as a writer.

Mrs Robbins, disapproving and ostentatiously unresponsive to her daughter's lover's badinage, was very much in his way on this holiday, even when she retired to her own room in dudgeon. Their landlady proved to be a trial. Prying into their belongings when they were out, she discovered the divorce papers from Isabel's solicitors which had been served on Wells just before they left London, learned that these two were not married, and was outraged. She did not dare attack her lodger openly, but she gossiped very audibly to her neighbours over the fence about the young pair who had taken advantage of her innocence, and the author records that he wrote the last manuscript pages of his first book on a hot August night at an open window, with the moths dashing themselves against the lamp, and the landlady in the garden below going on over the garden fence to her neighbour about people's morals and the wicked way in which she had been imposed upon. Wells, lost in his creative effort, could shut his mind against these disturbances, but Jane grew pale and depressed. They were all glad enough to return to town.

He could not afford to wait to see what kind of reception *The Time Machine* was to have. Full of energy and unleashed creative power, he threw himself upon his return to Mornington Road into completing *The Wonderful Visit*, which Mr Dent had commissioned. He wrote this book in six weeks of intensive work, enjoying every moment of it.

The Wonderful Visit is an essay in the ironical vein, a

polished and extended example of the kind of sketch with which he had pleased his fellow students in the *Science Schools Journal*, and which were now delighting the public who read the *Pall Mall Gazette*. The germ of the book had, in fact, appeared in an essay in the *Pall Mall Gazette* which took its point from Ruskin's remark that if an angel were to appear on earth, somebody would be sure to shoot it. In *The Time Machine* the Professor had gone off to see what life was like in the Fourth Dimension. In *The Wonderful Visit* the visitor comes from outside this world to see how we do here. An angel, pausing for a moment in contemplation of the world into which he has been hurled, is winged by an ornithological-specimen-hunting Vicar out with his gun, who has never seen such a large white bird and hopes to attain immortality in Saunders's *British Birds* with an account of his discovery. Science is employed only to set the score, like a preliminary roll of drums as the curtain goes up. On the night of the angel's arrival, disturbances in the upper atmosphere, particularly the colour of the sky, and mysterious noises in the heavens have been widely noted. These phenomena have prompted some learned and heavily explanatory letters to *Nature*. They have also disturbed the sleep of the villagers of Siddermorton, where the angel, alighting from his journey, touched down upon earth.

What makes *The Wonderful Visit* such a delightful book is its delicately ironical study of social life in the English countryside in the late nineteenth century. Thirty years later Wells explained: 'I tried to suggest to people the bitterness, the narrow horizon of their ordinary lives by bringing into sharp contrast with typical characters a being who is free from ordinary human limitations.' What he is also expressing is the resentment of an underprivileged boy brought up as the housekeeper's son in the great country house where Miss Fetherstonhaugh was mistress and the agent was Sir Edward King, and where there were places where you were allowed to go and others to which access was forbidden on pain of instant chastisement. The book is a satire on the squirearchy, still as dominating in the English countryside as it had been in the eighteenth century, Lady Hammerglow patronizing the angel, Sir John Gotch warning him off for trespassing and wanting to run him out of the village as a troublemaker, the village people militant against a stranger who cannot be explained or identified, the village doctor interested only in the angel's deformed shoulder-blades and expressing much medical abracadabra as he runs his hands scientifically over bones that supported wings, and the Vicar's troubled thoughts as his eyes are opened to the emptiness of the religious services he performs, all remind one that the setting is South Harting, while Miss Fetherstonhaugh, Sir Edward King, Dr Collins and the young curate at Up Park – the latter two the only ones other than servants and villagers with whom the tubercular young man who had been taught by Huxley could have any conversation – are being ironically depicted against a background which a resentful, observant youth had known in his most frustrated years.

This quickly finished and delivered to Mr Dent, he threw himself into completing *The Island of Dr Moreau*, a theme he had already sketched out but for which he had not yet found a publisher in advance. This book was very close to his heart. In it he was openly expressing for the first time what had only been implied in his first two books – open doubts about all the abundant benefits of science for a humanity which was not yet prepared for them. It was this dark shadow of a question which had given particular interest to his 'Rediscovery of the Unique' article in the *Fortnightly*. In *The Time Machine* there had been unforgettable pictures of the world running down to a stop, but the scene was generalized and remote in time. Here, in a book written only a few months later, we see in Dr Moreau a perverted scientist using his surgical skill to turn animals into the semblance of human beings. The delineation in *The Time Machine* of the baser of our remote descendants preying cannibalistically upon one another, and, further on in time, our familiar world, with all human life gone, dying in a desolation of cold and darkness, had been spine-chilling. But this was hundreds of centuries hence, and although the lesson was pointed as being an extension to ultimate barbarity of the contemporary division between capital and labour, such a remote degeneration of our species and our world aroused only fascinated interest, not alarm. This was evolution, perhaps, but the ultimate curve was lost in a futurity in which we felt no emotional part.

But Dr Moreau was here and now, and the evolutionary theory was still a very sore subject in contemporary terms with those who were ready to accept the gifts of science but unwilling to admit that its fundamental discoveries embraced human life and its origins as well as the world we lived in. Wells was now saying in terms which anybody could understand, in a novel open to anyone who could read what might be talked of in the laboratory but not in the drawing-room: that with a skill made possible by science – in this case, surgery – man could now parody creation. The effect was not spine-chilling so much as blood-curdling. Our remote descendants eating one another's flesh was nothing like so repulsive as animals here and now being turned into a travesty of human beings. Darwin's irrefutable proof of the origin of human existence could not be denied, but men generally were not yet ready to renounce the myth of a divine origin of the human spirit. Moreau's fiendish work of implanting human traits in animal forms seemed worse still because such traits were shown as ineradicable. When Moreau has been killed by an animal maddened by pain, and Pendrick is left alone on the island, he is forced to watch these animals, which have been made nearly human, reverting to something approximating their animal state: but retaining shreds of humanity.

Of course these creatures did not decline into such beasts as the reader has seen in zoological gardens – into ordinary bears, wolves, tigers, oxen, swine, and apes. There was still something strange about each; in each Moreau had blended this animal with that; one perhaps was ursine chiefly, another feline chiefly, another bovine chiefly, but each was tainted with other creatures – a kind of generalized animalism appeared through the specific dispositions. And the dwindling shreds of the humanity still startled me every now and then, a momentary recrudescence of speech perhaps, an unexpected dexterity of the fore-feet, a pitiful attempt to walk erect.

But worse still is the reverse implication. When Pendrick finally escapes and returns to London after his horrifying experiences, he cannot help seeing in the faces of the people he passes on the streets the likeness of this or that animal – 'Beast people, animals half-wrought into the outward image of human souls, . . . who would presently begin to revert, to show first this bestial mark and that.'

Wells tells us that the idea for the story was given to him by a case reported in the newspapers of the downfall of a man of science. It is more likely that he had begun the book two years before when Thomas Huxley, his hero, had given the Romanes Lecture at Oxford under the title *Evolution and Ethics*. In the lecture Huxley had made the point with which his biology students like Wells would have been familiar, that the cosmic process as evidenced in evolution is 'full of wonder, full of beauty, full of pain', for suffering, to use Huxley's phrase, 'is the badge of all the tribe of sentient things, attaining to its highest level in man'. Ethical progress can be made, not by imitating the cosmic process, still less in running away from it, but in combating it. Ethics demanded man's constant allegiance.

One sees why a character like Moreau might suddenly have sprung to Wells's creative mind as he read these dicta to which he had listened with such awe in his first year as a student. Moreau defends himself by saying, 'The study of nature makes man at last as remorseless as nature.' The dramatic promise in such a figure made an instant appeal to his imagination. Already at the age of twenty-nine the beginnings of a religion which might be called Wellsianity were taking vague shape in his mind, with science as its god, evolution its history, nature – including man – its congregation. Victorian rectitude, with most of the literary critics on guard, may have been shocked by the impiety of Moreau's actions, and the reviews expressed general alarm, but the upthrusting generation were excited and moved by Pendrick's story, sharing the drama in which he was involved on the island, and his strange illusions about the human faces he sees when he returns to the streets of London. At first Wells had not been able to find a publisher to take it. When Heinemann, emboldened by the reception his first books were getting, issued it a year after he had finished it, the sales did not match those of his two earlier novels, but Wells's reputation with the reading public as a writer of the unexpected and the shocking grew mightily.

The character of the author – it was always to be so – sticks out through everything that he writes. He was no scientist, but Darwin's and Wallace's patient explanation of the evolution of the species had caught at his imagination as something overwhelmingly dramatic. His storyteller's art rose instinctively to the majesty of the subject.

While the fate of *The Island of Dr Moreau* was still in suspense, four books – *The Time Machine, The Stolen Bacillus, The Wonderful Visit* and *Select Conversations with an Uncle* – by an author who had published only textbooks before, all came out within a few months in the late summer and autumn of 1895. *The Time Machine* and *The Wonderful Visit* both received striking notices. Critics with the weight of Edmund Gosse, Arthur Waugh and Robertson Nicholl reviewed them in highly favourable terms, and they were noticed at length in quality papers like the *Sunday Times* and the *Observer* which in those days customarily ignored novels unless they were by master hands like those of Henry James, Mrs Humphry Ward or Thomas Hardy. *The Time Machine* sold 60,000 copies before Christmas, and *The Wonderful Visit* was listed among the best-selling novels of the Christmas season. The volumes of stories and sketches received few notices, but those they did attract were encouraging, and with Mr Wells being loudly hailed as a genius by W. T. Stead, those publishers who had earlier been reluctant to offer contracts now fell over themselves in their anxiety to sign up his future work. Methuen offered to triple the advance and double the royalty for a second volume of stories, and Wells was able to write to his mother with justified pride: 'I have had letters from four publishers asking for my next book. It's rather pleasant to find oneself something in the world after all the years of trying and disappointment.'

Success had come just in time. For suddenly and, as always, without warning Fleet Street suffered one of its periodic hangovers from having taken on more material than it could digest, and hard times came for writers employed at space rates. But Wells was now well in with the *Pall Mall Gazette*. They suggested that he should review new plays for the paper, and he invested in his first evening suit and started spending his evenings at the theatre. It was in the course of these duties that he met and got to know Bernard Shaw, who was then doing the plays for Frank Harris's *Saturday Review*, in which Wells had occasionally been invited to do the novels. They both lived in North London, and frequently walked back there together after the theatre. Shaw had written five novels without finding a publisher for any of them, and had now turned his attention to writing plays. *Arms and the Man* had been produced in the previous year, but the others were awaiting production. This was the beginning of a wary friendship between absolute opposites who nevertheless respected each other's qualities, and who were both hungry for fame.

But Wells's career as a dramatic critic was brief. It was not long before the unaccustomed late hours and the cold wet winter nights, not enough to eat and too far to walk, combined to lay him out. First came a heavy cold, then the usual persistent racking cough, followed by the inevitable blood in the sputum. There was nothing for it but to put aside the dress suit, take to the country in earnest, and give all his time to authorship. It was almost a repetition of the events following the haemorrhage at Charing Cross Station, but this time Jane was in charge. With the capital raised from a mortgage on Mrs Robbins's Putney house, she took and furnished a small semi-detached villa in Woking in Surrey. Probably she chose the neighbourhood because W. E. Henley lived there.

Existence can be hard for a frail, testy genius, weighing next to nothing and resigned to the idea of an early death, conscious that he has not yet half begun to live. At every meal a sighing mother-in-law, whose widow's mite had purchased this freedom to survive a little longer in country air, whose resolute daughter kept the family peace, organized all this, and backed up with her mother's money her own faith in this cross little invalid with the bursting ambition and the hacking cough. It says a lot for Jane's resolute courage that she should have stood by him and seen him through.

Only at one point did he yield on the matter of principle. They celebrated the publication of *The Time Machine* by coming up to London in October to stay for a few weeks in their old rooms in Mornington Road, and they took the opportunity to get married. The divorce had gone through, and there was no longer any reason to put up with the disadvantages of free love, contributed by censorious landladies, impertinent servants, gossiping voices and the rest, which detracted from the high resolution and the freedom from bonds that were supposed to be the rewards of this unfettered state. This surrender to convention was greatly to the relief of Mrs Robbins and Mrs Sarah Wells, and even H.G. himself began to find consolations in respectability and success.

He did not need the sudden storm of applause that greeted *The Time Machine, The Wonderful Visit* and *The Invisible Man* to tell him that he was on to something important. His early self-confidence is amazing, considering how desperate his need for money was, and how long it had

taken him to hit the bull's eye. Here he was, at the beginning of his career, making daring predictions, attacking
church and squire, questioning man's complacent claims to
superiority in the world, knowing what this new public
would stand without flinching, and breaking daring new
ground with every book.

His singular success did not mean that everybody was
suddenly interested in science. The fundamental principles
of science, those discoveries which had led step to step from
Newton to Darwin, were then as much beyond the ordinary
novel-reader's comprehension and interest as Einstein's
Theory of Relativity has been to the ordinary man in our
time. But there was widespread interest in its marvels, and
curiosity about where it was all going to lead. What was
accepted without question was that science had worked
wonders, and it was assumed that it was going to go on
doing so, with material benefit to everybody. It had altered
the conditions and even the length of life. It was part of the
change that was in the air of the time, like the spread of
socialism, the weakening grip of established religion, the
emancipation of women, the rise of democracy. Wells made
science explicit for the ordinary man, and he did it with a
directness and a colloquial ease of style that made him
seem as fresh and modern as his subject. He had come on
the scene when the last of the great Victorian writers were
fading away. Their places were being taken by some very
remarkable new writers – Robert Louis Stevenson, Kipling,
Barrie, Conrad, Conan Doyle – who were providing plenty
of excitement for those who wanted that from their
reading.

What was it that Wells offered that none of these other
writers did? Creeps and spells and horrors? There was
something more than the scientific thriller-writer's tricks in
these early books and in *The Invisible Man*, *The War of the
Worlds* and *The First Men in the Moon*, which he completed in the Woking house. There was the steady reminder
that science is not always beneficent, that outside the little

envelope of our human life a great ordered universe swings through dimensions unimaginable to our minds, that outside the flickering glow by which science has enabled us to see something of its wonders, is ... 'darkness still'.

It was now 1897, the year of the great Jubilee, the high celebration of the Age of Victoria. But this was a memorial service, not the funeral pyre of a distinct age. The Victorian Age had really expired when the Prince Consort passed away and Darwin made his famous utterance and Marx mounted his attack on the social order in *Das Kapital*. That in 1897 Richard Gregory, the son of the boot-repairer at Clifton College, should have become the assistant to Sir Norman Lockyer, the editor of *Nature*, and that his friend and companion H.G., from his semi-detached villa in Woking, should be stirring into excitement with his myths the whole of a generation, were indications of a fundamental change of outlook. The new age of the common man had dawned in the Seventies and Eighties when Wells was a boy. Wells's singular feat was to be the total capture of this audience. Playing first on its fears and curiosities, he was to lead it on to examine its own shortcomings, and then attempt to elevate its mind and spirit to a higher level. The continuing struggle of man to adapt himself to his environment had taken on in this later scientific age the elements of a tragic drama. His storyteller's art rose instinctively to the challenge, and his success was fabulous. Unconsciously, he himself was the epitome of the common man.

By the end of 1896 the Wellses were prosperous enough to contemplate a move from the semi-detached villa facing the railway lines in Woking to a larger house with quite an extensive garden, where they could entertain, and where H.G. could have a study of his own instead of working on the dining-room table. Worcester Park, nearer London, was still quite rural at that time. It was probably because of their widening social interests that they moved to a centre where many contributors to the *Pall Mall Gazette* happened to be living. By any measure, he was now a success. His income had increased from £250 in 1894, the year before his first books appeared, nearly all of it earned from short stories and journalism, to well over £1500 in 1897, most of it earned from books. Money was becoming increasingly important to him, not for what it could buy – he had no extravagant tastes – but as a symbol of ground gained in the struggle for recognition as an author. His health was still a considerable handicap, and the oppressive sense of an early death hanging over him still made the struggle intense.

One other sense of strain also pressed on him painfully from time to time, shadowing an otherwise contented existence. He had recurrences of his vagrant mood – a longing to escape from what he called 'domestic claustrophobia', which came on him from time to time, arising, so he thought, from a not fully satisfied sex-life – which he was quite powerless to resist. He had the predatory urge of the highly sexed person, incapable of withstanding a blind attraction, and the attempts to control it were nearly always doomed to failure. Isabel was too innocent, perhaps too incurious, to be aware of being deceived. But Jane was different. Besides, Jane did not go out to work every day; she was always there. He respected her enormously, a respect and admiration for standing by him which amounted in the end to petulant, irascible, but deep affection. But always beyond was the unplumbed possibility, always behind was something that might have been missed, that should be turned back for. When these moods overcame him, and they did more frequently as the Wellses' lives turned outwards to meet others, he must have been very difficult to live with.

In 1898 a crisis of this sort seems to have occurred just when, both of them shy but enthusiastic and very likeable, they were making their first ventures into society, and it was probably stimulated by his contact with George Gissing, whom he first met at a dinner of the Omar Khayyam

Club in 1897. They sat next to one another, and Wells was immediately attracted by Gissing's good looks and air of distinction. He had read his books, and he knew something of Gissing's romantic story. No doubt Gissing was equally attracted by Wells's ebullience, his vivid sense of humour (which may well have been unrestrained in that singularly unrestrained society), and envious also perhaps of that aura of success beginning to accumulate about Wells, which had persistently avoided him. He was ten years Wells's senior, had been writing for much longer, was admired by everyone but read by few. Wells, with his ardent aptitude for sex, may well have envied Gissing his romantic appearance, as well as been excited by what he would certainly have known of Gissing's dramatic history as a lover.

While still a student at Owen College in Manchester, and one of the most brilliant ones there, Gissing had wrecked his career by stealing money to help a young prostitute, and had been sent to America by his family to make a fresh start in life. But he could not get out of his mind the face of the street-walker who had caused his ruin, and in 1878, at the age of twenty-one, he had returned to London, sought her out and married her. He had then set himself up with her in cheap lodgings in London in order to write novels. But the prostitute had found matrimony boring, and domesticity in a slum not at all to her vagrant inclinations. She had soon left him and taken to the streets again, and the next time Gissing saw her was when, a year later, he was summoned by the police to identify her corpse in a mortuary.

Within a year of that time Gissing had met a servant girl in Regent's Park one afternoon and had almost immediately proposed marriage to her. When Wells met him at the Omar Khayyam, Gissing and this second wife were living in lodgings in Wimbledon, quarrelling bitterly when they talked at all. Gissing was planning to escape from her. With his own innate tendency to flee from constrictive circumstances and his admiration for Gissing's romantic character, this situation was of the greatest interest to Wells. He invited Gissing to Worcester Park, and Wells was soon in Gissing's confidence. He and Jane went off with Gissing on bicycle tours. Gissing was a classicist, a man with a cultivated mind; Wells drank in from his friend some of the education he had missed or had got only from his reading, and soon they were planning a trip abroad.

The month the Wellses spent with Gissing in Rome was an education, but Gissing's matrimonial troubles pursued him even there, and the little party was continually plunged into gloom by the arrival of letters from Wimbledon, threatening suicide. They visited the famous sights, took long tramps in the Alban Hills, and dined and talked late of books and writing and life. Then, suddenly, H.G. had had enough of it. The familiar restlessness was upon him again. Leaving Gissing in Rome, he and Jane went on to Naples and Capri. Something then seemed to go wrong. He felt unwell and restless. They made their way back to England and he threw himself into *Love and Mr Lewisham*, which he had started just before he left for this holiday.

It was at this time, soon after his return from abroad, that restless, unhappy, and unable to get on with his work, he left Worcester Park one day and cycled across country to see Isabel at Virginia Water. Writing *Mr Lewisham* must have brought Isabel very keenly back to his mind, and the close confidences he had exchanged with Gissing during this holiday, when Gissing, driven frantic by wife number two, must have spoken often of his fatal passion for the prostitute who had ruined his life, must also have recalled for H.G. his own passion for Isabel.

Isabel, who had not yet remarried, was running a chicken-farm near Maidenhead. He had not seen her since their parting five years before, but they had had to correspond occasionally. Her letters were inexpressive, but her image had not vanished from his mind. They spent the day together in great amity, and then, his feeling aroused, he tried to make love to her. But she fought against him, not angrily but tenderly, as one would try to hush a protesting child that would not be restrained. 'How can things like that be now?' she asked.

I wept in her arms like a disappointed child, and then suddenly pulled myself together and went out into the summer dawn and mounted my bicycle and wandered off southward into a sunlit intensity of perplexity and frustration, unable to understand the peculiar keenness of my unhappiness. I felt like an automaton, I felt as though all purpose had been drained out of me and nothing remained worth while. The world was dead and I was dead and I had only just discovered it. [*Experiment in Autogiography*]

The encounter with Isabel, with all this emotional disturbance, brought on a breakdown. The doctor had to be called in, and it was July before he had recovered sufficiently to start work again. At the end of July he and Jane started off on their tandem bicycle for Seaford, where they meant to spend a few days before going on to stay with Dr Hick, the Medical Officer of Health for Romney, whom they had met through Gissing. H.G. felt and looked wretched. At Seaford Jane bought a thermometer and took his temperature; it registered 102 degrees, and he was obviously in no shape to continue the bicycle tour. He telegraphed to Hick 'Am ill. Can you take me in?' Then he and Jane made their way by train to Romney, and for the next two months he was a patient in Dr Hick's house. The cause of the illness was an abscessed kidney, that one which the lout at Holt had kicked when he had the young master from London on the ground.

Dr Hick's devoted nursing pulled him round without an operation, but once again he had received a reminder that he could not live as other men did. For two months he was able to do no work at all, but he was able to think, and, lying in bed in Romney, he planned out what was to be his greatest book, *Kipps*. To commemorate the birth of the idea, he drew a little sketch which has been preserved, showing Kipps breaking through from a hatched egg, with the date 'October 5th 1898, New Romney' in the corner. This was seven years before the book was published.

6

Building a Career

WHEN he was well enough to leave Dr Hick's home, they moved for his convalescence to a little furnished cottage at Sandgate, near Folkestone, with its back door opening directly on to the beach. ('The shrimps *will* come in and whack about on the dining-room oilcloth,' he wrote to Elizabeth Healey.) This provided a base from which Jane could sally forth each day to find an unfurnished villa, preferably on gravelly soil, which would fulfill Dr Hick's prescription for the right kind of dwelling for him. Plainly Worcester Park had to be abandoned.

H.G. was thus left to himself for long intervals during the day while Jane scoured the seaside villages and towns in either direction. Depressed and gloomy, his hopes of a literary career now dashed by the prospect of an early death, the little author of astounding scientific fantasies sat wrapped in blankets, gazing moodily at the sea. He felt quite unable to take up *Love and Mr Lewisham* where he had been forced to abandon it. All the go had gone out of him. Instead his mind dwelt insistently on what a bloody mess the world was in. With this, it was only a step for Wells to brood upon how greatly it might be improved if it could be reconditioned and redesigned along planetary lines. But there was nothing he could do about it. He wrote to J. V. Milne:

Valetudinarianism is my game for the next couple of years, and the confounded world must manage itself, until I am better at least. A man who would advise others must first diagnose himself and my abdomen is mystery enough for me, a strange region of which I am, I find, merely suserain. It's well the confounded viscus waited until I was prosperous enough to get advice and consultations and nursing and so on, or I should certainly by now have been getting myself unpopular in another world by frank criticism of the detailed management of heaven. But the gust has passed, and I still float in a shattered condition.

But it was during this brooding interval of solitude that the next stage in the author's career was being hatched. So far he had been proceeding by way of the thing he did best, stories with a scientific background. There could be no doubt of his success. The money was rolling in, the critics sang his praises; he was winning fame in America, and he was being translated into nearly every European language. But he was convinced that he had it in him to be more than a successful thriller-writer. He was a writer of comedy – witness *The Wheels of Chance* and *The Wonderful Visit*. *Love and Mr Lewisham* was not yet completed, but Chaffery had already been invented, and Kipps loomed in his mind. Under the beguiling veil of comedy, social criticism could be made, this damned world made to acknowledge its fatuous pride, its insolence and cruelty, just as the scientific books had insisted on the perils that could arise from the pride and power of science exercised by unprincipled hands.

He felt that he could get much nearer to the problems of life by writing about it in contemporary terms. Nevertheless, there had been something in his scientific books that singled them out. A few years later, writing to Arnold Bennett, he stated without false modesty what he believed made his books different:

There's a quality in the worst of my so-called 'pseudo-scientific' (imbecile adjective) stuff which differentiates it from Jules Verne, e.g. just as Swift is differentiated from fantasia – isn't there? There is something other than either story-writing or artistic merit which has emerged through the series of my books. Something one might regard as a new system of ideas – 'thought'. It's in *Anticipations*, especially chapter IX, and it's in my Royal Institution lecture, and it's also in *The First Men in the Moon* and *The Invisible Man*, and Chaffery's chapter in *Love and Mr Lewisham*.

By 'thought' he meant social criticism, and the particular references in his letter emphasize this. The habit of imagining consequences had taken deep root in the rich soil of the little scientific knowledge he had gained. The scientific method was to proceed step by step by the laws of strict causation, but the mythmaker's imagination leapt ahead to consequences that might follow if this strict line went momentarily out of true, if obstacles not yet overcome by science could be surmounted and progress continued beyond, if the power that science had put in men's hands got into the wrong hands, if the force of gravity could be overcome, if there was life on other worlds and the earth became a battlefield... From these suppositions had flowed his early books, *The Time Machine*, *The Island of Dr Moreau*, *The Invisible Man*, *The War of the Worlds*, *The First Men in the Moon* and *When the Sleeper Awakes*.

In *The Time Machine* science has merely provided the situation and, more doubtfully, the means of access to it. Then a whole new world is made open to the reader's imagination. This is not darkest Africa or the jungles of the East to which he may never hope to have access, but our own past, our own future, the very universe in which we have our being. Could we, by some trick of science, glimpse the world we live in dying at some time far ahead, this is how it would be. Fifty years before the first astronauts described the light of space, the bearded inventor, returned from his journey, could describe how:

Presently as I went on, still gaining velocity, the palpitation of night and day merged into one continuous greyness; the sky took on a wonderful deepness of blue, a splendid luminous colour like that of early twilight; the jerking sun became a streak of fire, a brilliant arch in space; the moon a fainter fluctuating band; and I could see nothing of the stars, save now and then a brighter circle flickering in the blue.

But *The Time Machine* is more than a description of what it is like to journey through the barrier of time. Congenial to the mythmaker's mind was what conditions would be like at some selected point in the future. How would mankind live? Would there still be good and evil, striving and rest, war and peace, hunger and love? Speculations of this nature had been the basis of many of his contributions to the *Science Schools Journal* – 'The Past and Present of the Human Race', for example.

What he finds forms the exciting substance of the story, but several things make these books different from anything written before or since, and mark them as the work of a mythmaker. One is the majestic sense of something greater than humanity overshadowing our familiar world. Another is the sweep and force of the descriptive writing, which rises at points to wonderful heights. There are moments of unsurpassable majesty – the death of the world in *The Time Machine*, the howling in the twilight on Primrose Hill of the last Martian left alive in devastated London, the death of the Invisible Man, the lunar landscapes of *The First Men on the Moon*, the chanting of the beasts in *The Island of Dr Moreau*. Moments, in fact, when the language becomes an incantation, and one is aware of surrendering to some emotion not ordinarily felt in reading. Language alone could not do this; it is the accompaniment to the theme. But it lifts the imagination to a level at which the reader not only surrenders disbelief, but positively wills belief, and is conscious of participating in the action, not just being an observer of it. All these books are about man and his place in a universe of which science has made him suddenly aware.

But when at Beach Cottage these doleful broodings were interrupted by an important call, Wells became his old combative self. Two majestic figures descended from bicycles and knocked at the door to inquire about his health: Mr Henry James and Mr Edmund Gosse. They had cycled over from Henry James's house at Rye, they explained, and entering and settling themselves for a talk, they inquired not only about his health but about his resources, and wished to know when he might expect to be able to take up his pen again. The talk was circuitous and tactful, but it came out that young and promising writers, by reason of illness or one thing or another, might need occasional help, was it not so? Wells had more than one thousand pounds in the bank. What he needed was health, not wealth. He allowed himself to contradict these great men. Once a man borrowed or was subsidized, the 'go' went out of his work; in his opinion it was a mistake to deprive a man of the sharp freshness of an earned cheque.

This visit was followed a week or so later by one from Mr J. M. Barrie, who took tea and reminisced, and spoke along the same lines as Henry James and Gosse had done. Only then did it come to Wells that the Royal Literary Fund, which dispenses pensions to literary figures in need, was instituting through these eminent men inquiries as to his condition, and he felt flattered. But a greater boon than mere cash was to flow from these visits. They were indirectly to be the means of introducing Wells to the large literary society to be found in this district, just at the time when he badly needed friends and cheering up.

Henry James must have been struck at their first meeting with the vigorous personality, lively mind and aggressive humour of this curious sickly young man whose work he genuinely admired. When he came to Beach Cottage, James invited Wells to visit him at Rye when he was strong enough to get out again, and it was James who in turn introduced him to Stephen Crane and Ford Madox Ford, both of whom had houses in the district. Joseph Conrad, with whom Wells had corresponded when he was reviewing novels for the *Saturday Review*, also rented a house in the neighbourhood. A good deal of week-end entertaining went on, and there was much coming and going. These were circles in which conversational skill was highly prized, and young H.G., with his gift for being amusing and stimulating, as he got out and about was soon welcomed everywhere. Prominent among the regular week-end visitors from London were younger intellectuals, writers and poets like the

Chesterton brothers, A. E. W. Mason, Jack Squire, Clifford Sharp – very lively and amusing fellows, great talkers and walkers, and drinkers in the robust fashion of the literary world of that time. H.G. was not up to all this, but his mental horizons broadened considerably in the relaxed hours spent with this company.

Leaving Beach Cottage, where spray from the sea some-times broke over the roof in rough weather, they took and furnished Arnold House on a three-year tenancy. It was a pleasant semi-detached villa with a narrow lawn in front running down to a tamarisk hedge which shielded the garden from the more boisterous weather. Living in this invigorating air, health flowed back into his frail frame like a tide returning over the bare sand, and soon he was hard at work. Here he took up *Love and Mr Lewisham* again and finished it with much care and elaboration. It was his first consciously written serious novel, and he was determined to make it as good as he could. 'Heaven knows when it will be done,' he wrote to Elizabeth Healey, 'for writing a fantasy romance is one thing, writing a novel is quite another.'

While still at Arnold House, the Wellses decided to build, and soon Spade House was rising, crowning the cliffs ninety feet above the sea, with its pergolas and lawns sweeping down to the beach, a far cry from the resolute little semi-detached villa in Maybury Road, Woking, with its small greenhouse pinned to its side; and unimaginable distances from the unhygienic miseries of Atlas House in Bromley High Street. Occupied in December 1900, Spade House was handsome, impressive and bang up-to-date. A photograph of its proprietor taken at that time shows him standing before the Gothic front door, hands thrust deep into his pockets, all five foot seven inches of him up-chested against the world: Kipps to the life.

At Spade House their two sons were born and the books of the next eight years – *Anticipations, Mankind in the Making, A Modern Utopia, Kipps, The Sea Lady, The*

Food of the Gods, In the Days of the Comet, Ann Veronica and *Tono-Bungay* – were written. He was settling down to the life of a successful author.

All should have been well, and the story should have ended happily with success achieved, health restored and a happy loving home from which to work. But with returning health and a sense of physical well-being came renewed agitations of the desire to wander. Here he was, immured in this fine house, while life and adventure swept tantalizingly by, beckoning him to follow. This is the central theme of the first novel he was to write in the new house, *The Sea Lady*, in which the setting is undisguisedly Sandgate, and Chatteris – who, trapped by his success, in the end yields to an overpowering sensuous demand – does what Wells himself longed to do.

Jane had kept up with him in his advance, perhaps in some respects had gone ahead of him. Spade House was rather a large and grand establishment for such a young author, even though his success had been remarkable. His income justified it, but it had the effect of tying him down, it built walls around him and agitated his intermittent sense of domestic claustrophobia. With all his success he missed what he most desired in life, a supreme sexual experience. The children, the large garden, the house opened always to guests, especially week-end guests from London, the domestic staff, all meant added expense and responsibility which could be met only by increased output. 'We feeds 'im and we fattens 'im, and he yields nigh two or three books a year': in this cry from the heart inserted in a presentation copy to a friend a few years later, he was more than jesting.

Jane had taken in his life the place his mother and his family had held. Bright individuals, conscious of their own cleverness, need an audience, and the Wells family had provided that for H.G. in his growing years. His humour and trick of mimicking people, and the funny little drawings he had made in his letters to his mother and brothers had been much treasured and admired. There seems no record of his having entertained Isabel in this way, and this says much for the difference in the sexual situation. With Isabel he dominated; with Jane he was dominated. These were not love gestures so much as propitiatory ones. Also they were a defence against an oppressive world in which they were fighting together for survival, and this shared laughter softened a little the harshness of his disappointment when he realized that his second marriage, as much as his first, failed to satisfy the raging hunger in him for the perfection his imagination had convinced him a sexual union between two people could be.

Ill-health only slowly relenting, poverty, a fierce, close application to work, and a sense of standing up to those oppressive forces with this fragile trusting little being who had put her life and happiness in his hands had kept him for a long time from straying. But strains were inevitable in a situation so precariously balanced. Such strains generally lead to cracks and to ultimate disaster; that they did not do so in this case, though they were to bring the marriage perilously near it several times, was because this association had from the start been a duologue. Jane, unlike Isabel, was articulate, and beneath the physical fragility was an iron will. H.G.'s volubility did not echo against a sounding-board; she had ideas, opinions of her own. The new woman stirred in this shy, inexperienced girl from Putney. She had not been content to be a 'typewriter' or a toucher-up of photographs. She had meant to get her degree and teach. Even if she had had the temperamental inclination physically to play Venus Urania to his overpowering personality, she would have demanded his attention and respect when those high passionate moments were over and life had to be got on with. Their discussions admitted a mutual recognition of the difference in their temperaments – as Wells describes it, a joint acknowledgement that fate had played a very scurvy trick on them in this respect, a confession of respect and love for each other in spite of this, and a determination to stick together and see their marriage through. A strong sexual instinct and a tendency to dominate go together, and there can be little doubt that the *modus vivendi* which a few years after their marriage they worked out, whereby each of them, recognizing their temperamental differences and the inequality of their bodily demands, might be free, without conscience or conflict, to balance and satisfy these by *passades* – momentary distractions for relief from intolerable pressure, not passionate affairs that engaged the heart and mind and spirit – was a plan evolved by H.G. and agreed to by Jane only as an alternative to a break-up of this second marriage. With this imperative satisfied, everything, they agreed, would go on as before. But, as he confesses in his autobiography, nothing ever is the same again. It takes two to make love, and love is a different thing for men and women. Jealousy and possessiveness are the natural accompaniment of any love affair, and *passades* cannot have limits set to them.

Jane would have known by this time what she had to deal with – an invalid doomed to recurrent bouts of invalidism, as it must then have seemed, and given also to bouts of 'domestic claustrophobia' which manifested itself in a restlessness which drove him away from home for days at a time, sometimes on his bicycle through the Kentish lanes, sometimes by train for unexplained absences in London. Given to stretches, too, of concentrated work that might last through several days and nights, to be followed by days of moodiness and despair if something did not come right. At such moments Isabel had lapsed into stony silence, unable to comprehend why he troubled so hard. This had made him add outright rudeness to cold withdrawal. Jane bore it all philosophically. With all his faults, you could not help loving him. Bursting with brains, bubbling with humour, he was full of a boisterous vital stimulating charm that made it nearly always a pleasure to be in his company, and you either rode the storm or were swept on to the rocks. Jane rode the storm.

7

From Anticipations to a
Modern Utopia

WHEN they moved into Spade House, he was writing the first chapters of *Kipps*, determined to follow up on *Love and Mr Lewisham* with the novel he had first thought of when lying ill in Dr Hick's house, and for which he meant to reach back into his own disordered past. But before going on with it, he was tempted into an enterprise that was to prove the beginning of a new line of activity for him altogether.

As the new century dawned, the idea came to him that an article anticipating what life would be like one hundred years ahead, when the practical application of the inventions of science would have altered it completely, might have some relevance and attraction in the year 1900. This was the sort of imaginative projection to which his particular cast of mind always responded vividly and enlargingly. The more he plotted it, the larger area the vision assumed. It was not a simple conception of an existence made easier by labour-saving devices. Emotions would also have freer play; there would be a loosening of restraints. Social behaviour would change, sexual repressions might be unlocked, the relations between men and women altered as the care of the home became easier and women, freed from menial tasks, used their liberty for constructive purposes. The whole fabric of social life would become unstitched and be knit up to new patterns.

W. L. Courtney, then editing the *Fortnightly Review* in succession to Frank Harris, was attracted by the idea when Wells raised it with him, and was ready to commission six articles on the subject. Wells was in his element, dredging up from those years of stimulating argument with his fellow students, and later with friends like Walter Low and Richard Gregory, the witty aphorisms and daring predictions they had exchanged, matured now by longer reflection and experience of life. These imaginings had always had the ring of truth to them. He had hammered away at this theme for so long. 'The Past and Present of the Human Race' had enormously amused his fellow students in 1885. Eight years later he had rewritten that piece for the *Pall Mall Gazette*, where, appearing under the title 'The Man of the Year Million', it had excited quite a lot of interest. This and other witty imaginings, aired at the College Debating Society or in the pages of the *Science Schools Journal*, were gropings towards the future, attempts to anticipate what life might be like ahead. Now he could drop the facetious air and write wholly seriously as a scientific thinker.

Anticipations, as the book which followed the articles came to be known, bears a much longer title: *Anticipations of the Reaction of Mechanical and Scientific Progress upon Human Life and Thought*. It set out soberly enough to consider the then current trends and developments of the main forces at work in society, the complete transformation of the whole idea of locomotion following the invention of the steam engine and the consequent effect on the diffusion of great cities, and the inevitable growth of a large and politically powerful skilled middle class in a society that in a scientific age was bound to become increasingly technological. Wells then examined the changes in the home and family life that this transformation in the movement of society was likely to bring about – the size of families, for example, and the position and authority of women in the home, and the kind of labour-saving homes there would be in a servantless age, leaving the women of the house even greater liberty; the effect this would be bound to have on the physical relations between the sexes, and the bringing up of children. From his skilled hand a picture emerged of what life has already become in the time we know, with spreading suburbs, crowded roads, and a house-owning, car-owning democracy which is not everyone's idea of perfect heaven. Seen through the mist of years from the class-ridden, slum-defiled England of 1900, however, it had redeeming features.

Wells described these articles as an anticipatory balance sheet, a prospectus of the joint undertaking of mankind in the years ahead. Risks must be considered as well as brighter prospects, and he correctly anticipated war as the main threat to the stability of the twentieth century. Writing before the end of the Boer War, he foresaw what army staffs then did not: the impact of scientific invention on the art of war, with machines, and especially the aeroplane, which was not then really off the ground, becoming so powerful that armies would be bogged down in defensive positions, cities razed to the ground, and the civilian population as much involved in the conflict as the soldiers.

He concentrated his attention on the triumphant emerging middle class. What was needed was a plan for their survival in the twentieth century, and with that 'impossible cheek' which Henry James was to come to admire in him, this comparatively unknown young man, who had written half-a-dozen well-thought-of scientific romances, had that ready to hand. Not only at hand, but passionately felt and fervently put forward as the only means of salvation from a doom otherwise unavoidable in a world in which science had released to humanity power that could lead to its own destruction. The day of sovereign states and empires was over; in a World State alone could salvation be found. He saw the World State as developing from a synthesis of larger groups in which the English-speaking nations, Britain and the United States, would play a commanding part, the final conversion being brought about by an open conspiracy on the part of *Übermensch* (not a term Wells used, but an exact description of his New Republicans).

A final essay on the Faith of the New Republic brought these *Anticipation* papers to a close. It was written with a passionate sense of urgency, and it evoked an equally passionate response from the great mass of the middle class to whom it was addressed. Did Wells know that there were so many waiting for just this lead? It is doubtful. He had had a very narrow experience of life; he himself had moved from the shop-keeping class of his youth, through London student life to teaching and journalism, and since then had led the solitary life of a writer, without money or health. His ideas had been debated with a few intelligent and lively friends of his own class, and had been aired in essays and stories in the *Science Schools Journal*. Now he burst with one bound into an open declaration of faith in the future.

The ethical system of these men of the New Republic, the system which would dominate the World State, would favour the procreation:

of what is fine and efficient and beautiful in humanity – beautiful and strong bodies, clear and powerful minds, and a growing body of knowledge and to check the procreation of base and servile types, of fear-driven and cowardly souls, of all that is mean and ugly and bestial in the souls, bodies and habits of men.

This doctrine of the repression of the unfit must have been less attractive than the frankness he expounded in dealing with the matter of sex. 'Our current civilization', said Wells emphatically, 'is a sexual lunatic', and had become so because of the prohibitions that prevented any discussion of the matter as a whole, the bashfulness that hampered what discussion there was, that permitted it only in a furtive silly sort of way, and had its ugly consequences in the production of countless needless and unhappy lives.

What he 'anticipated' beyond a period of disorder and hypocrisy in matters of sexual morality was something like free love (a subject to which he was to return with increasing ardour and explicitness in the years ahead), the state insisting on only one thing – the security and welfare of the child.

The programme was set out in detail. Education follows after birth; the programme was again revolutionary, for by then the whole world would be thinking and learning and the old idea of 'completing' one's education would have vanished with the fancy of a static universe. The economic aim of the new society would be directed against those who were parasitic.

In more than one aspect Wells's new society has an uncomfortable suggestion of strong-armed fascism about it, and with a sense of shock in the Sixties one is suddenly aware that the heaven Wells dreamed of in 1900 bears a distinct resemblance to the 1984 hell imagined half a century later by George Orwell. But Orwell was addressing himself to readers soured by disappointed hopes, Wells to readers newly liberated from old restrictions, tremulous with expectation of the wonders that lay in store for them. In Wells's vivid phrase, 'It is as if a hand had been put upon the head of a thoughtful man and had turned his eyes about from the past to the future.' It did not seem in 1900 beyond the bounds of possibility that a new society, all blemish washed away, could fructify the earth; that a specious scheme of events might be opening out with that inexplicable quality of design – to use Wells's metaphor – conveyed by one of Beethoven's symphonies; that 'presently, up out of the day-spring in the East, the sunlight will be pouring'. God would no longer be the mysteriously incompetent Deity, exasperated by an unsatisfactory creation. It would have been left at last for men to have wills that had caught a harmony with the universal will.

The old ethical principles, the various vague and arbitrary ideas of purity, chastity, and sexual 'sin', came like rays out of the theological and philosophical lanterns men carried in the darkness. ... But now there has come a new view of man's place in the scheme of time and space, a new illumination, dawn. ... The act of faith is no longer to follow your lantern. We can see about us, and by the landscape we must go.

The response was overwhelming. The effect was of someone anxious to get a hearing suddenly finding everyone listening. What had started as half-a-dozen articles which had been prompted by his journalist's instinct for the timely became, under the surge of his own eloquence and the stimulation of his own social and class resentment, a passionate declaration of faith in the sort of future he would like to see if he had the moulding of it. The nature of the response persuaded him that he had, in fact, something to offer humanity struggling along its difficult road.

At this moment what the public wanted to buy was visions and dreams, and *Anticipations* offered these, nobody appearing to notice the disharmony between the good life for those who qualified for it in Wells's picture of the future, and the position of those who for one reason or another did not qualify for it, whom he dismissed rather contemptuously as 'people of the abyss.'

No matter. At least he had succeeded in doing something which had not been done before outside the pages of a novel. He had made people aware of the social conditions in which they lived, the opportunities which had been put in their way as a result of the mechanical revolution, and the need in an entirely new world for new conceptions about God and religion, about sex and the relations generally between men and women, and about government and the authority which men set up to maintain order. Suddenly people were conscious that around them the social fabric which had lasted from the eighteenth century was breaking up, that new liberties were winging in and new responsibilities and disciplines were called for. There was the old mess to clear up, and then what beauty, what privileges, what a destiny awaited them.

Eight printings of *Anticipations* were called for in the first year of publication. The bookshops were full of it. In Europe it made the same tremendous impact as it did in England, the *Nouvelle Revue Française* acclaiming it *'une lampe qui éclaire la marche du XX siècle'*. In Germany and Italy it was the same. Wells, already admired there for his scientific romances, became a continental literary figure.

The genius of Wells was driving towards a point which all thinking people were fumbling for in that decade just before the outbreak of the First World War, a period which seems remote to us who have survived the two great wars of this century. We ourselves have grown sharp, bitter and wary from the very hell we have been through, but in that little sunlit patch of time everyone seems to have been as innocent as Adam not yet defiled by sin, and trembling with expectancy for some joyful experience that impended. It fell to this man, with his mythmaker's art, to awaken in a whole generation sensations they had not experienced before, making them conscious suddenly of 'possessing joys not promised them at their birth'.

Praise resounded from all quarters, even quite unlikely ones. Henry James, writing to H. G. Wells, acknowledging himself to be a little aloof from these 'social imaginings', as he fastidiously described *Anticipations* ('my world is somehow other'), nevertheless found the book 'full of truth and wit and sanity'. As he was always to do, he put his finger unerringly on what really constituted the triumph here: Wells's power of carrying his audience with him.

You really come beautifully out of your adventure, come out of it immensely augmented and extended, like a belligerent who has annexed half a kingdom, with drums and trumpets and banners all sounding and flying. And this is because the thing, in our deadly days, is such a charming exhibition of complete freedom of mind. That's what I enjoyed in it – your intellectual disencumberedness. [20 January 1902]

And Beatrice Webb noted in her diary for the last day of 1901 that *Anticipations* was the book of the year, 'full of luminous hypotheses and worth careful study by those who are trying to look forward'.

Meanwhile something flattering to his self-esteem happened. Almost certainly as a result of the publication of these articles in the *Fortnightly*, he was invited by the Royal Institution to give one of its famous Thursday evening discourses. The date set was 24 January 1902. This was an honour indeed. For one who had failed his scientific degree at first shot, who had been an undistinguished teacher and crammer since, who had made his way from the shops via Mornington Road, to be invited to address in Albermarle Street such a distinguished audience as that which gathered at intervals at the Royal Institution to listen to eminent specialists discoursing on high affairs established at once recognition of Wells's scientific rank.

His paper, *The Discovery of the Future*, was really an enlargement of *Anticipations*, with its political references muted, but the frankness about sexual matters daringly maintained. It was an undisguised attempt to enlist orthodox support for the doctrines addressed in *Anticipations* to the common man, on the grounds that as scientific experimentation was nothing more than forecast from proven fact, might not the path of human destiny, if not the individual life, be plotted by building up this growing body of scientific forecast into an ordered picture of the future just as detailed and exact as that which science had been able to build up from an examination of the geological past?

He went in for detailed prophecy, restating some of the propositions of *Anticipations* – the diffusion of populations, black and yellow peoples forced up the scale of efficiency, humanity – 'in a couple of hundred, or in a thousand years' – definitely and consciously organizing itself as a great world state.

But with man, in the end, we must go outside the sphere of reason and set our feet upon Faith:

One must admit that it is impossible to show why certain things should not utterly destroy and end the entire human race and story; why night should not presently came down and make all our dreams and efforts vain ... e.g. something from space, or pestilence, or some great disease of the atmosphere, some trailing cometary poison, some great emanation of vapour from the interior of the earth, or new animals to prey on us, or some drug or wrecking madness into the minds of men.

But one didn't believe it.

I have come to believe in other things: in the coherency and purpose in the world, and in the greatness of human destiny. Worlds may freeze and suns may perish, but believe there stirs something within us now that can never die again.

To this learned audience he could say something it was not possible to say in *Anticipations*, something utterly reve-latory of his feeling about his subject, man. 'I do not think I could possibly join in the worship of Humanity with any gravity or sanity. There are moods when one could join in the laughter of Democritus or share Swift's amazement that such a Being should deal in Pride.' But if the spectacle of human littleness was shot with pain, it was shot with pro-mise too. 'Small as our vanity and carnality make us, there has been a day of still smaller things. It is the long ascent of the past that gives the lie to our despair ...'

In the century just ended there had been more change in the conditions of human life than there had been in the past thousand years, and everything seemed pointing to the belief that the world was entering upon a progress that would go on with an ever widening and ever more confident stride:

It is possible to believe that all the past is but the beginning of a beginning, all that the human mind has accomplished is but the dream before the awakening. A day will come when beings now latent in our thoughts and hidden in our loins will stand upon this earth as one stands upon a footstool, and laugh, and reach out their hands amid the stars.

This was a majestic poetic vision, but some of the eminent scientists present may have seen the flaw in the analogy be-tween forecasting the next step in a scientific experiment, working from a confident and proved base, and prophesying an optimistic destiny for mankind from no sounder basis than faith that if he has come so far and so successfully he must go on in the same way. There is nothing wrong in professing such a faith, but it is not to be confused with science. Nevertheless the poetic concept was undeniable; it had the majesty of great myth, and Wells's new status as a scientific thinker was accepted in the scientific world when the paper was reprinted in full in *Nature*.

Prophets prophesying good things are generally welcome, and everybody rushed to make use of him for their particular purposes. Nobody stopped to ask what lay beneath these splendid remarks, how much concern for individual men, plainly still miserable in large numbers in spite of the developments of science, and whatever the ultimate happy destiny of their kind might be. Wells was courted particularly and immediately by Sidney and Beatrice Webb, who appeared on bicycles from the direction of London, breathless with admiration, earnest to enlist his support in the Fabian Society.

This strange couple, whose wedding rings were inscribed '*pro bono publico*', and who had spent their honeymoon inspecting trade societies in Ireland and attending the Trade Union Congress in Glasgow, were devoting their lives to remedying what could be remedied in the social organization by better administration. We owe them much, although it is difficult sometimes not to share H.G.'s impatience with such tireless busybodies. They were unconsciously to blame for leading Wells astray into fields which it would have been better for his fame as a writer if he had never penetrated.

Sidney Webb was small, bearded, solemn and fussy, and he came from a family on a social level with H.G.'s. Beatrice was tall and beautiful, well-bred and rich, and very clever and sharp in a day when such attributes were considered unbecoming in a woman. She seems early to have had an attack of conscience about the poor, and this had been aggravated when, in order to learn more about their condition, she had taken over the rent-collecting of some property her father had in the East End of London. From this experience had flowed the first article she wrote, published in the *Nineteenth Century* in 1887 (the very year in which H.G.'s career at South Kensington came to a disastrous close), entitled 'Some Enquiries into the Dock Life of East London'.

Sidney Webb had been a clerk in the Civil Service. He had met Bernard Shaw at a meeting of the Zetetical Society. Between the tall gaunt young Irishman with aristocratic connections and the undersized civil servant with a passion for detail, some deep attraction flowed – perhaps because they were both busybodies with an incurable interest in the minutiae of public affairs. Friendship and understanding grew up between them.* Shaw had got Webb into the Fabian Society, which the two of them, the one with facts, the other with oratory, now tended to dominate. It was Shaw who suggested to the Webbs that the much-talked-of author of *Anticipations* would be a useful recruit for the Fabians.

Shaw and the Webbs combined to persuade Wells to join. H.G. was flattered by the invitation. Besides, it fitted in very well with the need to escape at times from Spade House.

He was enormously busy – building his literary career with one hand, so to speak; continually at Mr Macmillan, who had now become his publisher, with helpful suggestions for getting some 'woosh' into the sales of his books; writing more rapidly than ever and with even greater power. This was partly because he was growing in assurance as an artist, partly because of the conviction settling in on him that it was open to him to influence men towards righteousness.

Not only up and down from Sandgate to London, but with occasional journeys across the Channel – now nothing out of the ordinary, but only a few years earlier an exciting adventure for young Mr and Mrs Wells. Hard at work in his study looking across the bay to the distant French coast, pouring out articles, short stories, novels, lectures, keeping

* 'He [Webb] was the ablest man in England. Quite the wisest thing I ever did was to force my friendship on him and to keep it.' Bernard Shaw, *Sixteen Self-Sketches*, (Constable, 1949).

up the large correspondence which arose from his books, ready in the midst of all this to collaborate with Arnold Bennett in a play which was to be 'the dramatic sensation of 1903'; in London, immersed in Fabian meetings, lunching and dining at his clubs or in private houses, addressing drawing-room meetings in the Fabian interest, talking, talking, talking ... always interestingly, always amusingly. He was a dynamo of energy, and he generated a desire in nearly everybody he met to be up and doing too.

One can plainly see him being carried away by the exuberance of his ideas. *Anticipations* and *Mankind in the Making*, which followed it, had been tentative outbursts; the spirit of prophecy that marked them had been the daring flights of a mind that, having moved in restricted spaces, had suddenly found freer air and whirled upwards. Even the formidably entitled 'The Question of Scientific Administrative Areas in Relation to Municipal Undertakings', the paper with which he read himself into the Fabian Society, had flashes of eloquence and humour in it.

Beatrice Webb, recording in her diary this first appearance of Wells at a Fabian meeting in which she was in the chair, noted proudly: 'Like ourselves, he is impressed with the need for some scientific adjustment of units of administration – to functions or services.'

One wonders what H.G. made of it all, and whether on that first night of his attendance he did not discern with that very blue piercing eye of his the fussiness and pettiness which was to break his temper in the end. Whatever he felt, the Webbs were very proud of their capture:

We like him much – absolutely genuine, full of inventiveness, a 'speculator' in ideas – somewhat of a gambler – in one sense a romancer spoilt by romancing, but in the present state of sociology he is useful to gradgrinds like ourselves in supplying us with loose generalizations which we can use as instruments of research, and we are useful to him in supplying an endless array of carefully sifted facts and broad administrative experience.

It was all to end in tears, but in 1904 he was the darling of the Fabians.

For the Wells's we had a little dinner – carefully selected – Mr Balfour, the Bishop of Stepney, the Bernard Shaws, Mrs Reeves, and a Mr Thesiger, a new L.C.C. Moderate.

In 1905:

H. G. Wells came for the night. He had sent us his *Utopia*. 'The chapters on the Samurai will pander to all your worst instincts,' he laughingly remarked when I congratulated him. He is full of intellectual courage and initiative, and has now settled down to psychological novels – I fancy somewhat inspired by H. James's late success.

Already, one can suspect, H.G. was enjoying pulling Beatrice's leg.*

---

* Wells had written her some months before this, while he was at work on *A Modern Utopia*:

'God is a coarse creature – a large part of civilization consists in man's strenuous efforts to correct the improprieties of Mr Balfour and your Divinity – and I think the steady abstinence from all forms of eating likely to provoke some gross form of retaliation upon God's part. My own experience of God, at any rate, points to that expectation. Besides, where is your advantage? Refinement doesn't tempt me: Intellectually I am already too refined as it is. I would rather be after God's pattern, gross, various, fecund and comprehensive, inexact and continually unexpected, and disciplined, specialized, determinate, inadaptable and expert. You must pardon me if I seem to be writing incoherently. I have been taking food.

You know it is quite dreadful to me to hear that Webb would have suppressed *Food of the Gods*. It shows how fearfully far you two have gone in pursuit of administrative efficiency. If I were a more authoritative person I should speak to you very seriously. I should implore you both not to think about Government for six months ...' [19 October, 1904]

8

Third Assault
on London

THE satisfaction of finding with *Anticipations* that his ideas were widely accepted, and the larger intellectual company in London to which he was introduced by the success of that book, did not divert him from his aim of becoming a serious novelist. The scientific fantasies had made his name and secured his financial position, but he had no intention of settling down as an English Jules Verne. With the same confidence and precision with which he predicted the future of mankind, he was prepared to forecast his own. It was that of a serious novelist who is going to write about life. Not simply reflecting, as in an old mirror, mankind at its endless struggle of adjusting itself to its environment, awakening the readers' sympathies to its miseries, humours and character. But showing life as it might be lived, but for the oppressions, the stultifying traditions and the follies that men had allowed like weeds to grow up and choke it. At last in 1901 he felt free, secure enough financially, with a young family now started and a new and fine home of his own, to devote himself solely to this task.

A change had come over him physically and psychologically. From being a rather sickly young man from the lower class, with gauche manners and somewhat furtive personality, by turns shrinking and assertive, he had in the last year or so become healthy in appearance and surprisingly assured in manner. Seaside living suited this London sparrow, washing away his pallor, softening the sharpness of his features, revealing a very good-looking young man beneath. The bicycle, wonderful invention, took him out into the Kentish hills in the afternoons, and put muscle on his frame where there had been only flabbiness before. Life was opening out for him. He was finding stimulating and sophisticated new friends in the populous literary circle of this corner of England, and they were in turn greatly taken with his cheery cockney disposition, his lack of 'side', his bubbling intelligence and his wit. He was making a conquest of this society just as he had done of his fellow students on the Exhibition Road. The tweed-capped, knickerbockered little figure leaning against his 'ironmongery' at the top the hill and looking down over the Channel to the coast of France on afternoon rides, really had the world at his feet in the early years of the new century.

He had arrived on the scene just at the right moment for the exercise of his particular gifts. Nearly everybody was discussing Life. Drawing-room meetings went on everywhere, decorous gatherings where somebody invited from one or another of the innumerable little societies which aimed at improving life got up and addressed the rest, questions following. Particularly the social conscience of the young of the middle class was aroused, and the same passionate desire to protest against the past made them eager to find an alternative programme for the future. What Shaw had been after, haunting society after society until he found in the young Fabian Society something that could be moulded to his conception of the Life Force, what Wells had been after in *Anticipations*, what Belloc and Chesterton were to be after in defending freedom and human responsibility from the designers of social Utopias, were all part of the splendid ferment.

They were all optimists. The only one in whose visionary splendours appeared occasional sombre streaks was Wells, but the doom that he saw throwing a threatening shadow across the future of humanity was aeons ahead, and if the New Republic he offered in *Anticipations* seems to us oppressive rather than free, with the privileged exercising dominance over the deprived, that is only because notions of equity and justice have changed. No one questioned as yet the fundamental separation of classes, and the conception of leaders and led had not got the sinister implication it has acquired in our time.

Elevated in a few years' time to middle-class status, warmly prosperous in place of the chill penury he had known all his life, bounding with energy and brimming over with ideas, Wells came with increasing frequency to London. He had been elected to the Reform Club, and he had been invited to join the Coefficients, a small circle of intellectuals and political figures who in 1902, at Beatrice Webb's suggestion, started to dine together once a month to discuss the affairs of the Empire. The membership was limited at first to twelve, and included such prominent figures as L. S. Amery, Edward Grey, J. B. S. Haldane, Henry Newbolt, Lord Milner, Bertrand Russell and Sidney Webb. But not, noticeably, Sidney's great friend Bernard Shaw, for whom the pleasures of the table had nothing to offer and political discussion about the Empire was barren. But Wells was in his element argy-barging away in such company, as keen for Empire as any of them, though he professed republicanism and socialism and had already declared himself for a World State. The inconsistency did not bother him, or seem to bother him. At first he was a little shy and subdued in this company, but he soon started to cascade.

He had not changed as much as the outward circumstances of his life and his altered appearance suggested. Always a realist when it came down to money matters, though he could not help being flattered by the attention being paid to him by important people, he knew that the essential thing was to establish a position as a novelist, and he never for a moment lost sight of this, even when his battle with the Fabian Old Guard was taking up all his time.

Arnold Bennett was his confidant in his desire to get on.

With the Coefficients he could be statesmanlike, with the Webbs and Shaw earnest for the coming of socialism, with Henry James serious about the novel, though with all of them his 'cheek' was likely to show through now and then. But with Enoch Arnold Bennett he could let down the pretence.

Bennett came from the provincial north. They had both attacked London at the same time, Bennett first as a solicitor's clerk, while Wells had begun as a teacher. Each was determined to make his name as a writer, and in both cases it took some years of arduous work before the bull's-eye of publication was hit. Bennett's first contribution to letters appeared in *Tit-Bits*, a very low-brow weekly, just about the time H.G. began in the *Pall Mall Gazette*. Wells never looked back, but Bennett accumulated rejection slips as fast as he did acceptances, and with that passionate interest in money details that was to mark him always, he worked out at this time that he was earning an average of threepence an hour. Persistence was his great virtue, and he was to persist until he became the highest-paid journalist in England, as well as a successful novelist. But it took years of hard labour, and his first firm start in life was his appointment as assistant editor of a dying periodical called *Woman* in which his father had been persuaded to invest £300.

The contrast between these two young men is constantly interesting. Wells, the Huck Finn of letters, lighting out for Indian territory; Bennett the good boy, whose first appearance in print had been a poem entitled 'Courage'. The cheerful Sam Wellerism of Wells contrasts sharply with the earnestness and steady plodding of Bennett: Wells handsome and flushed with success, full of bounce; Bennett with the handicap of his stutter, his protruding teeth, bulging eyes and quiff of hair, his delayed sexual development markedly different from Wells's defiant lustiness. The comparison was all in Wells's favour.

Yet like spoke to like between them. Their letters, admir-

ably collected in a fascinating book,* reveal their undisguised conspiracy to get each other on, the devil take the
rest. It was not truth so much as a spreading of suggestive
ideas that Wells put before his fellow diners at the Coefficients, or offered up to Henry James when the great pundit
discoursed learnedly on the English novel. But it was utter
truth that he and Bennett spoke and wrote to each other;
even the occasional covert boast, lightly disguised in irony,
is truth.

Bennett to Wells:

I have read *Anticipations* in the *Fortnightly*, and hasten to
say that I have been absolutely overwhelmed by the sheer intellectual vigour of them, not to mention the imaginative power.
These articles really have made me a little afraid of you. Either
you have in supreme degree the journalistic trick of seeming
omniscience, or you are one of the most remarkable men alive ...

Wells to Bennett:

I am glad to tell you that your modest surmise is correct.
There is no illusion. I am great. And the detached reading of
Anticipations gives you no inkling of the massive culminating
effect of the book as a whole. I am asking C&H [Chapman and
Hall, the publishers] to send you a copy, but the mean suspicion
of publishers that authors use their numerous presentation
copies as personal gifts may stand in the way. In which case I
will honestly get the book and send it to you myself. I want you
to read it very much *and*, if it takes you, to do something to
propagate my gospel. I believe quite simply that a first-class
boom and uproar and discussion about this book will do an
infinite amount of good in the country and to you at least there
is no need to put my belief in breeches. I think I am safe to get
most of the comfortable *educated* London public but I dream
of getting it read by parsons and country doctors and all that
sort and going much wider than my publishers dream. I think

* *Arnold Bennett and H. G. Wells: A Record of Their Personal and
Literary Friendship*, edited by Harris Wilson, Hart-Davies, 1960.

there are a multitude of interesting quotes to be dug out of the book, about home conveniences, the status of unmarried girls, cooking in the future, building, dress, etc, that ought to be *groundbait* for the big public – even the Corellian public ...

Here spake, not the prophet, but the earnest young seeker after a market for his wares, appealing to a friend before whom he need strike no false attitudes, and who, if he wished, might do him some good. Bennett was by no means yet well known, nothing of his that is remembered today had yet been published, but he had now become a successful journalist whose contributions were welcomed as much in the American press as in England, and who had a very well-developed sense of the value of publicity. He, or his agent, Pinker – whom Wells had put on to Bennett, much to Pinker's subsequent profit – persuaded the *Cosmopolitan Magazine* that an article on H. G. Wells, the brilliant young author of *Anticipations* and much-talked-of scientific fantasies, by his friend Enoch Arnold Bennett, might be timely.

The article duly appeared in the *Cosmopolitan* for August. It is a masterly summary of all that Wells had produced to date. It makes the point that his scientific fantasies, under the guise of romance, offer a serious criticism of life; that in *The Wonderful Visit*, the record of the sojourn of an angel in a convention-ridden village, and in *The Sea Lady*, the sojourn of a mermaid in a convention-ridden seaside town, there are apparent moral and imaginative qualities which demonstrate that he had the gift of seeing things afresh, of – Bennett's illuminating phrase – 'approaching the investigation of phenomena with senses absolutely virginal'.

Bennett then goes in for prophecy himself. In his view, Wells will go on to work still more strenuously in the field of *Anticipations*; he will deal with futures less and less remote, and, with his gifts of imagination, fancy, huomur, satire, irony, develop into an actual, prevalent political force. Bennett sums up: 'His strongest points are his clear vision and his intellectual courage and honesty; his weakest point is his instinctive antipathy to any static condition.'

It was well said, and the extent of the article, and the affectionate care with which it had been fashioned, pleased Wells enormously. Except the prophecy. *Mankind in the Making* was already being written, but, like a man tempted to drink who swears that this will be positively the last, he wrote to Bennett:

I want to write novels, and before God I *will* write novels. They are the proper stuff for my everyday work, a methodical careful distillation of one's thoughts and sentiments and experiences and impressions.

Bennett was to stand by him and remain his confidant throughout the ups and downs of his reputation and through his scandals of the next twenty years, and Wells was to stand by Bennett throughout his two unsuccessful attempts at matrimony. It is strange that Wells can do the most outrageous things and never forfeit our sympathy but there is something odiously self-satisfied and money-grubbing about Bennett which makes it hard to like him. He knew so many secrets, and confided them all to his journal. He seems to have shown a fondness for Jane, and she for him, which at first sight is surprising, considering his lack of physical appeal, until one realizes that what joined them together was their joint fascination with H.G.

The first fruits of this dedication to serious novel-writing had been *Love and Mr Lewisham*, a novel which Wells had started to write in 1896, but had had to put aside at intervals during the ill-health of the past few years. It was to be his *magnum opus*, and he was determined not to let it go until he was absolutely satisfied with it. As he wrote to Elizabeth Healey, 'There is really more work in that book [*Mr Lewisham*] than in many a first-class F.R.S. research thesis, and stagnant days and desert journeys beyond imagining.'

Love and Mr Lewisham is Wells's own story of his

student days at South Kensington and the failure of his
first marriage. Some of its detail is borrowed from the experiences of Richard Gregory, who had done in fact what
Lewisham does in this fiction – married a girl on his guinea-
a-week student's allowance. But mainly it is Wells's own
story of the frustrations of love and the manner in which
this sexual imperative gets in the way of a man's career.

It is his first novel of character; his first attempt to get on
terms with the art of the novel. The scientific romances had
depended on incident and description; the human personality had no effect upon the flow of incident. Except that
he has the courage to venture, the Professor in *The Time
Machine*, for example, is an automaton, an observer, a recorder of wonders which are not influenced at all by his
human will. The same is true of Pendrick in *The Island of
Dr Moreau*, though he registers shock and exhibits human
endurance. *The Invisible Man* has an invisible character; all
that we are aware of is his petulance and exasperation at
the fix he has got himself into, and his horrifying end does
not touch the springs of our sympathy, which are moved by
the plight of Thomas Marvel, who becomes the invisible
man's hostage. The same is true of the narrator in *The
War of the Worlds*, though here, for Wells's narrative skill
was increasing fast, we begin to see a figure more recognizably like Wells than Pendrick in *Dr Moreau*; the narrator
still and the observer, but a man who engages our curiosity
if not our sympathy, someone we try to identify with the
writer.

But Mr Lewisham is very different. Here is a man, a victim of life's unhappy chances. Lewisham fights back, and we
are totally on his side; his final surrender calls for our tears.
Poor Lewisham has so desperately wanted to get on in life,
and he has been betrayed and tripped up by such a very
human failing, falling in love. All our sympathies are with
this most ordinary hero, this Lucky Jim of the Nineties,
bursting with ideals, defrauded by a rogue like the medium
Chaffrey, seduced from the 'Schema' with which he has re-

gulated his life by a chance encounter with a pretty face which set glands working, the possible uprising of which had never occurred to Mr Lewisham when planning his road to success. The very courage with which he accepts not only matrimony but the burden of a mother-in-law who has been deserted by the rogue Chaffrey, abandoning in the end his dreams of a scientific career, touches our sympathy and arouses our admiration. It was a whole world away from Henry James's experience, but James called it 'in short, a bloody little chunk of life'. That indeed it is.

But its reception was disappointing. The public were not much amused by Lewisham's earnest struggle to come to terms with life. Wells had offered them a brilliant self-portrait, but nobody then knew the details of his life, and to the class-conscious readers of those days Lewisham seemed rather a presumptuous, vulgar young fellow, and his being put in his place by fate a not unmerited rebuke. What they wanted was another *War of the Worlds* with legless and noseless Martians equipped with whip-like tentacles – eight of them each side of the mouth-slit – who kept themselves going with human blood run directly into their veins by means of a little pipette. They wanted more of this stuff – familiar London laid waste with the heat-ray, as the Martians moved crab-wise, encased in Handling Machines – not young Mr Lewisham interviewing the scholastic agents or surrendering himself cautiously to passionate love.

Wells could have responded to this check by turning back to science fantasies. They were easy to write, and the 'price per thou.', in which he had an abiding interest, was highly satisfying, but what he wanted more than money was recognition. Good though he knew *The Time Machine* and *The Invisible Man* and *The Island of Dr Moreau* to be, they were not novels of character; they did not reflect life so much as show the effects of an eccentric deviation from it. They were profitable, but they did not put him where he wanted to be, where he knew he could be if he tried: with Kipling and Stevenson; or, to go back a bit, with

Hardy; to go even further back, with Dickens and Sterne. The power was stirring in him, *Kipps* was under way, and he knew it was going to be a great book, but it took time. His was not the sort of nature to draw itself apart from the world, feed upon the imagination and give birth to something splendid. He needed human contact and applause or criticism; he had the clever man's need of an audience.

It says something for the firmness of his aim that he should have resisted the temptation to turn back to the profitable vein of fantasy. He had dedicated himself to the task of being a novelist, and he wrote quite severely to Arnold Bennett, who had just given up the editorship of *Woman* to launch out as an author himself, and who had written to congratulate him on what he had read of *Love and Mr Lewisham* in serial extracts, at the same time questioning the commercial wisdom of abandoning a line for which his name was known.

A year later he wrote again to Bennett, a letter marked 'Private and Abusive', complaining at being left out of the contemporary writers considered in Bennett's *Fame and Fiction: An Enquiry into Certain Popularities*, which had just been published. He concluded bitterly:

For me, you are part of the great Public, I perceive I am doomed to write scientific romances and short stories for you creatures of the mob, and my novels must be my private dissipation. [19 August 1901]

Bennett took two months to answer, and then, in that chaffing vein with the underlying note of deep seriousness when it touches on the great subject of Getting On which marks the whole of the corespondence between these young men struggling to make names for themselves in the world of the novel, he replied:

I sent you my 'bright' and amusing book as a return – feeble, but the best I could do – for the copy of *Love and Mr Lewisham* which you caused to be sent to me. I hesitated seven days and seven nights before sending it. I kept saying to myself: 'now will the incurable and amazing modesty of this great man prevent him from guessing the true reason why I have left him out of this my book?' (which however does not pretend to be a 'review of the state of contemporary fiction'.) I at last resolved to send it and hope for the best. Alas! The worst has happened. You will have to see a doctor about that modesty of yours. Can you not see that I left you out

- a)   Because I felt incompetent to assess you
- b)   Because nothing less than a whole book could contain you
- c)   Because your popularity needs no explaining
- d)   Because it was my ambition, after 25 years of study, meditation and prayer, to attempt an elaborate monograph on you, and let this be the climax of my career.
[16 October 1901]

Wells meant to make *Kipps*, on which he was now hard at work, the immediate successor to *Love and Mr Lewisham*, but being Wells, he was restless, ambitious, supercharged with energy. *Mankind in the Making* seemed a necessary follow-up to *Anticipations*. He could not hasten *Kipps*, but he needed to follow up *Lewisham* with another novel, especially as *The First Men in the Moon*, the last (for some time) of his scientific romances, was coming out that year. So he turned to something which was begun lightly, but which ended again in a personal statement – the anguish of the sensual man who has to conform to the hard rigour of life.

What he plainly intended in *The Sea Lady* was a social comedy mocking the pretensions of the English middle class. Wells himself describes this as a parallel story to *Love and Mr Lewisham*, with the variation that in *Lewisham* love leads to settling down and in *The Sea Lady* it breaks things up. But Mr Lewisham may be said to have settled down as martyrs do to their fires: Chatteris, in *The Sea Lady*, surrenders himself thrillingly to the sensuous dream, forfeiting his life as the price.

Love and Mr Lewisham is much the more undisguisedly autobiographical of the two novels. But *The Sea Lady* wears only a thin disguise. It is a parable, dressed in irony, which reflects one of the main preoccupations of Wells's mind as a novelist – the perplexity of the drive and urge of sex upon human relations. As yet he dared only to speak in parables, but soon this preoccupation was to impinge on all his writings, even speculative books like *A Modern Utopia* and visionary novels like *In the Days of the Comet.*

The Sea Lady has the supreme merit of seeming actual, not fictional. The Sandgate beach is the locale of the story, and the Pophams, the Wellses' next-door neighbours in Arnold House, if not the originals of the Buntings, must have been in on the joke and supplied, consciously or unconsciously, many of the features of this splendidly solid British middle-class household into which on a summer's day, in the arms of Fred Bunting, comes a mermaid for what proves an extensive stay and one severely and fatally disrupting to the even tenor of the Bunting existence. Across the bridge of the years we catch again the sunlight of that Edwardian morning when Mrs Bunting's two daughters are disporting themselves genteelly in the waves while their father and Fred, their brother, are mooching about at a polite distance. Suddenly a lady, swimming in towards the shore, disappears. Dad and Fred, borrowing a ladder, plunge to the rescue, and Fred, not much of a swimmer, is under the impression that he has rescued her and brings her ashore in his arms. She is beautiful and her lips brush his ears and Fred's heart thumps; and then, as everyone crowds round, it is noticed that she has a tail. A mermaid! The immediate Edwardian middle-class reaction is not to attract attention, especially as some low excursionists are approaching with genial inquiries as to 'What's up 'ere?' Before anything more can be said, Mrs Bunting has bundled her up the garden and into the house: the Sea Lady has come to stay.

The Sea Lady had the same attraction for the early-middle-aged Wells that the figures of France and Columbia in the cartoons in *Punch* had had on the imagination of the infant Wells. She is Beauty, Venus Andromyne, for which we are all searching. Staying with the Buntings are the Glendower girls, and the older Miss Glendower is a figure who was always to haunt Wells's imagination in another way. A beautiful but passionless blue-stocking, she regards sex as a momentary and rather shameful little intimacy necessary for procreation, to be carried out essentially in a spirit of earnestness, the whole aim of matrimony being to 'get on'. Adeline Glendower reappears in *Kipps* as Helen Walsingham, who nearly catches Kipps in his climb up the social ladder. She is the young woman *with something gone out of her*, in Wells's view. From *Kipps* onwards, greater injuries provide the tensions in his novels, but in these early books the sense of social deprivation which no doubt stung him and his Jane in real life comes only too clearly through.

If *The Sea Lady* started as an amusing joke, in the end it became a low passionate cry of distress for beauty lost and pleasures forgone in the line of duty. Wells becomes Chatteris. Chatteris, the young man who is nursing the local parliamentary seat and is engaged to Adeline Glendower, falls in love with the Sea Lady. Something in him that craves sensuous love responds to the Sea Lady's allurement. In the end, she returns to the sea and Chatteris goes down with her beneath the waters. On the beach, where the Buntings once disported on a summer morning, only the policeman is left, holding a wrap found lying there, the beam from his lantern searching over the gently breathing sea, 'a stain of faint pink curiosity upon the mysterious vast serenity of night'.

What had started out as an entertaining comedy, dealing ironically and resentfully with some of the stiffer and sillier conventions of English middle-class life, took on a deeper, more poignant note of regret for sensuous beauty lost in the relentless pressure to 'get on'. Something had 'gone out of'

Adeline Glendower which was only quiescent in Chatteris,
in spite of Chatteris's vehement intention to 'go a man's
way', avoiding desire:

The light and guide of the world, a beacon on a headland
blazing out. Let it burn! Let it burn! I make my choice ...
Renunciation! Always renunciation! That is life for all of us.
We have desires, only to deny them, senses that we all must
starve. We can live only as part of ourselves. Why should *I* be
exempt? For me she is evil, for me she is death. ... Only, why
have I seen her face? Why have I heard her voice ...?

The cry broke from Chatteris, but it broke from the very
being of Wells. One clear strain is evident in nearly all his
novels, and Wells himself admits its presence and its significance in *Experiment in Autobiography*, acknowledges,
too, that it was often reflected in his fiction. His heroes always escape from the net which imprisoned them – Chatteris to drowning, Ramage in *The New Machiavelli* to exile
in Italy. But the end of the escape is the death of hopes,
ambitions, even life itself. It was what young Lewisham had
escaped to. But to withstand the temptation to escape, to
turn resolutely aside from desire, not to know the glorious
swift rushing imaginative passion – that is the beginning of
death in life. Wells was settled now with a wife and family
and herded into that narrow road bounded by high walls
that leads steadily upwards to success. The next few years
were to test his resolution to withstand desire and the unrelenting pressure of success.

The Sea Lady was published in August 1902, and again
without pause he turned to the subject that more and more
was to take possession of his imagination, the thinking-out
of the problem of human will and government. Looking
back in his autobiography, he sees himself in his early years
as disentangling himself from his family and origins and
making himself a citizen of the world. 'I move from a back-
yard to Cosmopolis; from Atlas House to the burthens of
Atlas.' He sees himself as becoming the conscious common

man of his time and culture, 'a specimen drop from the changing ocean of general political opinions'.

His second open assault on this subject, *Mankind in the Making*, is less successful than *Anticipations* partly because it is more wordy. Partly, also, because it deals too exclusively with the need of education in reaching Utopia, a subject less exhilarating than some of the visions of a looser sex-life hinted at in *Anticipations*. Before he had finished that book he was at work on *The Food of the Gods*, a fictional counterpart of *Mankind in the Making*, and the first of the novels to be published under the contract he was about to sign with Frederick Macmillan for the publication of all his future work. *The Food of the Gods* starts humorously and vigorously. What makes Wells's early books so attractive is the ease with which he slips into the story. This humorous observation of everyday life and character was native to his genius; what was foreign to it, although congenial to his reforming mind, was the effort to establish on such a foundation a meaningful allegory. The native wit of the Cockney and the didactic assertion of the teacher sometimes clashed painfully. 'Boomfood' is a joke when it is first introduced. When it gets out of hand and children grow into giants, it is still quite funny. But when they are presented as the supermen of the future, the allegory becomes caricature and the wit is lost.

As we shall see later, when he began his long argument with Frederick Macmillan, Wells regarded *The Food of the Gods* as a fantasia on bigness, a subject which always fascinated him, perhaps because he was below the normal height himself . By 1903, when this book appeared, he was so firmly established that a novel which seems to us to lose its brilliant opening by tasteless exaggeration later, was treated with considerable respect by the critics. He was beginning to be the most talked-about writer of the time, and men of letters, scientists, political leaders like Balfour, and political activists planning the perfect state, like the Webbs, Bernard Shaw and the leading Fabians, all discussed his views

with great earnestness and solemnity; though someone very
clear-eyed like Beatrice Webb could confide to her diary
the weakness of his case:

A world run by the physical science man straight from his
laboratory is his ideal: he does not see that specialized faculty
and knowledge are needed for administration exactly as they
are needed for the manipulation of machinery or natural forces.
But he is extraordinarily quick in his apprehensions and took
up all the points we gave him in our 48 hours talk with him,
first at his own house and then here. He is a good instrument
for popularizing ideas, and he gives as many ideas as he receives.
... Altogether it is refreshing to talk to a man who has shaken
himself loose from so many of the current assumptions, and is
looking at life as the explorer of a new world.

Few seemed to notice at first the growing emphasis upon
freedom of conduct and the loosening of restraints,
especially in moral matters. Or see that beneath his impatience with the muddle and wrongness of so much in life
was a desire not only to mend these matters but to dominate
the reconstruction himself. Or see that the prophetic mind,
performing so brilliantly, was governed at times by some
smaller, more fleshly and vulgar emotions. The subtle and
searching brain had its disablements: it was dominated by
three great mythologies, sex, science and religion, which
were in the forefront of everyone's mind, young as well as
old, at this time of swift social change. But Wells sought to
teach, expound and proclaim, and to relate these myths to
the world's experience, and he lacked the qualities the task
called for. He was not a reasoner or a scientist. He was a
creative artist whose imagination had awoken to the tremendous possibilities of science for mankind. He yearned to be
a thinker, a sage, a prophet, and he thought that the visions
for the betterment of man's lot that crowded through his
active brain were indications that he was cast for that role,
whereas they were the processes of the creative imagination
engaged in generating visions, and were of little practical

use in the world of affairs, except to stimulate men to action or to thought.

But this was not immediately apparent when, flattered by the Webbs and persuaded by Shaw, he left his study to join the Fabian Society. The manner of thought and even the conduct of a whole generation were affected by this decision to break out and reach a wider audience, and, in the process, a novelist of great powers was lost to English literature.

9

The Fabian Battle
and Its Consequences

ONE has to make an effort to get back into the frame of mind of those Edwardian years, so different from ours. The first impression left by the plays and books and memoirs of the time is of a young society, carefree and rich on the one hand, and poor but happy on the other, which has thrown off the repressions of the long Victorian age, playing like children in the sunlight before the shadows of evening fall. But seriousness was in the air too. The brief span of years between the 1880s and the First World War saw considerable wealth accumulate in many more hands, and the luxuries of life, once the privilege of the aristocratic few, made available to nearly the whole of the middle section of the population. For this they had to thank the scientists and the engineers, who had taken over where the researchers left off, and who were busy applying the possibilities of earlier scientific work to practical affairs. The great engine of progress which had been started up by the Industrial Revolution was accelerating, and everything was moving at a giddier and giddier pace. This was exhilarating, but to many serious-minded people the accumulation of wealth at the expense of social progress was a doubtful blessing. Consciences were being smitten, and 'Where is all this leading us?' became a not unusual cry.

In such an atmosphere ethical groups tend to flourish, and the Fabian Society, which was born in an upper room at 17 Osnaburgh Place, Regent's Park, on an evening in October 1883, was typical of its time. A small gathering of educated men and women, sharing two main assumptions – that human life should not consist in the accumulation of material possessions only, and that the exercise of spiritual activity is essential to the full life – met together and set up the Fellowship of the New Life. Their goal was the cultivation of a perfect character. Far from aiming at reform, they dreamt rather of withdrawal from the world because of its wickedness, and they even discussed setting up a community to show by example how a higher life might be lived.

The gentle posturings of the Fellowship of the New Life were soon activated to a brisker pace and more clearly defined objectives by the addition to the membership of a talkative, white-faced, purposeful young Irishman, Bernard Shaw, not long arrived in London from Dublin, and haunting societies where he could speak. Finding this little group's headquarters just opposite in the street where he lived, Shaw joined it. Within a very short time, and chiefly under his masterful direction, the Fellowship had not only changed its name to the Fabian Society, but passed swiftly from its pristine state of pious contemplation to a programme aimed at no less than reconstructing human life. But its intentions were still far from revolutionary, and talk was preferred to action. The small membership was composed of like-minded men who recognized the muddle into which society after a century of industrialism had got itself and thought the way to clear up the muddle was to redesign the essential apparatus of daily life: the way taxes were paid, better housing, insurance benefits – essential matters enough, but not to be fought for behind barricades. The very title which the renamed Society took to itself was indicative of its cautious approach to these problems. Conquest was to be by permeation of the existing political parties with the Society's enlightened ideas, not by setting up a party of its own or joining one of the existing socialist organizations which aimed at democratic freedom. Besides Shaw, the leading figures in the Society were civil servants like Sidney Webb and Sydney Olivier, and the small membership was essentially middle and upper middle class; they worked on blueprints, not close to the breath of life.

A *sine qua non* of admission to the Society had been from the beginning what was called the Basis, which all members were required to sign. This set out the Society's aim in six short paragraphs which plainly bore the mark of Shaw's style and Sidney Webb's thought, Webb from the beginning being the planner behind this reanimated and renamed Society. Quite simply, the Basis said that the Fabian aim was the reorganization of society by the emancipation of land and industrial capital from individual and class ownership, and the vesting of these in the community for the general benefit. For the attainment of this object it looked to the spread of socialist opinions and the general dissemination of knowledge about the relation between the individual and society. As might be expected in such a Society, the Basis had been the subject of frequent dispute, and committee after committee had been set up over the years to revise it and bring it up to date. But little was ever done about it, and the Basis remained the test of a candidate's fitness for admission.

The messianic tables of the Society might be said to be *Fabian Essays*, seven essays discussing the Fabian viewpoint, which had had a considerable success when published in book form in 1890. Like most well-meaning, intellectual discussion groups of its kind, the Society was dominated by a few forceful characters; otherwise the membership was woolly-minded, humanitarian, even vegetarian – just nice middle-class people. And not very many of them. By the time *Fabian Essays* was published in 1890 the membership was only 150, and in spite of the entertainment offered by Shaw's witty eloquence, members seem to have continued to belong out of conscience rather than conviction. By the time Wells joined, the number had climbed to 730, but the Society was in the doldrums. The lectures and meetings were rarely attended by more than twenty people. The Webbs knew what they were doing when they seized on the author of *Anticipations* and *Mankind in the Making* and persuaded him to throw in his lot with them.

Wells came in as a Very Important Person, and the effect on this small circle was rather as though a large object had been dropped into a small pool. There was considerable commotion, a sudden increase in wider activity, and the Society found to its gratified surprise that its meetings were becoming well attended, and its membership immediately began to increase rapidly. This was not wholly, though it was largely, due to Wells's fame.

The end of the Boer War, and a growing feeling of dis-enchantment with the two main political parties, a desire to be modern and 'with it' that comes over society every now and then – all these things had contributed to the growth of a middle-class interest in socialism. The particular Fabian appeal was its inherent gentility; it offered all the sense of adventuring into the future thoughtfully, positively and constructively, in the right company, in one's own class. It became at this time especially attractive to younger intelligent people anxious to throw off the restrictions of the past and come to terms with the twentieth century. *Anticipations, Mankind in the Making* and *A Modern Utopia* fitted exactly into their mood, so that when it was known that the author of these books had joined the Fabians, a ground-swell of interest in the Society mounted and, in the words of its secretary and historian, Edward Pease, 'membership grew at an unprecedented rate'.

It was the quality and enthusiasm of this new member-ship that lifted the Society out of obscurity and made it the most influential body in England outside the conventional political parties. The new members included such men as Granville Barker, Aylmer Maude, Arnold Bennett, Lau-rence Irving, Edgar Jepson, Reginald Bray, Sir Leo Chiozza Money, Dr Stanton Coit, Hamilton Fyfe, A. R. Orage, G. T. Trevelyan, Edward Garnett, Philip Snowden, Clutton Brock and many others who were drawn into the movement because Wells was there. Edward Pease, who was himself no unqualified admirer of H.G., recorded that 'The meetings were crowded, and we were driven out of one hall after another. Moreover the propagandist enthusiasm of Mr Wells and the glamour of his name helped to attract a large number of distinguished persons into our ranks . . .'

Wells read himself in modestly enough with a paper on 'The Question of Scientific Administrative Areas in Relation to Municipal Undertakings'. Under this formidable title he dealt amusingly with the troubles he had had with local authority in building Spade House. He was never to be a speaker. His voice tended to shrillness, and his delivery was muffled and deprecating in tone, although the matter of it was usually aggressive enough. But it was what he said that counted, and there were enough Wellsian ideas bubbling up even in this first paper to excite the members used to a much duller diet.

In such confined circles a conflict of personalities was bound to develop. The Fabian Society had for long been the private preserve of a few dominant personalities. Wells was a dominating personality himself, and one, moreover, who had a chip on his shoulder about his underprivileged beginnings, which carried with it a resentment against the middle class to which the original Fabians, as well as nearly all these recruits, belonged. With Shaw and Wells as members of any small group, no matter what its composition or its aims, collision was inevitable. Shaw fancied himself, quite justifiably, as an orator; he was proud of his ability to think on his feet as another man might be of his skill as a musician. He had an exceptional clarity of mind, and it was constructive as well as analytical; he could analyse with the skill of a chemist the weak parts of someone else's argument and put forward his own ideas with an impressive lucidity and conviction.

What a disadvantage this put Wells at! Although he was not as deep a thinker as he would have liked to be taken for, his ideas could reach beyond the limited vision of ordinary men and sweep them up with enthusiasm. His mind was like a lamp shining into the blackness ahead. Many felt they saw by it, and the feeling was exhilarating.

But this depended upon unquestioning assent. Shaw questioned, and Wells blustered in reply.

Without Wells's presence and the excitement aroused as the duel between him and Shaw developed, the Society would have gone on, but it would not have attracted the wide notice this struggle between two very articulate men gave it. Wells could not suppress his desire to dominate this group of intellectuals, and Shaw could not allow a Society which he had himself largely shaped to give its allegiance to another. The clash, when it came, began quietly enough, after Wells had been a member for more than two years. Wells was to have read a paper on 12 January 1906, but as a General Election was then in progress he substituted for it a brilliant and moving little autobiographical fragment called *This Misery of Boots*.

Although this is all Fabian doctrine – it advocates the national ownership of leather so that all, and not merely the rich, may have decent boots, and very vividly contrasts his own unprivileged youth, when he saw the boots of the passing world through the grating in the pavement above the basement kitchen, with his own present comfort, which includes boots made for him that fit – the signs of a rebel-in-the-making are apparent in the closing section:

Let us be clear about one thing: that Socialism means revolution, that it means a change in the everyday texture of life. It may be a very gradual change but it will be a very complete one. You cannot change the world, and at the same time not change the world. You will find Socialists about, or at any rate men calling themselves Socialists, who will pretend that this is not so, who will assure you that some odd little jobbing about municipal gas and water is Socialism, and backstairs intervention between Conservative and Liberal is the way to the millennium. You might as well call a gas jet in the lobby of a meeting-house the glory of God in heaven.

This was a savage jab at the Executive of the Fabian Society. It cut at the very root of the policy of permeation of existing political parties from which the Society took its name, and the slighting reference to 'little jobbing about municipal gas and water' must have been specially painful to Sidney Webb, whose devouring hobby this subject was. The London County Council had been born almost at the same time as the Fabian Society, and municipal societies bulked very largely in the Fabians' early programme. What Sidney Webb, with his passion for detail, cherished as a worthy work was boring and banal to the visionary mind of Wells. He was throwing down a challenge to the Old Guard, and as the enthusiastic response to this emotional appeal assured him that he had members' support, he was not long in following it up with a more direct challenge. He asked leave to deliver another paper, and a month later presented to a crowded meeting one entitled *The Faults of the Fabian*.

Only gradually, after a beginning which praised the high-minded purpose of the Society, were members made aware that he was criticizing them for lack of imagination, lack of 'go'. The picture he drew was far from flattering, but painfully true. The Society was small, 'still half a drawing-room society', lodged in 'an underground apartment, or cellar, with one secretary and one assistant'. It had set out on the great task of the alteration of the economic basis of life, but if it was demonstrably incapable of mending its own condition, what hope had it of reaching the greater aim? He flung comparisons at them:

Measure with your eye this little meeting, this little hall: look at that little stall of not very powerful tracts: think of the scattered members, one here, one there. Then go out into the Strand. Note the size of the buildings and business places, note the glare of the advertisements, note the abundance of traffic and the multitudes of people. That is the world whose very foundations you are attempting to change. How does this little dribble of activities look then?

Then he threw down his challenge. Abandon the tentative tactics of Fabius for the incisive action of Scipio. Don't

wait to permeate. Go out and convert. Don't make it difficult to become a member. Alter the Basis so that it is easy.
'Make Socialists and you will achieve Socialism; there is no
other way.' And how to go about it? Simple. Raise an income of £1,000 a year, take bigger premises, increase the
staff, prepare well-written literature for the conversion of
unbelievers (not tracts to fortify the faithful); enroll young
men and women, some paid, some volunteers, to carry on
the propaganda and the administrative work. Go out to the
attack, seek out the coming generation at high school, technical college and university. 'Unless I am the most insub-
stantial of dreamers, such a programme as I am now putting
before you ought to carry our number up towards ten thousand within a year or so of its commencement.'

One is irresistibly reminded of Edward Ponderevo's complaint about Wimblehurst. At this very moment his character was being shaped in *Tono-Bungay*, and he was complaining to George's mother about the deadening effect of
Wimblehurst on a chemist with go-ahead ideas:

> 'They've no capacity for ideas. They don't catch on; no Jump
> about the place, no Life. Live! – they trickle, and what one has
> to do here is trickle too – Zzzzzz.'
> 'Ah,' said my mother.
> 'It doesn't suit me,' said my uncle. 'I'm the cascading sort.'

Swept away by enthusiasm, the meeting unanimously
agreed that 'the Executive Committee be instructed to ap-
point a Committee consisting of members and non-
members of the Executive to consider what measures should
be taken to increase the scope, influence, income and activity
of the Society', and a further resolution instructed the
Executive to defer the Annual General Meeting and the
election of a new Executive Committee until the Committee
had reported.

Wells had started something. He had also provoked the
opposition of the Old Guard, and Shaw, chief spokesman
always for the Elders who ran the Society, must have been

longing for the matter to come to debate. What it came
down to in the end, in fact, was a duel between Shaw and
Wells, between two types of mind, the remorseless, steady
instigator of reform against the flinger of phrases, the ut-
terer of battle cries, the fighter ready to storm the citadel.
Shaw had given Fabianism an intellectual air; without him
it might have abandoned itself to the vain dreams of a
Fellowship of the New Life on the one hand, or busied
itself only with pettifogging municipal socialism on the
other. It owed him much. Yet if Wells had not blown in,
the Society would have languished unnoticed by the wider
world.

The General Election of 1906 had resulted in an overwhelming victory for the Liberal Party. But what made the
result of extraordinary significance was not the near-
annihilating defeat suffered by the Conservatives – the worst
they had known for three-quarters of a century – but the
first notable success of the Labour party under the leadership of Keir Hardie. They had put fifty candidates in the
field, and succeeded in having no less than thirty of them
elected, four of them being Fabians. Suddenly it was seen
that the Labour party did not consist of a few cloth-capped
fanatics but was a political force supported actively or pas-
sively by the great organizations of Labour throughout the
country; that they had a programme, not just an account of
resentments to settle; and that, in fact, a new era in
Britain's political life had begun. Suddenly everyone was
talking socialism, wanting to be informed about it, anxious
to join the swelling throng on its triumphant march to the
New Jerusalem. Wells's *Faults of the Fabian*, written while
the General Election was in progress, was delivered just at
the moment when England was waking up. It was exactly
attuned to the general thought and inclination, and once
again, either with incredible luck or incredible foresight, he
had caught the public interest when it was at the point of
being aroused.

That was his good luck. Less good was it that he had

arranged a lecture tour in the United States – it was to be his first visit there – for March, a month after he had delivered this paper. The Committee, appointed at the meeting when he read his paper, was sitting during this time, preparing the Report, but he was not at hand to attend the meetings. Jane Wells was its secretary, and he peppered the members of the Committee with exhortatory and sometimes abusive notes from abroad.

A third factor which increased the excitement was a paper which Wells was asked to give in the autumn of 1907 for a series of meetings which Mrs Bernard Shaw was arranging in the Society. The paper proved too long for one meeting. Entitled *First and Last Things*, it was a deeply emotional, candidly autobiographical statement of his own faith and opinions, and it was aimed at the younger members over the head of the Old Gang. Much extended from its original draft, it was given in the form of three lectures to the Nursery Group of the Society, which had been organized by one of Hubert Bland's daughters. This junior section of the Fabian Society was immensely serious and constructive, but devoted to dancing and picnics too, some of the young members falling in love and eventually marrying each other – 'no better security for prolonged happiness in marriage than sympathy in regard to the larger issues of life', comments the secretary, Edward Pease, who had himself married a Fabian in 1889.

First and Last Things is sub-titled *A Confession of Faith and a Rule of Life*. One senses across the years the excitement of those meetings, and imagines that earnest, tubby figure delivering in that high-pitched voice the burning words. One can visualize Wells in the very act of delivering it, much as he depicts himself in the introduction to *A Modern Utopia*.

The Owner of the Voice you must figure to yourself as a whitish plump man, a little under the middle size and age, with such blue eyes as many Irishmen have, and agile in his movements and with a slight tonsorial baldness – a penny might cover it – of the crown. Its front is convex. He droops at times like most of us, but for the greater part he bears himself as valiantly as a sparrow. Occasionally his hand flies out with a fluttering gesture of illustration. And his Voice (which is our medium henceforth) is an unattractive tenor that becomes at times aggressive. Him you must imagine as sitting at a table reading a manuscript about Utopias, a manuscript he holds in two hands that are just a little fat at the wrists. The curtain rises upon him so.

One sees the eager young faces upturned to his, listening to a confession which rings with truth. It is a personal confession, but it is at the same time an appeal to others to join him in a life-faith, and across the bridge of the years comes the very essence of this man, dominated by the myths that possessed him, radiating the power of his ideas into a whole generation.

What is he saying? That the race, not the individual, is important. The race flows through the individual. In so far as we realize ourselves as experiments of the species for the Species, just so far do we escape from the accidental and its chaotics. Out of the whole living creation rises the Spirit of Man beginning to realize at last his synthetical purpose, to increase Power and realize Beauty. The speaker does not believe that he has any personal immortality. Believing in the great and growing Being of the species from which he comes, to which he will return, he can only believe that the peculiar little thread that is his individual life will undergo synthesis and vanish as a separate thing.

He defines his attitude to Christianity. It is not antagonistic, but he cannot give himself to it utterly as a believer. The great and very definite personality of Christ living for centuries in the hearts and imaginations of mankind does not and never has attracted him. The Christian Christ is too fine for him; he had no petty weaknesses. The speaker's own uncertainties and heartaches, his doubts and tears, have been confirmed by another figure – and strangely his name must have fallen on Fabian ears: Oliver Goldsmith, the gentle creator of *The Vicar of Wakefield*.

In all this there must have been complete conviction. Something revelatory of a gentle emotional side of H.G.'s character emerges from this confession. One senses the agony of the slights he had suffered as a clever boy brought up amidst the ignorant. He had a fellow feeling for Oliver Goldsmith, for

his blunders and troubles, his vices and vanities, seized and still hold my imagination. The slights of Boswell, the contempt of Gibbon and all his company save Johnson, the exquisite fineness of spirit in his *Vicar of Wakefield* and that green suit of his, and the doctor's cane and the love despised, these things together made him a congenial saint and hero for me, so that I thought of him as others pray. When I think of that youthful feeling for Goldsmith, I know what I need in a personal saviour, as a troglodyte who has seen a candle can imagine the sun.

Conduct follows necessarily from belief. What, then, is the good life? That which contributes most effectively to the collective growth. Through subordinating oneself and all one's motives to the awakening and the development of the consciousness and will of our species one attains Salvation. Right living is in doing that for the general good of the race which one does best. Setting oneself apart, turning one's back on the others, is the waste of life; it is sin. What we work towards is synthesis, and this communal effort is the adventure of humanity, the enterprise of God, the captain of mankind.

How odd all this sounds now, sixty years later. These declamatory sentences, calling men away from selfishness to work for the common good. God regarded as a Captain at the head of an heroic army struggling sternly to reach that ultimate haven where the storms of competition shall rage no more and the Spirit of Mankind, cleansed, synthesized, whiter than white, shall, like a zephyr on a fresh spring day, play lightly for evermore. One understands fanatics like Karl Marx; one can allow for the blind enthusiasms of dedicated men like H. M. Hyndman or William Morris, Keir Hardie or Robert Blatchford. But what were clever men like Shaw and Wells doing talking of the New Jerusalem, speaking of armies commanded by God the Captain marching on the world city of mankind?

It is a mistake to scoff. Every age has its brief-note, and that by which the 1960s may be judged in 2060 might well make us feel foolish and hot-eared and inarticulate with embarrassment if we were alive to hear it. Socialism was no longer the hope of the oppressed only. Into the hearts and minds of millions a little light was breaking, and it must have seemed to them that not since the birth of Christ, which heralded the defeat of old barbarism and oppressions, had such a dramatic change for the condition of man been promised.

This is where the message of Wells differed from that propounded by other prophets of the hour. He spoke to the intelligent young, not in England only but all over the world. It was not a limited class, for nearly half the world was under middle age when normal death came at forty-four or forty-five. The greater part of mankind, therefore, was green and fresh to new ideas. The appeal he made was physical as well as intellectual; for the achievement of the human synthesis, he asked them to submit not only their general activities and intellectual life, but their bodies and emotional possibilities, so as to make a new world bodily and spiritually.

This was not a rousing call for everyone to abandon all restraint and straightaway embrace where desire drove them. Nevertheless, it was a far cry from the original Fabian programme. The Basis had not considered sexual relations as part of the design for reconstructing life. But Wells was cunningly introducing a subject which he knew was coming to the forefront of everyone's mind, especially the minds of the younger members now thronging into the Society.

It was a sensible appeal to discuss sexual matters without

prejudice and with frankness, accepting that the subject is an extraordinarily complex one in which individuality must play a great part. Some sexual intercourse, he said to these young, is a necessary phase in existence; without it there is an incompleteness, a failure in the life cycle, a real wilting and failure of energy and vitality and the development of morbid states. And since half the friendships and intimacies that make life interesting draw something from the mysterious elements of sexual attraction, a discussion of them is important.

The effect must have been startling, and it says something for the courage with which H.G. held these convictions, and for the broad free sweep of his mind, as also for the enthusiastic response he drew from his young audience, that he should have turned an eloquent and emotional declaration of the socialist purpose into a frank and fearless advocacy of the need to break down our individual separations, cast aside our reserve so that in the end the Believer will also be the Lover. For love breaks down the boundaries of self, and true love is the individualized correlative of Salvation. In the end, words are not enough.

I am trying to be as explicit as possible in this writing about Love. But the substance in which one works here is emotion that evades definition; poetic flashes and figures of speech are truer than prosaic statements. Body and the most sublimated ecstasy pass into one another, exchange themselves and elude every net of words we cast . . .

He can only sum it up by saying:

To love is to go living radiantly through the world. To love and be loved is to be fearless of experience and 'rich' in the power to give.

He knew, of course, that his own conduct from time to time – and this was in the general knowledge – could be quoted against the views he pressed here on his excited audience. He knew the duality of much of human nature, and how his own professions were belied and contradicted often by his own actions. In the last resort:

> I do not care whether I am seated on a throne or drunk or dying in the gutter. I follow my leading. I am more than myself, for I myself am Man. In the ultimate I know, though I cannot prove my knowledge in any way whatever, that everything is right and all things mine.

The lectures scored a tremendous success amongst those ardent young members, and must have done much to induce in H.G. a dangerous estimation of the support he enjoyed. Everything was going his way except fate and Bernard Shaw.

There was naturally a good deal of opposition among the Executive to the direction in which Wells was proposing to lead the Society, but if it had not been for Shaw the opposition would have been swept along with everybody else to support Wells's large ideas for expansion. As it was, the Old Guard, dominated by Shaw, played the Fabian game to perfection. When Wells returned from America it was to the destruction of a love-affair growing increasingly beyond the limits of the *passade* which had been agreed upon between him and Jane, and especially embarrassing and dangerous because it could not be kept secret in this small gossiping Society. His natural impatience with committees and procedure made him unhelpful to those who were trying to help him. But finally the Report was ready. It was circulated to all members at the end of the year, together with the reply to it from the Executive, a document clearly written by Shaw himself, for there was no mistaking his style. The reply said simply that Mr Wells's proposals were impracticable, and as long as the Executive remained in office any attempt to pass them would be regarded as a vote of lack of confidence and the Executive would promptly resign. The issue was plainly joined. Either the Fabian Society as it was, or a Wells Society professing doctrines not written into the constitution.

At the meeting in December the issue was debated, with Shaw naturally the principal spokesman for the Old Guard. But everybody had to have a say, and in his autobiography Wells perfectly conveys the crowded scenes in Cliffords Inn as the members, buoyed up by the excitement aroused by this battle between the giants, thronged the meetings – the first had to be adjourned to give all the leaders a chance to speak. The excitement was so great, the atmosphere so confusing, that Mrs Shaw found herself voting for instead of against the amendments proposed by Wells. The eye of the novelist caught all the leaders in their characteristic attitudes:

the fine speeches of Shaw; Sidney Webb, with his head down talking with a fast lisp, terribly like a Civil Servant dispensing information; the magnificent Bland in a frock-coat and a black-ribboned monocle, debating, really debating, Sir, in a rococo variation of the parliamentary front bench manner; red-haired Haden Guest, being mercurial, and Edward Pease, the secretary, invincibly dry; myself speaking haltingly on the verge of the inaudible, addressing my tie through a cascade moustache that was no sort of help at all, correcting myself as though I were a manuscript under treatment, making ill-judged departures into parentheses; the motions, the amendments, the disputes with the chairman, the show of hands, the storms of applause ...

Shaw had never been in better form; cold, clear, persuasive, chaffing his old friend Wells for misguided enthusiasm, and doing some very neat footwork by trapping Wells into an undertaking to remain on the Executive even if his proposals were defeated. Having extracted that undertaking, he said: 'Very well, then, I may pitch into Mr Wells without regard.' And did so, mercilessly. He showed that Wells's proposals were a dreamer's fancies. The handsome offices must be produced by the large income, not the large income by the handsome offices. The brilliant pamphlets by practised authors, not by the meagre talents of hard-working members. He dealt in turn with each of Wells's proposals, showing some to be mere baseless visions which the reality of the facts made quite impossible, and of others that the Executive had already taken steps to implement them; they were not to be rushed into them by the methods suggested by Wells. He wove confusing circles round Wells's intentions, and Wells, shrill, denunciatory, overemphatic when it would have been politic to be subtle, and fatally given to vagueness when precise details were needed, cut a poor figure. At the adjourned Annual Meeting in March he failed to carry the Executive with the nominations of supporters whose names he had proposed, though he himself was re-elected. He had lost the battle. What remained was the bitter memory of a high aim debated into the ground. His undertaking to Shaw forced him to sit there for another year at least, like a bird with clipped wings. It cannot have been an easy year, and his conduct, as we shall see, was doing nothing to endear him to the Old Gang who had triumphed.

Yet Shaw was right: Wells's life had been 'one long promotion', with never a set-back until this one occurred. From the beginning his story had been one of self-assertion. At first this had just been a matter of achieving literary success and getting money and fame. Then when it became apparent that men were highly receptive to dreams, he had thought he saw wider possibilities, a real 'Hitler' future before him. When that prospect was denied him by the ill-luck of running up against someone, in the person of Shaw, who was just as clever as he was, and who was immeasurably superior at the art of persuasion by eloquence, Wells fell into a display of tantrums that was to alter for the worse the direction, the temper and the character of his work.

How these fools talked! What a contrast they must have offered to his fine, clean, imagined Order of Samurai. In the New Republic of his dreams such gas-and-water matters, such parish-pump affairs, which they thought to be socialism, would have been dealt with by small officials, under the command and inspiration of the Samurai.

This order, which is fully pictured in *A Modern Utopia*, had seized the imagination of many of the younger Fabians, and Wells had an eager and passionate following, without power but very earnest. The Samurai was to have been a voluntary nobility, an order into which entry was theoretically open to everyone, but was made difficult by qualifications and severe disciplinary tests. Which would you have? Pettifogging municipalization on the one hand, epitomized for Wells in the Civil Service figure of Sidney Webb; or the alternative he offered, the young and the strong and the beautiful, the Order of the Samurai, perhaps wearing uniforms, anyhow bearing faces strengthened by discipline and touched by devotion? To us, survivors of another age, it is all reminiscent of rallies at Nuremberg and torchlight processions in Rome, but there can be little doubt of the appeal it made for a time to the imaginations of young Edwardians.

In the following September, Wells resigned, giving as his reasons in a letter in the *Fabian News*, 'disagreement with the Basis which forms the Confessions of Faith of the Society, and discontent with the general form of its activities, together with a desire to concentrate on the writing of novels'. To him, the dreamer, who had foreseen an Order of Samurai rising from among these intelligent young people to fashion the New Republic, the thing had become dust. Bitterness, disillusion, despair rushed in to fill the vacuum from which all his energetic dreams had vanished at the cold touch of reason. Years after, reflecting on this issue, and on the time and thought he had given to it, he was conscious only of how silly and inept he had been, remembering only how badly he had played his hand. 'At last I suddenly became aware of the disproportionate waste of my energy in those disputes, and abandoned my attack. Not there was the New Republic to be discovered. By me at any rate.'

He was to have his revenge on those 'prigs at play' later

in *The New Machavelli*. Looking back from a distance of sixty years, it does seem now, as it seemed to Wells in retrospect, to have been a petty conflict about issues that have not really mattered. Our world was born on larger and bloodier battlefields than the cellars of that building in Cliffords Inn. In retrospect the Fabians seem to have been far off from where the pain and the struggle of social justice were being felt. In this year, 1908, the unemployed in Glasgow attempted to storm the City Council Chamber and were stopped by the police. Hunger marchers who had walked from Manchester to London held a protest meeting on Tower Hill. And in September, while the Fabians were busily engaged in their exciting procedural battle, the old-age pension came into effect for the first time. The maximum pension was five shillings a week, but this was reduced by a shilling a week according to any other means of support that might be provided, and it came down to a shilling a month if by one means or another – by gift, allowance or your own labour – you were in receipt of an income as little as £2 12s. 6d. a month. When the Old Age Pension Act came into force on 24 September there were heartbreaking scenes all over the country. Many of those entitled to the pittance could not read, and most of them could not write. Too often they had not had the benefit of baptism, so there was no true record of their age. Even when their names appeared in parish registers they could not afford the cost of a proved extract. A month later in Trafalgar Square there were demonstrations of hunger marchers. The length of the Strand away, the excited Fabians, bursting from their crowded meetings, chattering like starlings, converged on Appenrodts for coffee and talk and intrigue, for gossip and scandal, for arguments about the shape of the world to come, while the hungry marchers resisted the efforts of the police to move them on from Trafalgar Square, and an unseasonable heat-wave, with temperatures of eighty degrees on the first four days of October, at least made it easy for them to sleep out of doors.

While all this was happening, Wells was putting himself into a very tricky position in another matter. Gossip about his private life was becoming very sibilant, and not helping his cause in some quarters. The excited response of the younger members of the Society to his ideas had been soothing to his vanity. At a senior level the Fabian Society was acting as the standard-bearer of socialism in Britain, with serious intellectuals like Philip Snowden, who was later to become Chancellor of the Exchequer in the Labour Government, William Temple, who was to become Archbishop of Canterbury, L. S. Amery, Harold Laski, R. H. Tawney and others, giving to Fabian socialism a constructive air. At a junior level the Fabian Nursery were reflecting this seriousness, with youthful touches to make it all interesting. They formed separate discussion groups, where very enlivening topics were frankly discussed, and some of the liberties tasted, new to that time, of mixing with the opposite sex and having some fun, all under the guise of educating themselves in serious social questions. Under the chaperonage of the wives of the Elders, they met one another at dances, and at the Fabian Summer Schools. When out of their chaperones' hearing, they discussed the forbidden subject of sex; in many cases they fell in love, in a few became engaged, and in some even married. It was this very active younger group which had listened avidly to Wells's *First and Last Things*, and they admired him enormously. All this he found comforting to his hurt pride, and *Ann Veronica*, which seemed so daring to the general public, took shape in his mind as he watched these fair young men and women at their venturesome play, to which his own ardent temperament so sympathetically responded.

One of the finest passages of character dissection done in *Experiment in Autobiography* is the one Wells does on Hubert Bland, a founder member of the Fabian Society, and his wife, who was E. Nesbit, the famous writer of children's books. The distinction Wells is plainly trying to make in this passage is that which lay between his own open and liberal attitude towards sex, and Bland's furtive but immensely active interest in the subject:

> He [Bland] was under an inner compulsion to be a Seducer – on the best eighteenth-century lines. . . . He was, he claimed to me at least, not so much Don Juan as Professor Juan. 'I am a student, an experimentalist,' he announced, 'in illicit love.'

These confidences had been exchanged when the Wellses had first moved into Spade House and had been invited to Dymchurch, only a bicycle ride away, where the Blands kept open house. The contrast between Hubert Bland, who affected city clothes even in the country and wore a monocle attached to his waistcoat by a broad ribbon and confided in him the secrets of his numerous conquests, and the tall, restless, good-looking woman, rather absent-minded, who was his wife and who wrote sentimental stories for adults but wonderful books for children, was fascinating to the novelist's eye of Wells. The house was always full of visitors, long-haired intellectuals mostly, fascinating to him too because he and Jane were just beginning to emerge from the solitude of their existence while he had been making his name and he had never before met these theorizers, themselves impotent creatively but very vocal about what was needed. Included in the crowded company at week-ends was generally the latest of Bland's conquests. And unexplained and numerous children – until the secret of the household became clear to him.

The astonished visitor came to realize that most of the children of the household were not E. Nesbit's but the result of Bland's conquests, that the friend and companion who ran the household was the mother of one of these young people, that young Miss So-and-so, who played Badminton with a preoccupied air, was the last captive of Hubert's accomplished sex-appeal. All this E. Nesbit not only detested and mitigated and tolerated, but presided over and I think found exceedingly interesting.

Wells introduces the Blands in his autobiography chiefly to point out what was wrong with the direction of the Fabian

Society. In his view, the dominant personalities managing its affairs were themselves so mixed-up, jealous of one another, and activated by selfish desire and obscure plots and strategies, that the Society as a whole was in urgent need of a searching psychoanalysis.

What he does not confess to in this engaging pastiche of some of the chief figures is that his own conduct was unifying the opposition against him. One of the mysterious Miss Blands, an active member of the Nursery of the Fabian Society, was so carried away by his eloquence that she was prepared to run off with him, and was stopped only at the last moment when she was plucked from his side in a railway carriage at Paddington Station. Whispers of this escapade circulated in the Society; while Bland, in the guise now of an outraged parent, pressed for Wells's prompt expulsion from the Executive. As always it fell on Shaw to remonstrate, and he wrote to reprove Wells for such unsocial behaviour. Wells replied, quite unrepentant about his part in the escapade:

Spade House
1909

Dear Shaw

The more I think you over the more it comes home to me what an unmitigated middle-Victorian ass you are. You play about with ideas like a daring garrulous maiden aunt, but when it comes to an affair like the Bland affair you show the instincts of conscious gentility and the judgement of a hen. You write of Bland in a strain of sentimental exaltation. You explain his beautiful & romantic character to me – as though I didnt know the man to his bones. You might be dear Mrs Bland herself in a paroxysm of romantic invention. And all this twaddle about the 'innocent little person'. If she is innocent it isn't her parents' fault anyhow.

The fact is yours is a flimsy intellectual acquisitive sort of mind adrift & chattering brightly in a world you dont understand. You dont know, as I do, in blood & substance, lust, failure, shame, hate, love & creative passion. You dont understand & you cant understand the right & wrongs of the case into which you stick your maiden judgement – any more than you can understand the aims in the Fabian Society that your vanity has wrecked.

> Now go on being amusing.
> Yours ever
> H. G. Wells

Ann Veronica had started off as a major novel, and Geoffrey West declares that it was cut short only because it developed unsatisfactorily. Wells himself says 'it was only a slight reflection of anything that actually occurred', but he acknowledges that Ann Veronica came as near to being a living character as anyone in his earlier love stories because in some particulars she was drawn from life. In Mr Stanley, Ann Veronica's father, there are unmistakable echoes of Hubert Bland; from Mr Stanley come phrases that Bland must have used when his own daughter ventured on a little free love herself. Mr Stanley says that people who wrote novels ought to be strung up, and 'pernicious rascals' was the mildest term he used for them.

But the figure drawn from life in *Ann Veronica* is not Miss Bland, who subsequently married Clifford Sharp, the first editor of the *New Statesman*, but a much more interesting, beautiful and attractive character with whom Wells now fell passionately in love. Amber Reeves was the daughter of parents who were prominent in intellectual and political circles in London. Her father, the Hon. William Pember Reeves, had been a newspaper editor in New Zealand, and subsequently a member of the New Zealand Cabinet before being appointed Agent-General for New Zealand in London, an office which he was just on the point of resigning at this time to become a Director of the London School of Economics. Mrs Pember Reeves had been a prominent member of the Fabian Society for many years. She was head of the Women's Section, held advanced views on women's rights, and was an admirer of Ibsen and other continental dramatists long before their work became well known in England.

Not surprisingly, the two daughters of such a marriage were brilliant and unconventional. Amber Reeves had taken a first-class degree at Cambridge, but before this had already followed her mother into the Fabian Society. Wells's behaviour with Miss Bland had been prompted by his own vanity and, one suspects, an irresistible desire to revenge himself in this outrageous way on the Old Gang. But in the months following this notorious escapade his attention was first caught and then held by this beautiful, witty, intelligent young Cambridge blue-stocking – his Venus Urania come to life, but twenty years younger than he was.

It was in the summer of 1908, after he had been re-elected to the Executive of the Fabian Society but deprived of any hopes of reforming it, and while in an angry and embittered mood ('The soul goes out to that mighty Being, to apprehend it and serve and possess', as he had proclaimed to the young Fabians in *First and Last Things*, but 'the Soul's desire suddenly turns to presumption and hypocrisy upon the lips. One grasps at the universe and attains – Bathos') that he began to write *Ann Veronica*.

10

Macmillan and Wells

WHILE all this had been going on, Wells had been as highly productive as ever. Between 1903, when he joined the Fabian Society, and 1908, when he left it, he wrote not only two of his greatest novels – *Kipps*, which appeared in 1905, and *Tono-Bungay*, which came out in 1908 – but three other novels in between – *In the Days of the Comet* (1906), *The War in the Air* (1908) and *Ann Veronica* (1909).

Nor was this all. *A Modern Utopia*, written while *Kipps* was being written and coming out in the same year, put the crown on the design for modern living first sketched in *Anticipations* and developed in *Mankind in the Making*. *The Future in America* was the fruit of his tour there in 1906. *New Worlds for Old* (1908) was an extensive and well-developed argument for enlightened socialism. There were pamphlets like *Socialism and the Family* and *Will Socialism Destroy the Home?*; there were extended essays like *First and Last Things*, and Fabian pamphlets like *Reconstruction of the Fabian Society* and *This Misery of Boots*; and there was all the jockeying of influential members and the innumerable letters written by hand to encourage his supporters in the mounting struggle for the soul of the Fabian Society. The amount of words poured out by Wells in the five years between 1903 and 1908, some representing the highest flights of his genius, some the most aggressive of his career, but all requiring intense concentration, exceeds a million. And as the struggle in the Fabian Society mounted to a climax, he was deeply involved in a passionate love affair which also demanded its medium of words and its hours of distraction.

With Frederick Macmillan, who became the publisher of all his books from 1903 onwards, his relations were never entirely easy. Each respected the other's skill and needed him for what he could offer. In 1903, when they came together, Wells had written a dozen books, but in spite of laudatory reviews and the wide discussion and interest they had evoked, not one had sold more than 10,000 copies, which was an insignificant sale compared with Marie Corelli's or Hall Caine's on the one hand, and Rudyard Kipling's on the other. Wells thought that his mistake lay in having his books scattered: if they were all in the hands of one publisher who could issue a collected edition, it would be worth that publisher's while to advertise the lot, not only the latest.

Macmillan's American branch had published *The Wheels of Chance* in 1896, and Wells had had at that time some correspondence with Frederick Macmillan over American copyright,* which was ensured by simultaneous publication. The American market was a valuable one, but although by 1903 Wells was greatly admired in France, Germany and Italy, and flourished there in translations, in America, he complained to Arnold Bennett, '"English Jules Verne" is my utmost glory, reviews of my books appear among the dentifrice advertisements, while paragraphs circulate to the effect that the author of these wild pseudo-scientific extravaganzas is a "dry goods clerk".'

In 1900 he would have laughed at his own concern about recognition, though he would have wanted it no less. But in 1903 he had joined the Reform Club, the Fabian Society and the Coefficients. He was beginning to take himself seriously. Macmillan seemed to be the publisher best equipped to gather his works together, arrange his American publication, and lead him on to the greatness which he believed awaited him.

*It is interesting to read H.G.'s own description of the book to Macmillan: '. . . deals in a humorous and at last slightly pathetic way with the cycling holiday of a half-educated, imaginative and well-meaning draper's assistant and his adventure with a girl, chock full of "advanced" views (also cycles), with whom he becomes involved'.

Macmillan needed Wells almost as much as Wells needed him. His firm had become, with Longmans and Murray, the leading publishers of the day, but with the new public had come in a wave of new publishers – the firms so familiar to us today, Heinemann, John Lane, Dent, Cassell, Methuen, all having begun business in the 1890s – and they were bringing in new writers and making the older-established fiction lists look stuffy and unadventurous. Macmillan knew that it was not enough to have Kipling and Hardy if he did not also have H. G. Wells or Somerset Maugham or Joseph Conrad, and he was quite prepared to meet the terms asked by Wells, a £500 advance against a 25-per cent royalty for each book for a three-book contract, with an option to continue on the same terms in the future. At the regular price of novels, six shillings, allowing for perhaps one in five copies to be sold in the colonies at a royalty of fourpence or sixpence, he would have to sell about 7,500 copies to recover this advance. This did not look out of the way. Methuen had printed 8,000 of *The Sea Lady* and had sold over 5,000 in the first few months. Everyone was talking of Wells, and his sales were bound to go higher. It looked like a profitable investment, and each side came to it in the beginning with satisfaction and with a high regard for the other's capabilities. It was only as they got going that they began to have some personal reservations about each other. Wells thought Macmillan's manner rather autocratic; the chip on Wells's shoulder about being lower middle class became very evident, and the struggle in Macmillan's soul between his commercial instincts as a publisher and his dislike of bounderish behaviour became all too evident, as time went on.

Frederick Macmillan was a notable figure on the publishing scene, having been the instigator of the Net Book Agreement, which, by making it an offence to sell books at less than their published price, had avoided suicidal price-cutting and saved bookselling from bankruptcy at the end of the century. He was now President of the Publishers

Association. He had lived in a publishing atmosphere from the cradle. His father, Daniel, one of the founders of the firm, had died at the early age of forty-three, and Alexander, the surviving brother, had taken Daniel's children into his home and brought them up as his own. The present partners of Macmillans, therefore, although cousins, had lived with each other from nursery days on; and when, in the large Victorian home in which they were brought up, they were allowed at table, great men were usually assembled there. The talk was of nothing but books and ideas – not always as to how many copies a book might sell, but how it might influence and teach, or glorify the Lord, for the Macmillans were strong broad Churchmen.

Alexander Macmillan was robust in character as well as health, and intellectually enormously vigorous. He was to become a leading publisher of the late Victorian age, a friend and confidant of Gladstone and of many other great men outside literary circles. John Morley was his chief literary adviser, and in the scientific world which came to flower in the years following the publication of Darwin's *Origin of Species*, Alexander took the advice of scientists like Norman Lockyer, the astronomer, and Thomas Huxley, Darwin's friend, who was to become Wells's admired teacher.

In fact, this stalwart survivor of the two Scottish brothers lived for his business day and night. In the old building in Bedford Street, smoking evenings were held weekly, and authors of fame, not only those published by Macmillan, gathered to smoke churchwarden pipes, drink, and make merry in the rather bantering way that Victorians favoured. I remember the pipes being still on the mantelpiece in the dining-room when I joined the firm sixty years later, and an armchair I often sat in had fixed to it a brass plate which was inscribed to commemorate Wordsworth's visit to the office. An old oak table bore the autographs of Tennyson, Herbert Spencer, Coventry Patmore and other great men who used to sit round it on those smoking evenings to which

came not only writers like Tennyson and Matthew Arnold
and Charles Kingsley, but scientists who were coming up
fast, and statesmen like Gladstone, and visiting Americans
like Mark Twain. These were not all old men, as we think
of them today: Gladstone and Tennyson were in their fifties.
Alexander had just turned fifty on the night when in the
dining-room they discussed the foundation of a weekly journal which should be the supreme means of communication
between the scientists, and *Nature* was born in a haze of
smoke, amid the excited murmur of voices prophesying the
future. The others present on such evenings, though bearded
like the pard, were bright-eyed young intellectuals sucking
on long clay pipes, many of them at the beginning of
famous careers.

On Alexander's death in 1896, Frederick succeeded as
head of the firm, and by the time that Wells came on the
scene in 1903, Frederick, his brother Maurice, who had
begun his career as a master at St Paul's, and Daniel's son
George were in control of the business. Something else had
happened to them. They had become upper middle class.
Expensively educated, scholarly in temperament, refined in
manner, growing rich and powerful and sure of themselves,
they faced a world in which men like Wells were coming up,
and tried to control it as they controlled their business.

Control is the proper word. This was a family business,
expanding overseas, employing more and more people every
year, but these three ran it, and there was no nonsense with
boards of directors or shareholders. The partners met each
morning, shook hands gravely, discussed the letters, gossiped in a lordly way, bickered a little with each other,
revealed what they were at that moment up to; then re-
paired to their rooms and their ledgers, their calculations
and designs, and kept at it often until late at night, and did
this for a full six days a week.

It was into this atmosphere that Wells bounced in 1903
with all the confidence in the world, and so much did he
count on Macmillan's active cooperation that within a

month or two of signing the new agreement he was suggesting that Macmillan take over all his earlier books from the publishers who had issued them.

At present I am not very conspicuously before the public, there is a speculative element in my future, and I suggest to you that if you are going to put your money upon me to the extent of £1,500, that you would do well to put down another hundred or so to secure the 'dissipated' books while they are at this level. Dispersed they do little good, but brought together they could be kept before the bookselling trade and advertised with a maximum of economy, and their constant presence on sale would be most excellent permanent advertisement. Now they ought to come cheap, but a time will come when the bookseller and publisher will develop their opinion of me – at least we go on that assumption. [31 July 1903]

Macmillan saw the point, and entered into negotiations with Methuen, Dent, Chapman & Hall, Lane, and Harpers, who had published the earlier books. Chapman & Hall were reluctant to give up *Anticipations* and *Mankind in the Making*, and Dent clung tenaciously to *The Wonderful Visit*. But the others were willing to deal, and soon Macmillan found himself in possession of the publishing rights and plates of a dozen books, and the publisher of an author with very aggressive intentions towards capturing the public an author who bombarded him with letters and was constantly in and out of the office. What a contrast he offered to Mr Rudyard Kipling, who never called and never complained.

The correspondence gets into its stride with the first novel Macmillans were to publish, *The Food of the Gods*. This title, it turned out, had been used for a small book on cocoa published by Elkin Mathews, and it emerged that Wells had known all along of the existence of the Elkin Mathews book and had given an undertaking that he would not use the same title for his. At first Wells protested that he did not remember having made any such promise, and instructed Macmillan:

You really must get evidence that I made the promise. I really do not remember anything about the correspondence and these little publishers are equal to anything. It's quite possible of course that I gave the promise. The plain fact is that when a man is thinking hard about some particular piece of work (and I must have been upon *The Modern Utopia*) he hasn't the reserve energy to be also his own solicitor and his own businessman. I ought to have sent B.J.'s letter to you. If he really has got my promise then I think we must make the title

> *The Food of Gods on Earth*

though it's a clumsy, silly addition. [25 June 1904]

Two days later he wrote again:

The Food of Gods on Earth is so detestable a title it keeps me awake at nights. ... What do you say to *Heraklephorbia: The Food of the Gods*, making the former title a sort of second title? That 'On Earth' is intolerably weak. 'Heraklephorbia' is no doubt a hard-looking word, but it's not too difficult to pronounce. It arrests attention. The French title is to be '*Place Aux Géants*', the Italian '*Ecco i Giganti*', neither of which gives any tolerable English equivalent. The plain fact is that *The Food of the Gods* is *the* title and I can't stand the idea of any other. Suppose we were to give the book a long title:

> *The Food of the Gods*
> *and how it Came to Earth*

and trust people to drop the last six words. I really think that is quite the best thing to do – far better than adding 'on earth'. Why 'on earth'? You will be wishing it anywhere else very soon. [27 June 1904]

When *The Food of the Gods, and How It Came to Earth* finally appeared at the end of September, the reviews were extensive rather than enthusiastic, and the sales were disappointing. H.G. comforted Macmillan:

Of course in many ways I am repulsively new and difficult for people, and that is why I've tried to fix up things with you in such a way that you will have every reason for patience and persistence in getting together a public for me. It is only undistinguished work that sells in mechanical ways, but strongly individualized work, as mine is, though it is much more difficult to handle at first, does often in the long run have a better sale. [28 October 1904]

But at the same time he tried to arouse Macmillan to be more adventurous. 'I like your firm in many ways. I don't think you advertise well, and I think you are out of touch with the contemporary movement in literature. I don't think you have any idea of what could be done for me (but that you will, of course, ascribe to the vanity of authors)' was one of his earliest shafts.

On this particular subject of advertisement Wells always showed an unfailing ardour and expertise, and it is easy to see where Edward Ponderevo in *Tono-Bungay* came by his stimulating and unorthodox ideas. Macmillan was constantly resisting. Outside Macmillan's private office and along the boardroom corridors, there hung against the panelled walls the portraits of some of the great Victorian writers whose work the firm had published: Tennyson, Matthew Arnold, John Richard Green, J. Henry Shorthouse, Dean Westcott, Lord Morley, Dean Church, James Russell Lowell: poets, historians, theologians and philosophers who had been responsible for so much of the Victorian grandeur in literature, and who had brought the firm profit and a great name. From in most cases a luxuriance of whiskers, their likenesses gazed down from their expensive frames on this beautiful broad corridor, and managed to give an unforgettable impression of dignity, solidity and richness to the business of publishing books.

Macmillan was not someone always looking back to the past. On the contrary, he was considered to have rather advanced views; he was an innovator and not a traditionalist, as witness the Net Book Agreement, which transformed the whole world of bookselling, but which was initiated by him personally at great risk.

So he was very far from being a stick-in-the-mud; but he was someone who hated extremes, and Wells was, it is plain from the letters, a continual trouble to him. Wells's books were well reviewed, though they did not sell as much as Macmillan had hoped. Nor enough to satisfy the author, who was continually reproachful, bustling into the building with new and wholly unacceptable ideas as to what might be done to promote the sale, or writing from Sandgate long lectures on the art of publishing or short barbed notes obviously meant to stimulate the recipient to further action. When Macmillan read the manuscript of *Tono-Bungay*, he must have known what Ponderevo meant by 'woosh', a vulgar word for a manner he found displeasing. He tried, when he could, to pass Wells on to the advertisement manager, Mr Ratcliffe, and Wells fell upon Ratcliffe, addressing him as 'Dear Fame-Maker', soliciting his opinion of titles and even of a plot, until he saw that Ratcliffe was really a senior clerk who had been deputed to look after press advertisements and who was under Mr Macmillan's thumb. Whereupon Ratcliffe became, in a letter to Bennett, 'Macmillan's advertisement imbecile'.

At this stage Wells was happy to lean heavily on his publisher; Macmillan was the recipient of all his confidences and ambitions about getting on as a writer. From news of the dramatization of *The Wheels of Chance* to moans about Newnes & Co., who had published *The First Men in the Moon*, had overprinted, and were now remaindering some of their surplus stock, he told all with the frankness and charm of a small boy, but a small boy who knows what he wants and is adept at the art of wheedling:

This is the first time I have been remaindered. If only they had consulted me, there is no doubt you would have taken over plates and stock. Still, there it is, and the mischief is done. The book is entirely at your service . . . [6 August 1904]

Have you noticed the controversy in the *Westminster Gazette* upon stile [*sic*] apropos of an article in the *Nouvelle Revue* attacking my English? I enclose the cuttings for you to see what is happening. The passage under criticism was taken by M. Bluet from the serial in *Pearson's Magazine*, and none of these people has discovered that the passage has undergone considerable modification in the book. It would be an unbecoming thing for me to enter the lists in this affair but I think someone in your office might very conceivably point that out without offence. And I think this very vigorous ventilation of my name in the *Westminster* justifies your drawing attention by a special advertisement to the existence of my book. I hope your attention has been called to the excellent notice of *The Food of the Gods* in the *Monthly Review,* and the long article by Reja in the October *Mercure de France* on *H. G. Wells et les merveilleux Scientifique.* What an admirable little magazine the *Mercure* is! I wish you or someone would give us one like it over here. In France it's becoming a power to reckon with. [30 September 1904]

Then he suggested sandwich men in Oxford Street, pointing out that this had served W. W. Jacobs's publisher very well. Macmillan rejected the suggestion curtly with 'We must draw the line somewhere.' Wells refused to accept a rebuff from his new friend. 'Very well,' he said gaily, 'but you really ought to try it. It is the only way of getting at the new middle-class public.'

Within a week or two he was back at the subject again, longing for Macmillan to 'get a move on'.

I am sending you with this a couple of fascicles of matter that may be of use in advertising my work. This is but a selection of passages from press cuttings that my father has dug out for me, and secondly a very good little article on my work by E. A. Bennett which appeared in the American *Cosmopolitan* two years ago. I have thought if you made up all or most of this matter into a little pamphlet that could be printed abundantly and cheaply, and if you sent it out with your Autumn Announcements, and used it *copiously* for advertisements, it would be of very great benefit in many ways. The notices cover books not in your hands but I think you will agree with me that as matters stand, it is quite to your advantage to advertise my works *as a whole,* in spite of this fact. [6 August 1904]

With *Kipps,* he felt that the moment had come for a special effort.

It is, I feel, the most considerable book (from the point of view of a possible popularity) that you have so far published for me, and I think that now is the time for a very special effort to improve my position with the booksellers and book-buyers, an effort that, by the nature of my agreement with you, will count not only in relation to my preceding books but to all my subsequent ones, to your advantage. I look to you now for some able and sustained advertisement and I will confess that I shall feel it is you and not me to blame if *Kipps* is not carried well over 10,000 copies. I designed our agreement to ensure you the fullest security for any special outlay you might incur in pushing my books, and I do think it is in the spirit of our under-standing that you should now not simply spend money but time and attention in making the book commercially a success. It is not as if I were asking you to push rubbish. *Kipps* is good and amusing and as well written as any contemporary novel. It is not as if I asked you to stake your enterprise on an unknown man. My reputation is out of all proportion greater than my book sales. But it is a special and personal reputation, you have to educate your booksellers to it, you have any profit in cul-tivating it, and you will I know forgive me if I remind you as emphatically as possible of the necessity of doing so ... [9 August 1905]

Once more he descended on Mr Macmillan, passing along the board-room corridor between the paintings of past great authors to beard in his office the publisher who had his books but was not doing enough with them. One pictures him, a little bundle of energy, facing the suave presiding genius of this publishing machine. One pictures Mr Macmillan, too, and one sees all too clearly what each disliked and distrusted in the other.

No record of the conversation exists, but that the inter-view was stormy and that there was a certain adamancy in Mr Macmillan's attitude may be guessed from the two letters with which Wells the same day followed up this interview. The first was written from the Savile Club after luncheon, 'thinking further of our conversation'.

There lies at home the project, and some passages and chap-ters of a long novel that I hope will appear in 1907.* It is a large

* This was *Tono-Bungay*.

scheme, and I do not want to set it aside. But the completion of it depends very largely on the success or failure of *Kipps* and *In the Days of the Comet*. I don't want to hurry the thing, and if *Kipps* fails to sell pretty heavily I do not see how I can give myself unreservedly to it. In which case I shall probably have to propose some work of a slight and less sustained character for 1907 ...

I do not know how you feel in the matter of my books but if you really have no confidence in my literary pretensions, I do not see why you should not cut the whole business at this stage. If you feel disposed to make me a fair offer, a firm and detailed offer, I will consider what I can do to take the whole enterprise off your hands. Tastes differ, and I do not see why we should not bring off a transaction of this sort in an entirely amiable spirit and with perfect frankness on both sides. It will be better than drifting along in a state of mutual criticism and injury.

On the late evening of the same day, flushed perhaps with wine, and certainly with the praise that had been showered on him at a dinner party by leading men who were reading the serial extracts, he pressed home the attack and wrote again to Macmillan, setting out what Kipps was aimed to do, and how it might best be put over.

Kipps is essentially a novel, built on modern lines, about the development of a single character. The older type of novel was held together as a rule by a complex *plot*, and was ampler and *looser* in form than its successor. Here the interest is concentrated entirely upon a single amusing individual and *often* on what he says and does on this or that occasion. *Kipps* is designed to present a typical member of the English lower middle class in all its pitiful limitation and feebleness, and beneath a treatment deliberately kindly and general provides a sustained and fairly exhaustive criticism of the ideals and ways of life of the great mass of middle-class English people. The other characters grouped about him present contrasted influences in the commonplace English environment. They are all based on the most careful and exhaustive study of living types: you must judge for yourself how far they are alive. The effects sought are a subdued humour and the unforced pathos of feebleness and inadequacy. There has been the most strenuous effort to avoid pushing the jokes home or any vulgar insistence upon the emotion of the situations. I have sought before all things the glow of reality. It's an infernally good book as a matter of fact. I have had it praised tonight by Barrie, Arthur Morrison, Jeremy Jacobs, and Sidney Lee, who have all been reading it serially, and I refuse absolutely to be modest about it, after this outburst of approval in a dinner party of less than twenty men. I've been aiming at the interest of character, the same interest that gives Dickens his value, that gives value to all good novels, and I do not believe there is a single figure in the whole story that is conventional and unreal. I do not believe there is a sentence in all the dialogue that is out of character or a single event that is not natural and as it might have happened. So much for *Kipps*. I don't think your criticism of *The Food of the Gods* quite hits the mark. You simply miss the drift of the later parts, but a certain number of people don't, and more will come round to it as time goes on. You judge the book as a story merely, whereas it is a sort of fantasia in *bigness* – a thing in three movements, with a variation in treatment in each movement. I suppose you will smile if I compare one of my books to a symphony, because you are I think of that type that does not readily perceive that living men are as good as the dead. You are sceptical about me as you would have been sceptical about Coleridge if you had been his contemporary, or about Goldsmith, and you force me to unbecoming lengths of self-assertion. You don't believe that literature is still going on and that, I think, is not a good habit of mind for a publisher of contemporary writers.

This was a bit hard on the publisher of Kipling and Yeats and Hardy and young Winston Churchill's life of his father, of Maurice Hewlett and Henry James. But the storm blew over.

Soon Wells was again at his self-appointed task of putting 'go' into his publishers. By November, in spite of excellent reviews, *Kipps* had not sold 10,000 copies, and now was the moment 'to shove the thing into a sale of five figures'.

I should doubt if there remains any section of the inner educated reading public that has not heard of *Kipps*. But now I think is the time to push the attack upon the larger less literary middle-class public. For them I think something a little more urgent, something a little more in the manner of *The Times* advertisement is needed. I would suggest a heading 'Have you read *Kipps*? It is the most amusing and human novel of the year!' and then a volley of short quotes ...

I do hope the book keeps on the move. When will the 'second large impression' come?

He was fertile with suggestions about advertising in theatre programmes, about the design of showcards, about leaflets to go out with The Times Book Club lists, about posters at Portsmouth Station saying simply KIPPS WORKED HERE. He raised again enthusiastically the question of sandwich men, and was not rebuffed when Macmillan again stiffly refused.

All's well, but I wish I could make you think differently about those sandwich men. If you had them for a week of the shopping season, round and about The Times Bookshop region during the afternoon, and in the City about midday I am certain that at just the present time it would give the book a huge lift. You know it was the making of *Many Cargoes* and Jacob's reputation. After all, why should not all the people who are buying *Captains All* buy *Kipps*? It's just as amusing and much fresher. Only the point is that people who buy Jacobs don't read the *Athenaeum* and have to be got at through the shop window. Have you noticed the way Hodder & Stoughton are advertising Jacobs? It's the way to the drawing rooms of the suburban middle class, I'm certain.

Don't think I'm not pleased with all you are doing. It has answered, hasn't it? But I feel that this is a chance to experiment boldly. Now the book is on the move, and well on the move, it seems a pity not to try everything that will drive it home.

Try sandwich men the second week in December – good simple boards – and you'll put up the sales 2,000 a week.

In November and December sales accelerated, and the book was reprinted three times. By Christmas 12,000 of *Kipps* had been sold. These were the best sales Wells had had with any book, and he felt justifiably pleased, and inclined to be rather didn't-I-tell-you-so-ish in his attitude to Macmillan, and especially with Ratcliffe, with whom he could be more familiar. Of all his books, *Kipps* meant most to him. It was the first long novel of character he had embarked on, and it was about himself and the things he knew of. The thought that it might perish of neglect was sharp pain to him.

He wanted to be accepted not only as an entertainer but as a teacher; he wanted to use the novel form to discuss love and science and religion 'as Pope in his time used poetry to discuss natural Theology'.* This was what he had been getting at in *Love and Mr Lewisham*, where a serious question was posed: 'How far does matrimony interrupt a career?' The artistic form of the novel could and should enclose a question about life as a nut encloses the kernel.

Kipps asked no practical question, but it posed something deeper, an attitude to life. In this 'Story of a Simple Soul', Kipps and his Ann survive, if not exactly triumphantly, at least unvanquished by the superior accents and the social condescension bent upon them when Kipps comes into his legacy and emerges like a bubble from the depths beneath to explode on the bright surface of life. Although for the purposes of the comedy Kipps's ignorance and the deformity of his accent and the deficiencies of his manner set against middle-class respectable Folkestone are exaggerated compared with those that marked Mr and Mrs Wells as they entered upon the social scene at Sandgate, there is no doubt that H.G.'s experiences in the drapery at Portsmouth are faithfully reflected in Kipps's at Folkestone, and the building of Spade House is mirrored in Kipps's adventures in the same field. How far is it meant to be comedy, which it most exquisitely is, ranking high among the comic creations in English literature, and how far did Wells mean it to be a protest against the settled English habit of finding their social inferiors laughable? When he was writing *Kipps* in 1903 and 1904, Wells did not stand very far off from the

* *Experiment in Autobiography.*

events he was describing. His own legacy of brains and talent had given him an opportunity to break free of the world of shops, build his own house, penetrate a new social class; he looked back in wonder and love to the class he had left, the narrowness and drabness of their lives, the pitiful deprivations imposed on them, and remembered the simple joys that even this poor existence afforded. The satire in *Kipps* is directed not against Kipps's and Ann's gaucheries, but against Mrs Bindon Botting's oppression, Helen Walsingham's pretensions, Mr Chester Coote's pompous snobbery signified in his characteristic reproving cough – 'a sound rather more like a very, very old sheep a quarter of a mile away being blown to pieces by a small charge of gunpowder'. Comic touches had been a distinguishing feature of Wells's work from the beginning, and comic characters and comic scenes had appeared in his earlier books. But *Kipps* was the first novel in which the comedy was sustained throughout, even through the moments when the author's mood is darkened temporarily as he cries out against those social forces that overshadow people like his Kipps and are responsible for 'the stupid little tragedies of these clipped and limited lives'. But for once, for just this moment of slackwater in his life, when he was balanced between what he had been and what he was to become, he looked back in loving regard to what he had come from, the preacher and reformer momentarily subdued to the creator of character. Wells withdrew behind little Kipps, who at the end of the book is rowing his wife upon the Hythe Canal at the end of a summer's day.

He had ceased from rowing and rested on his oars, and suddenly he was touched by the wonder of life – the strangeness that is a presence stood again by his side.

Out of the darkness beneath the shallow, weedy stream of his being rose a question, a question that looked up dimly and never reached the surface. It was the question of the wonder of the beauty, the purposeless inconsecutive beauty, that falls so strangely among the happenings and memories of life. It never reached the surface of his mind, it never took to itself substance or form; it looked up merely as the phantom of a face might look out of deep waters, and sank again into nothingness.

'Artie', said Ann. 'Penny for your thoughts, Artie.'

He considered.

'I reely don't think I was thinking of anything', he said at last with a smile. 'No.'

He still rested on his oars.

'I expect', he said, 'I was thinking just what a Rum Go everything is. I expect it was something like that.'

'Queer old Artie.'

'Ain't I? I don't suppose there ever was a chap like me before.'

He reflected for another moment.

'Oo, I don't know', he said at last, and roused himself to pull.

It *was* 'an infernally good book', and one understands Wells's protest to Macmillan: 'I refuse absolutely to be modest about it'.

Early in January 1906 he wrote to Macmillan that he would be in London on a Saturday about 2.30 and would like to call and discuss three important matters with him. Three of his early books, *The Time Machine, Select Conversations with an Uncle* and *Certain Personal Matters*, had come back into his hands from their respective publishers (they had been published on time-expiring agreements) and he wanted to know if Macmillan would reissue them. Next he announced that he was going on with his big novel for 1907 – this was *Tono-Bungay*, though he did not mention it by name, merely saying that he had a very good title for it. The book was in fact well beyond the planning stage, for the first part was already written, and he put forward the proposition that these early chapters should be set up in galley proof so that he could take them with him to America when he went there to lecture in March, to help his negotiations with American publishers. 'I think it ought to make a much bigger splash than *Kipps*', he concluded.

The date of this letter is 11 January 1906, and although he did not mention this to Macmillan, he was coming up to London to give the Fabian Society his lecture on *This Misery of Boots*. He told Macmillan that he might be reached, to confirm this appointment, c/o Sidney Webb, Esq., 41 Grosvenor Road, S.W.

The third point on which he wished to see Macmillan was the title of the comet book, which Macmillan already had at the printer:

I'm still bothered about the title of the Comet Story. We *must* have a good title for that, I feel, and one that calls attention to the fact that it is an emotional and passionate story with a good deal of love in it. Otherwise it will start off in the hands of the wrong people. If it is backed up I think it ought to beat *Kipps*, but it will need a certain amount of explaining. When it is near publication I think it would be a great help if I lent proofs about, and set people discussing it. Have you read it yet?

And he ended with a postscript listing several alternative titles: *The Lovers' Comet*, *The Comet of the Opened Hearts*, *The Comet of the New Birth*. He had already in a previous letter suggested *The Comet of the Sweeter Air*, 'to distinguish it from books of *The First Men in the Moon* class'.

This letter reveals a great deal about Wells. Not only his immense energy and fertility as an author at this period, but the way his mind was working, and the direction in which his talent was turning. In one year he had published two books as different in kind as *Kipps* and *A Modern Utopia*, each of which was at this moment being eagerly read and praised and discussed. *Kipps* had been reprinted several times since publication, and Chapman & Hall were having a field day with *A Modern Utopia*, the reviews of which had been so ecstatic that the word 'rave' seems an understatement. To the *Athenaeum* there had been no work of this importance published for the last thirty years, while the *Outlook* thought that it challenged comparison with Plato's *Republic* and More's *Utopia*.

At the end of such a year there might have been pause for rest, particularly as he was to leave in March for an American tour lasting several months,* and he already had *In the Days of the Comet* in the press and was about to launch an all-out attack on the Fabian Old Guard. But, far from resting, he had written *This Misery of Boots* and was knocking up *The Faults of the Fabians*, a more extensive lecture and his opening barrage on the Old Guard, and he was deep in *Tono-Bungay*, intending to finish it before the end of the year.

His energy was boundless and so was the intoxication produced by all his success. It was as though 1905 marked a continental divide in his life, looking back with *Kipps* nostalgically to the past, and with *A Modern Utopia* adopting a brisk and practical pose towards the future. But Wells was not a practical man: he was a visionary. He could see the end, all right, but he was quite incapable of lowering his gaze to take account of the obstructions that had to be overcome, the detours that must necessarily be made, to reach it. Nothing demonstrates this better than *In the Days of the Comet*, and his fussing about the title was a symptom of what was bothering him.

Since much of the wrath and opprobrium that was going to fall on H.G.'s shoulders during the next few years was caused by his combative attitude towards those who opposed his views as much as by his own outrageous behaviour, and since the first danger signals were fired in *In the Days of the Comet*, this book, which came between his two great successes, *Kipps* and *Tono-Bungay*, deserves special attention. It is a story of how our earth came under the benign influence of a comet and the Great Change took place. The old world, the dark world we still know – 'full of preventable disorders, preventable diseases, and preventable pain, of harshness and stupid unpremeditated cruelties' – yielded unconsciously to the Great Change, to the happiness and beauty of the atmosphere that now bathed it, in which all evil had been washed away. But in Leadford's, the narra-

* 'I am going to write loose articles mingled with impressions of The Future in America (no less).' Letter to Henry James, 25 January 1906.

tor's, memory there lingered the recollection of moments
of bliss in the olden times, when the grey was stabbed
through and through by joys of an intensity, by perceptions
of a keenness, that had now gone out of life.

Parload is his friend, and Parload is an amateur astronomer, plainly based both in physical appearance and in other
detail on Wells's old friend Richard Gregory. Gregory had
specialized in astronomy, and, industrious as ever on his
friend's behalf, provided the little scientific background
necessary for this story, which is not very much. Halley's
Comet was due to make its regular seventy-five-year appearance about 1908, and a year or so before then its predictable
return would certainly have occurred to H.G.'s fertile mind
as providing just the right background for a novel that
might have the wide appeal of one of his old scientific
fantasies, but which might include a prophetic vision of
what the world was coming to, along with some constructive
ideas for remaking society, the Fabian idea being strong in
him at the moment.

This novel is a first draft of some of the features elabor-
ated in *Tono-Bungay* and *The New Machiavelli*. The physical ugliness of the industrial landscape is here, and Nettie
is a first cast of Isabel, to be much more deeply studied,
though not altered in character, in Marion in *Tono-Bungay*.
Wells's mother is here as the work-ridden figure, fearing
God and man. In Leadford, the narrator, there is the proto-
type of George Ponderevo in *Tono-Bungay*, and of Remington in *The New Machiavelli*, who had momentarily flashed
out also in Chatteris in *The Sea Lady*: the reasonable man
who yet cannot deny his own sensuality. Wells himself.

After the Great Change, socialism prevails, humanity is
released from its old bondage, everyone is free. Alas, too
free for the tastes of those readers who saw the value of
order and the advantages yielded to society as a whole by
decent repressions. For what Wells pictures amounts to free
love, though he was vigorously to deny this, and the first
crack in the mutual admiration which he and the leading

Fabians had felt for each other is visible in the entry which Beatrice Webb made in her diary after reading *In the Days of the Comet*:

H. G. Wells gave an address to the Fabian Society on Socialism for the middle classes, ending up with an attack on the family. Some of the new members welcomed his denunciation, but the meeting, which was crowded, was against him, for the simple reason that he had nothing constructive to suggest. Since then I have read *In the Days of the Comet*, which ends with a glowing anticipation of promiscuity in sexual relationships. The argument is one that is familiar to most intellectuals – it has often cropped up in my own mind and has seemed to have some validity. Friendship between particular men and women has an enormous educational value to both (especially to the woman). Such a friendship is practically impossible (or at any rate, impossible between persons who are attractive to each other – and therefore most remunerative as friends) without physical intimacy; you do not as a matter of fact, get to know any man thoroughly except as his beloved and his lover – if you could have been the beloved of the dozen ablest men you have known it would have greatly extended your knowledge of human nature and human affairs. This I believe is true of our present rather gross state of body and mind. But there remains the question whether, with all the perturbation caused by such intimacies, you would have any brain left to think with? I know that I should not – and I fancy that other women would be even worse off in that particular. Moreover, it would mean a great increase in sexual emotion for its own sake and not for the sake of bearing children. And that way madness lies. This is omitting the whole social argument against promiscuity which is the strongest. Regarding each individual as living in a vacuum with no other obligations than the forming of his or her own character, I still reject 'free love' as a method of development. I suggested to Sidney for consideration whether our philosophy was not tending to the restriction of all desires to the maintenance of health in the individual and the race – meaning by health, the longest continued and greatest intensity of mental activity – and to the continuance of the species at the highest level of quality?

H. G. Wells is, I believe, merely gambling with the idea of

free love – throwing it out to see what sort of reception it gets – without responsibility for its effect on the character of hearers. It is this recklessness that makes Sidney dislike him. I think it is important *not* to dislike him: he is going through an ugly time, and we must stand by him for his own sake and for the good cause of collectivism. If he will let us – that is to say. I am not sure he is not getting to dislike us in our well-regulated prosperity.

What was the ugly time he was going through, noted confidentially by this very perceptive, clear-eyed woman? There was no trace of it in his outward fortunes; he was riding high in popular esteem, but the first outburst of criticism was then starting, and he was fighting back desperately and vindictively, asserting that he was no prophet of 'free love', but only an advocate of 'freer love' and of a remission of the accepted view of the masculine proprietorship of wives and daughters.

Frederick Macmillan does not seem to have been unduly perturbed by the book; at least, he did not suggest any changes. When Wells saw him on this Saturday in January, the General Election which was going to seat thirty socialists in the House of Commons for the first time was in progress. Mr Macmillan would have disliked Wells's socialist views, but this was a work of imagination, not a sociological study. There is no record that he disapproved of the book or regretted his undertaking to publish it. When he read the first chapters of *Tono-Bungay*, left with him that day, with their masterly evocation of a poor boyhood, the publisher's instinct in him must have responded to this demonstration of a great book in the making. *Kipps* had pleased him; *Tono-Bungay* excited him. He could not like the man, but as partner–publisher he responded to the author's work, and the question of free love did not bother him as it did Mr and Mrs Sidney Webb, whose missionary zeal was irritated by these fanciful flights which attracted the wrong kind of convert. It says something for H.G.'s magic with women that he could arouse in Beatrice Webb the thought that 'you do not, as a matter of fact, get to know any man thoroughly except as his beloved and his lover', even though she hastily called herself to order with the question whether 'with all the perturbation caused by such intimacies, you would have any brain left to think with'.

The meeting with Macmillan on that Saturday afternoon in January 1906 settled the title of the comet book: it was to be *In the Days of the Comet*, and Macmillan agreed to set up the first chapters of *Tono-Bungay*. Off went H.G. to America, taking the galleys with him. He spent two months there, visiting New York, Boston, Chicago and Washington, where he met President Roosevelt. Out of this came *The Future in America*. Henry James, to whom a copy was sent, found it 'overwhelmingly beguiling', but with his usual perception he penetrated the book's weakness:

I think you, frankly, – or think the whole thing too *loud*, as if the country shouted at you, hurrying past, every hint it had to give and you yelled back your comment on it; but also, frankly, I think the only way to utter many things you are delivered of *is* to yell them – it's a yelling country, and the voice must pierce or dominate; and *my* semitones, in your splendid clashing of the cymbals (and *theirs*), will never be heard. [8 November 1906]

James himself had revisited America the year before, and his *The American Scene* came out from the same publisher, Chapman & Hall, a few months afterwards. His gift copy to Wells was acknowledged by Wells, who found it 'one of the most wonderful things you have done', but ended:

You take the thing at the opposite pole of my attack, you make it a criticism of life and manners – things I have had only incidental dealings with – you take the whole thing as an ineffectual civilization and judge it with so informed and temperate a decisiveness. But I wish there was a public worthy of you – and me. After the book is closed and I have gloated again at the still almost incredible marvel of a cover 'uniform' with mine, I do get this gleam of discontent. How much will they get out of what you have got in? [20 March 1907]

The claws were being bared for the dispute that was going to come into the open five years later. Wells's impatience had some excuse. He was at the high peak of his quarrel with the Old Guard of the Fabian Society, and he was being defeated on the very grounds that James put his finger on in his criticisms of the book.

Tono-Bungay occupied all his time that could be spared from the Fabian quarrel on his return from America. In the spring of 1908 it was finished, and Wells was convinced that he had written his masterpiece, that never would he do anything better. It is the most autobiographical of all his novels, for it recounts in beautiful detail not only his childhood days below stairs at Up Park, but his period at Midhurst as a chemist's apprentice and his classes at Midhurst Grammar School, his student days in London, his falling in love with his cousin, his marriage, and the unhappy outcome.

George Ponderevo is H. G. Wells not only in the incidental details of his life, but in the expression of his views. All the books he was to write hereafter were to have biographical references, but George Ponderevo in *Tono-Bungay* is a self-portrait of the matured Wells, as Lewisham represented the young, ardent, questioning Wells. 'A certain innate scepticism – and a certain inaptitude for sympathetic assimilation': thus he was while a little boy at Up Park listening to the talk of the servants. Then, 'I am certain I knew quite a lot about love at fourteen', and he tells of his passionate youthful ardour for Beatrice, the daughter of the house, who flirted with him, the housekeeper's son. This early glimpse he gives us is of a girl astride the wall of the park while he was outside. The same girl scene is repeated in *The History of Mr Polly*, and it must reflect something that had left a strong mark on the mind of the young Wells. The depiction is not so much of strong passions stirred as of social barriers only momentarily withdrawn, to be interposed again the moment his passion made him daring.

Then the growing awareness of the ugliness of industrialized England that is not Bladesover, festering spots that
had the colours and even the smells of a well-packed dust-
bin, and wandering about this wilderness of crowded dingi-
ness with young receptive wide-open eyes, the clever boy,
nursing his resentment, and asking, 'But after all, why?'

Learning to hate authority and learning to detest submis-
siveness, too clever for his class in a class-ridden England
in which God was on the side of the squire and his lackey,
the priest. Defying God, and getting away with it, no thunderbolts or visitations of plagues, no hell-fire or punishment
of any kind. Finding out that cleverness paid; it got him on.
Making his rat-like raids on libraries and feeling himself
the last dwindled representative of such a man of letters as
Swift. Escaping to London, and finding there elements in
his nature that responded to its mysteries and enticements;
discipline falling from him like a garment, the raptures that
the body can feel suddenly overwhelming him. His marriage
to Marion and the breaking of a dream.

It all comes clear. In this beautifully observed study of a
clever boy with an emotional sensuous nature, coming from
a mean home in an outer-suburban background into the
teeming London world, with his imagination, with his
hidden power to express himself, we see why he should have
become the writer, socialist, planner, reconstructor of
society, sensualist and seducer he did become. George Ponderevo, with his socialist ideas for reforming the world,
became his uncle's chief lieutenant in the racketeering business of supplying a gullible public with perfectly worthless
pills and making an immense profit out of it.

There were scenes in this book that might have bothered
Mr Macmillan, for Beatrice is certainly a very uninhibited
heroine, but they did not. Nor were the critics, who, after
In the Days of the Comet, were on the lookout for any repetition of the suggestion of free or even freer love, perturbed by this aspect. Perhaps the book was too evidently
a masterpiece and too plainly set against a background of

social England in a time of change, and the moral – the undeniable wickedness of immoral commercial enterprise –
too plainly driven home, for the underlying flashes of liber-
tarian exercise to attract attention. As the admirable Raknem reminds us, in *First and Last Things* Wells had already expressed the central theme of *Tono-Bungay*:

> I see ... tens of thousands of wealthy people wasting lives in
> vulgar and unsatisfying trivialities, hundreds of thousands
> meanly chaffering themselves, rich and poor, in the wasteful
> byways of trade. ... All these people reflect and are part of the
> waste and discontent of life.

It was this central theme of *Tono-Bungay* which held the
attention of critics and readers when it appeared. But before
it was even serialized, when this masterpiece of a great
writer's work was still in the press, he was at work, swiftly,
indignantly and passionately, bruised by his quarrel with
the Fabians, on a book, *Ann Veronica*, that was to mark a
turning-point in his career.

11

Ann Veronica and
the Consequences

Ann Veronica is not one of Wells's most highly regarded books, although Ann Veronica as a character is one of the most attractive of Wells's heroines, and the book has an assured place in the emancipation of the modern novel from the inhibitions of Victorianism.

Ann Veronica shows a girl of the new age, beautiful, clever, thrusting at life, bursting out of the bonds that kept young maidens tethered, whether they had brains or not, until a suitable young man came along to release them by marriage into another form of bondage, that of the wife and mother subservient and obedient in all things to her husband and her lord. Ann Veronica will not accept this. She does not want marriage, although a respectable suitor is at hand. She will not submit to her father's domineering commands. She walks out, takes a room in London, borrows money from an older man who is trying to seduce her, joins the Fabian Society and becomes a suffragette, is arrested and imprisoned for civil disobedience, falls in love with a much older and already married man who is her biology instructor, and – not waiting to be seduced – seduces him and runs off with him for an illicit holiday in Switzerland, as a result of which she becomes pregnant.

It is a far cry indeed from the late Victorian love stories, and in 1909, when fathers of families were fighting strenuously to maintain the old standards of obedience and purity, when suffragettes and socialists were making confounded nuisances of themselves, stirring up political and social troubles, it came as a distinct shock when one of the leading novelists of the day not only portrayed this unedifying situation in all its details but plainly said that this was the way things were going, and cast Ann Veronica in the part of a heroine struggling against out-of-date restrictions and oppressions.

H. G. Wells was a name that ranked with the first half-dozen then writing, and in 1909 his fame and popularity were at their high-water mark. But already eyebrows were being raised. *In the Days of the Comet*, in 1906, had set up a quiver of alarm in some quarters. The *Times Literary Supplement* had drawn attention to the fact that in *Socialism and the Family* (1906) 'Socialistic men's wives, we gather, are, no less than their goods, to be held in common. Free love, according to Mr Wells, is to be the essence of the new Social Contract ...', while the *Spectator* charged that 'Free Love' was to be the dominant principle for the regulation of sexual ties in Mr Wells's regenerated state.

That was not at all what he had meant. Of course, he believed in free love, but he was not yet ready to say so in plain terms. What he could and did say was that Socialism was more than just a matter of tinkering with economic factors; properly and naturally it invaded the family as well, and inevitably the renuclearation (his term) of society would involve a greater degree of sexual freedom on the one hand, and collective family responsibility on the other. But this is very far from saying that in a socialist world wives would be held in common. He was always a poor hand at defending his beliefs, and now he denied hotly that he advocated free love, without making it clear that what he denied was his critics' interpretation of what he meant. He was merely bringing the relation between the sexes into the open. He was saying that this was the important thing in life. What should have been said proudly now had to be admitted defensively. He even had to threaten legal proceedings for misrepresentation of his views at one stage.

The female figure that haunted Wells's imagination was that of the 'young lady' (as distinct from Ann Pornick or the servant girl in *The Wonderful Visit*) who combines a forwardness about sex with an intellectual curiosity about life. Such figures excite the sensuous admiration of young George Ponderevo in *Tono-Bungay*, struggling with Beatrice in the bracken, and of Mr Polly, enraptured by Christabel on the school wall. Ann Veronica Stanley is the enlargement of those fleeting glimpses of perfection, with

black hair, fine eyebrows, and a clear complexion; and the forces that had modelled her fatures had loved and lingered at their work and made them subtle and fine. She was slender, and sometimes she seemed tall, and walked and carried herself lightly and joyfully as one who habitually and commonly feels well, and sometimes she stooped a little and was preoccupied. Her lips came together with an expression between contentment and the faintest shadow of a smile, her manner was one of great reserve, and behind this mask she was wildly discontented and eager for freedom and life.

Ann Veronica defies her father's command. 'What is the good of talking?' cries Mr Stanley. 'A man's children nowadays are not his own. That's the fact of the matter. Their minds are turned against him. ... Rubbishy novels and pernicious rascals. We can't even protect them from themselves.' An immense gulf seems to open between her father and daughter as he says these words. 'I don't see', says Ann Veronica, 'why parents and children ... shouldn't be friends.'

Very delicately and subtly, having drawn in such bold suggestive strokes the impression of a beautiful girl thrusting at life, Wells shows her wanting 'to know', and her world saying, 'Shush, it is indelicate to think of such things.' Then, because her father disapproves of the effect that universities have on young women and refuses her Cambridge, she goes to the local women's college and lives on at home, but, being intelligent, and moving with her age, she badgers for latch-key privileges. 'Shamefaced curiosities began to come back into her mind, thinly disguised as literature and art ...'

She rebels over her father's refusal to allow her to go to a fancy-dress ball, leaves home and takes a room in London.

She is taken to a meeting of the Fabian Society, and observes from the back seats of the gallery at Essex Hall

the giant leaders of the Fabian Society who are remaking the world: Bernard Shaw and Toomer and Dr Tumbay and Wilkins the author, all displayed upon a platform. The place was crowded and the people about her were almost equally made up of very good-looking and enthusiastic young people and a great variety of Goopes-like types.

(Those Goopeses, in *Ann Veronica*, are typical earnest Fabians, he a mathematical tutor, a small dark reserved man with a large inflexible forehead, his wife very pink and high-spirited, with one of those chins that pass insensibly into a full, strong neck; a swift and unkind caricature, this, of the not uncommon types of earnest middle-class social reformers, who one suspects often irritated the creator of Utopian Samurais. Wilkins is Wells, the public figure. As Wilkins, he was to pass in and out of other of his novels. He appears later in *Ann Veronica* in *propria persona* as Capes, the middle-aged biology tutor who becomes Ann Veronica's lover.) Afterwards she attends larger and more enthusiastic gatherings of the socialist brethren, a meeting of the advanced section of the women's movement in Caxton Hall ... and then other exhibitions and meetings until she is aware

not so much of a system of ideas as of a big diffused impulse towards change, a great discontent and criticism of life as it is lived, of a clamorous confusion of ideas for reconstruction – of the methods of business, of economic development, of the rules of property, of the status of children, of the clothing and feeding and teaching of everyone.

None of which gives the answer to a young heart – and this is what Wells is saying in this novel and making it believable – none of these manifold and worthy aims gives the answer to a young girl reaching out for life.

The whisperings of scandalized observers were already beginning to circulate in the Society when Wells suddenly shaped *Ann Veronica* to a conclusion that fixed the identification of the girl unmistakeably. When he must have been at the point in the story where Ann Veronica declares her love for Capes, for we know that he finished the book at the end of July, something occurred which altered his intention with the story and forced, or perhaps inspired, him to bring it to a sudden and explosive close. The evidence for this is an event explicitly described in the book and forming the turning-point to the climax: a suffragette raid on the House of Commons which took place on 30 June. A crowded and excited meeting of suffragettes had been held at Caxton Hall as a prelude to an attempt to convey personally to the Prime Minister, Asquith, a resolution demanding votes for women. Printed bills had been issued days before, inviting the people of London to attend in their thousands outside the House of Commons. A deputation of thirteen women left the Hall for the House, where a large crowd, consisting of sightseers and roughs as well as sympathizers, had gathered in response to the hand-bills. The deputation, however, was refused admittance to Palace Yard by the police. When they returned to Caxton Hall to report their failure, the meeting there broke up, and the women then tried to force their way into the House, singly and in groups, affording the crowd considerable entertainment. Amid the *mêlée* a furniture van drove into Palace Yard with a pass that was in order, but from it, when the doors were opened, streamed a body of suffragettes making for the Chamber. They were arrested, and their wooden horse was dragged, by young policemen perspiring on the warm summer's night, to the accompaniment of jeers from the crowd, into a corner of the yard.

Of the twenty-seven women who were arrested, twenty-six next morning, after a night in the cells, refused to be bound over and were given prison sentences of up to three months. Wells makes Ann Veronica one of these.

The raid on the House of Commons made the headlines; it was one of the boldest strokes yet of the militant suffragettes, and Wells used every detail of it for his story. Suddenly he is telling no longer the story of Jane and himself, but of Amber Reeves and himself. Whether Amber Reeves was in fact one of the group who made the raid is uncertain, but Wells uses the night's events to provide the experience which turns Ann Veronica from a restless discontented young girl chafing against the conventional restrictions of her time into a determined young woman who comes out of her prison experience unchastened and unremorseful and fully awake to what she wants.

From this point on there is no mistaking the identity of the Ann Veronica who runs off with the married Capes. The liveliness of the dialogue, the accelerated pace of the story, the direct forthrightness with which Ann Veronica takes over the command of their situation all reflect what we know of Amber Reeves, and of the impact this love affair had on Wells just at the time when the Fabian Society had spurned his proposals and Shaw, with diabolical cleverness, had trapped him into being 'bound over' to be of good behaviour. The contrast between his own weak submission and the courageous attitude of these defiant spinsters must have struck him very forcibly. Besides, he was in love for the first time with someone who approximated to his ideal of perfect physical response with perfect intellectual companionship. The very disparity in their ages, the danger to her and to him of an affair which could hardly be kept concealed in the small and gossipy Fabian circle, only served to fan his ardour and make him behave recklessly. Over two years of trial were ahead of him. This affair was to spread over not only *Ann Veronica* but the novel which followed it, *The New Machiavelli*, where the story is told again in the love affair between Richard Remington and Isabel Rivers. It was nearly to wreck Wells's career, but, passionately in love, he was blind to all the consequences as he seized on the House of Commons incident to turn his story to a rapid conclusion.

Ann Veronica and her lover, on an illicit honeymoon in

the Alps, exchange views on morality which may well have been struggling for expression in many intelligent young people of the time but which had not appeared in serious novels before. Capes says:

'Life is two things, that's how I see it, two things mixed and muddled up together. Life is morality – life is adventure. Squire and Master. Adventure rules, – and morality looks up the trains in Bradshaw. Morality tells you what is right, and adventure moves you. If morality means anything it means keeping bounds, respecting implications, respecting implicit bounds. If individuality means anything it means breaking bounds – adventure. Will you be moral and your species, or immoral and yourself?'

Shocking question! It does not seem to have occurred to him that some people – Mr Macmillan amongst them – might be appalled by such attitudes, as well as by the implications of the story, or that the identity of the main figures might be so easily apparent. One is reminded of Somerset Maugham's *Cakes and Ale,* and the surprise, not altogether affected, which Maugham expressed that anyone should think Alroy Kear was Hugh Walpole.

The events leading up to the publication of *Ann Veronica* by a publisher other than Macmillan and the outburst that followed its appearance are foreshadowed in the correspondence that passed between Macmillan and Wells in the autumn of 1908 while *Tono-Bungay* was still in proof. On 15 September 1908, Wells wrote to Mr Macmillan:

I have now under revision a second novel, *Ann Veronica,* which I propose you should publish in the autumn of 1909. It is shorter than *Tono-Bungay,* about 80,000 words, but it is, I think, the best love story I have ever done. I will send you the MS. in a few weeks' time. Behind the cover of these two books I want now to get on with a third one which I have planned out in the last few weeks and which is to be a modern political novel. I want it to be big and various in the same way that *Tono-Bungay* is, and to give Westminster, a big north country election, a country house party, and at the same time a lot of the subordinate life, Socialist meetings at powerful shops, political paragraphers, and so on and so on. I would like to give what is left of this year and all 1909 to that, and if the sales of these other two novels justify, to put it out as a book right away in 1910.

There are my plans. Have you read through *Tono-Bungay?* I hope you have, and I hope still more that you like it and believe in it. As I told you long ago I want to specialize as a novelist. I think now my opportunity is ripe, and that if new novel follows novel without anything to distract people's attention – any other sort of work by me, I mean – it will be possible to consolidate the large confused reputation I have at the present time. Are you game to back up the idea?

Two weeks later he sent the completed manuscript of *Ann Veronica* to Macmillan, and on 7 October Macmillan wrote:

Dear Mr Wells,

I have read *Ann Veronica,* but before deciding definitely as to whether we can fall in with your suggestion that it should appear under our Agreement in the Autumn of 1909 I should like to get one of my partners to read it, and I will therefore ask you to leave the matter open for a few days. I am going to Scotland on Friday but shall be back in the middle of next week and will write to you again as soon as I return.

When Macmillan did write again on 16 October it was to refuse the book, a blow which no author takes lightly, particularly one so established in the public recognition and his own esteem as Wells was.

Dear Mr Wells,

I am sorry to say that after very careful consideration, we do not see our way to undertake the publication of *Ann Veronica*. I could give you the reasons, but as I know you resent literary criticism from a publisher – I refrain from doing so.

I regret exceedingly that we feel obliged to come to this decision, particularly as I suppose our refusal puts an end to our contract with you, unless, as I hope may be the case, you are inclined to consider this book as outside it.

Yours sincerely,
Frederick Macmillan

To which Wells replied the next day:

Dear Mr Macmillan,

I'm very sorry too, for I wanted my novels now to come one after the other from the same house and in the same form. I should really be glad to have your criticisms. It's quite a fancy of yours that I resent criticism from a publisher, and anything that comes from you would, I am sure, be illuminating.

I think this must end our contract. I only entered into that in order to secure just what this breaks up, and that is the steady succession of my books. But I hope this will not prevent your negotiating for some of my future books. Your contract has complicated my negotiations for serial rights very greatly, but I do not regret the experiment we have made. I think you have a fairly considerable book in *Tono-Bungay*, and I am only sorry that you will not have the book that will follow *Tono-Bungay*.

Yours sincerely,

H. G. Wells

This was not the letter of a man appalled at a disastrous turn in his fortunes just at a moment when his own private affairs were in considerable disarray. Wells had reason for his cockiness of which Mr Macmillan was ignorant.

On 19 October Macmillan obliged with some criticisms; they were not, however, criticisms of the literary content, which was pretty well unassailable, but a perfectly justifiable dissent from handling goods which, as a tradesman, he thought not suitable for his customers. In this Macmillan correctly anticipated many of the criticisms that were going to be made of the book.

I regret that we cannot publish *Ann Veronica* as it seems to me a very well written book and there is a great deal in it that is attractive, but the plot develops on lines that would be exceedingly distasteful to the public which buys books published by our firm. The early part of the book with the picture of middle-class suburban life is very entertaining, indeed up to and including the episode of the suffragette girl there is nothing to object to. When, however, Ann Veronica begins her pursuit of the Professor at the International College, offers herself to him as a mistress and almost forces herself into his arms, the story ceases to be amusing and is certainly not edifying.

I can't help thinking that all this part of the book is a mistake and the moral of the book, if there be one, is not such as will commend itself to the majority of people.

> I am,
>> Yours very sincerely,
>>> Frederick Macmillan

Wells had reason for his confidence. Luck had played into his hands. Just at this time an intelligent and ambitious young man, Stanley Unwin, destined to become a leading figure in the publishing world, had joined his uncle, T. Fisher Unwin, to begin his publishing career. Casting about to develop the Fisher Unwin list, young Stanley Unwin got his uncle's permission to send letters round, signed by Fisher Unwin, to a number of well-known authors asking them if they had anything on the stocks for which publication was not already arranged, and expressing the interest of his firm in any such items. H. G. Wells was one of the names and it must have come as a considerable surprise when so famous an author as Wells started to talk business by return. Fisher Unwin's letter had chanced to arrive on the same day as Macmillan's letter rejecting *Ann Veronica*.

17 Oct. 1908

Dear Fisher Unwin,

You say you are disposed to speculate in *futures*. Very well, what will you give for all rights, serial and book, American, British and Colonial of the version in English of a novel by me which I have in hand, more or less, at the present time?

It is to be called *Ann Veronica*. It is to be the love-story of an energetic modern girl who goes suffragetting and quarrels with her parents. It is to be over 70,000 and under 90,000 words in length. It can be delivered in a state fit for negotiation before the end of the year, and it is to be published in book form between September 30th and Dec. 25th 1909.

Next, as to the state of my books in the market. *Kipps* did just 10,000 at 6/–, and has since yielded a handsome price from Nelson for a 1/– edition. The Socialist book of the summer,

New Worlds for Old is about 100 under 5,000 at 6/–. It stands
high in British advanced circles.

The novel is fairly advanced. It is also humorous and passionate. My last two books, sold and forthcoming in America, got
£500 and £300 in advance royalties respectively. Tauchnitz
pays usually £40, sometimes £50. I have a book, *The War in
the Air*, just coming from Bell, which is bound to do well with
the booksellers, and my next novel * is to be the chief item of
the new *English Review*, which has a successful air about it, and
is to be published by Macmillan in the Spring.

Put up a firm offer of £1,500, payable Oct. 1, 1909, and *Ann
Veronica* is yours, free of royalty. We will eliminate the Agent,
and you shall be absolutely unhampered by accounts, and free
to sublet rights to Nelson for the Shilling fiction series, or anything of that sort to any extent. No other new book by me shall
appear between Sept. 1st and the end of the year 1909. And
this offer is made without prejudice to the negotiations I am
carrying on elsewhere. I don't bind myself to keep it open for
you.

Yours very sincerely,
H. G. Wells

The negotiations took some time. Fisher Unwin was not
used to these substantial terms for a novel, and he was an
old hand at worrying away at a bargain, like a dog with a
bone. One sees his desire to conclude the deal grow as
he worried over point after point, but Wells played an astute
game and gave nothing away – in fact, took something
back, the translation rights, which he recalled had always
been the property of Mrs Wells, also the American

---

* *Tono-Bungay*. Although Wells was having an argument with Ford
Madox Ford about terms for the serialization, he was active at this
time in urging his friends to support the new *English Review* by
offering their work for serialization. The mechanics of payment were
not easy for authors to comprehend, but the novelty and ingenuity
of the offer was the very thing that appealed to Wells: two-fifths of
the net proceeds of the first four numbers were to be divided between
the contributors according to the number of pages filled. 'If this
Review comes off, English literature will be saved. Arise! Awake! Or
be for ever fallen!' he wrote to Vernon Lee in October 1908.

rights, which he had meanwhile disposed of. The offer in the end was not for all rights 'lock, stock and barrel', but Fisher Unwin was ready to settle, and sent urgent notes to H.G. begging him to meet him at his club or office to conclude the matter. The first number of the new *English Review* had already appeared with the early chapters of *Tono-Bungay*, and everybody was beginning to talk about the book. Wells proved hard to nail down, and now it was Fisher Unwin who was desperate, not the author who in October had been shocked by the refusal of *Ann Veronica* by the publisher who had agreed to 'back him up', 'with new novel following novel without anything to distract people's attention'. Finally the contract was signed.

Wells was passing through a difficult time. His love affair could no longer be kept secret. He had resigned from the Fabian Executive, ostensibly because he wanted to devote all his time to writing, but actually because it was not possible to sit there with the outraged mother of the girl he had wronged.

The financial crisis was over, but not the love affair. That this was a very powerful thing in Wells's life is beyond dispute. The glimpses of it that appear in his correspondence or can be extracted from the brief mention of it in such gossipy books as Arnold Bennett's *Journal* do not show him in a very favourable light, but middle-aged men with family responsibilities make awkward-looking lovers, especially when matched with young, beautiful, intelligent and daring girls.

He must have been an ardent lover, and he was always a wonderful companion. It is quite certain that this was not a one-sided affair, and that the girl was as much in love with him as he was with her. For some time she had been trying to withdraw from a love affair into which she had entered with her whole heart and soul. She loved H.G. with all the ardour of a young and passionate nature, and it was an ill chance that just when she had made up her mind to give him up, she should have found herself pregnant. All the ardour, the pressing demands, were now on H.G.'s side, and it was he who was anxious for marriage, and she who saw that their association could not be continued without pain and distress to everyone. The baby seemed to him not a threat to his marriage with Jane, but an excuse to escape it, just as the severe haemorrhage he had had when he was at the coaching establishment had presented itself not as a threat to his own survival, but an excuse for leaving Isabel and throwing himself on the world as a writer.

In all this drama, only the girl comes through clearly and nobly. She did not lack suitors; it would have been easy enough to marry, but she loved H.G. She returned from France, where H.G. had taken a villa for her outside Paris. On the channel boat she thought of suicide, but was much too healthy-minded to give this more than a desperate passing thought. She had been brought up in a home where advanced magazines lay about on the tables and advanced topics were freely and openly discussed, so to her mother she confessed everything in the assurance that someone who had talked so much about freedom for women would understand her dash for it. But, like Hubert Bland, Mrs Pember Reeves took a very different view when the precepts she had advocated were put into practice by one of her own children. Soon afterwards, she accepted a suitor who had been pressing her to marry him for many years, someone her own age whom she had known well in the Fabian Summer Schools. They were married in July, and the baby was born in December.

Throughout these months of crisis H.G. had led a harrassed life. In May, Spade House was sold, and during the summer he bought in Jane Wells's name the leasehold of 17 Church Row in Hampstead, one of a beautiful terrace of eighteenth-century houses looking from its garden windows over the valley in which London lies to the Surrey hills on the other side, and from the front overlooking an old church-yard in which many famous stage and literary figures are buried, a very different graveyard from that which the china shop in Bromley had lain close to. The family moved into the house in August, and in October *Ann Veronica* appeared.

Between May, when they left Spade House, and December, when a vindictive campaign against the book was being waged chiefly in the columns of the *Spectator*, Wells must have known the sufferings of the damned. Hardly a day can have passed in which he was not reminded of his folly, and he might be left by his biographers to mourn this in privacy were it not that what he was to become as a novelist and as an artist was shaped to some extent by his experiences during this period of stress. He was not one to shrug off his resentments or to shrink from argument.

To those he loved or admired or trusted, he could show a very appealing side of his nature, the good man who has momentarily faltered but is not rotten to the core. To Maurice Baring he wrote in September: 'Don't listen to evil stories about me for even if the facts were right the values are wrong'; and to Elizabeth Healey, who had remained such a faithful and affectionate friend, he wrote in January:

All the rumours are true or false in various measure. Mrs Blanco White has got a jolly little daughter anyhow. I'm afraid I've behaved rather scandalous, but nohow mean in the past year. Believe everything scandalous but nothing mean about me, and you'll be fairly right.

To Edwin Pugh, another old friend, he could smile at the turn fortune had served him:

The Lord deals gently with me. My personal unpopularity is immense but amusing, and people listen with blanched faces to the tale of my vices, and go and buy my books.

But with the 'whisperers' and 'scandalizers' he could be very fierce. He saw all the scandal as emanating from the Old Gang in the Fabian Society – not surprisingly, since he had succeeded in seducing the daughters of two of its most eminent members. He saw the Webbs as industriously as always circulating tales of his misdemeanours, and in September 1909 he wrote fiercely to Beatrice Webb, threatening 'a public smash' to clear up 'the untraceable soaking nastiness about us. But when people of your sort act as channels for the inventions of the Bland–Colgate * type, there's nothing else possible but the open.'

But at the same time he could boast to Arnold Bennett rather jauntily of the fact that the affair continued even after the marriage, which was untrue. It is extraordinary how these two characters who had boasted to and joked with one another could continue to do so long after there was any need for it.

And by the bye, it may interest you to know that that affair of philoprogenitive passion isn't over. (You will remember the affair.) Interesting and remarkable psychological reactions followed. The two principals appear to have underestimated the web of affections and memories that held them together. The husband, a perfectly admirable man, being married, attempted to play a husband's part (which was asinine of him). Violent emotional storms have ensued and there is a separation and I think it will be necessary out of common fairness to him to give him grounds and have a divorce – and run a country cottage in the sight of all mankind. I tell you these things to strain your continence, knowing you will tell no-one and suffer dreadful things not doing so. I have sold Spade House and got a delightful house in Church Row, Hampstead for Jane. We shall go there in August, I expect. I am extremely happy and have never worked so well.

To Bennett he could write in this rather odious vein of the seducer revelling in the satisfaction of sin, but to Vernon Lee,† who had been a guest in his home, an admirer of his Utopian ideas, and particularly a friend of his wife, his tone was very different – no more remorseful but definitely less brazen.

---

* Colgate was a secretary employed by the Webbs.
† Vernon Lee was the pseudonym of Violet Paget.

Dear 'Sister-in-Utopia',

This world is very resonant and transparent and I perceive you have been listening to scandal about me and avoiding me, instead of coming to me to find out just what the moral values were, as I think you ought to have done. I am very sorry for I wanted to talk to you – very sorry indeed. And it was not kind to my wife who likes and admires you beyond measure. Well, I forgive you, because I know the complications of life, and if at any time you would like to know me again I'm altogether at your service. I've done nothing I am ashamed of. I had meant to write you a long letter against your symbol of the laurel bough – it would have been very long if I had written all I meant to do.

Goodbye for a time,
Very sincerely yours,
H. G. Wells

Vernon Lee acknowledged this letter with sympathy and understanding, and he replied:

I can't talk about things now. It's vital to us all that we should be left alone to straighten out our own affairs in our own way – and thought of and dealt with generously. So – until we can talk next year let us leave this. Will you, if you can, silence talkers and hasty judges, and believe me always

Very much yours,
H. G. Wells

Something moved him at the end of November – perhaps the harassment of the ridiculous campaign being waged against him in the *Spectator*, and the volume of talk in clubland and in literary London, which must by this time have been extensive – to write to this woman who was by ten years his elder, a sensitive, an intelligent and, above all, a just woman, to confess his love for the girl, and to confide in her that, although now married, she was to bear his child. It was a courageous thing to do, for it invited criticism from someone whom he respected, but H.G. was never one to turn aside from a blow.

Vernon Lee's view, gently but firmly expressed, was that in such a case, with a girl so young, an experienced man owes her protection from himself – and herself. What concerned her was that part of the price for such a misdemeanour has to be paid by those who had *not* drunk the wine and eaten the cake:

In all this story the really interesting person seems to me to be your wife, and it is *her* future, her happiness for which I am concerned. And I cannot help also thinking of the damage which this business has done to Utopia and Utopians; above all, the recrudescence of prejudice and horrid suspiciousness which will come in the way of the possible comradeship of so many men and girls.

Vernon Lee hoped, in conclusion, that 'impossible as it may be for you to show or me to see, there yet remains an explanation of all this matter which – both the point of view and the actual facts – may be worthy of what I have imagined you to be and am still willing to give you credit for'.

The blend of real affection and understanding of his difficult position with restrained reproof for his weakness which this admirable woman revealed in her letters to him must have touched him. It was a far cry from the vulgarity shown in the attitude of someone of commoner mould like Arnold Bennett and the side of H.G.'s character which came uppermost when he was with his common friend. It was in December that Arnold Bennett recorded in his journal that he had been to lunch with the Wells's – 'talked H.G.'s scandal from 12.15 to 1', presumably secluded with a decanter in H.G.'s study before joining a larger party for lunch, at which that inveterate and kindly gossip William Rothenstein was one of the guests. A few nights later Arnold Bennett was there for dinner; a large party, with Hampstead neighbours, and parlour games after dinner. All was lighthearted, Christmas was coming, the wine flowed.

And on New Year's Eve, within a few hours of the event, Wells was writing to Vernon Lee that a little daughter had been born to him and his mistress. What did he betray in that letter that called forth this in reply?

Dear Mr Wells,

Thanks for your letter. I still am, and perhaps shall always be, deeply perplexed before your personality as a human being, or rather by that dualism (which is so often a discord), the human being who teaches other people. Perhaps this perplexity is due to the inventor of the Samurai being a 'poietic' man, and the disbeliever in Samurai and the Samuraidom on the whole a rather Samurai-ish woman.*

She concluded by offering up prayers for the little daughter, as well as his two sons, for their happiness, and that they might make others happy.

Two weeks later she wrote again, as though by an after-thought, urging upon him advice that he was not to take, for neither his passion nor his resentment could be contained.

Dear Mr Wells, dear friend –

I don't know exactly what it is I meant to write, except that what I wrote last represented only one half of me, and represented it in a cut-and-dried, pedantic, self-righteous form. I *do* think all that. But I think and feel that you are one of the greatest and dearest of living persons, and that your books, even your worst, are far above the best thought and will of those who fall foul of them.

And, dear Mr Wells, and since I speak of falling foul (and in the literal sense 'foul') of your books, I want to say again – and after all such sickening discussions of *Ann Veronica* – that you *must not* give us who are faithful to you the misery of the discussions that will ensue if at this moment you write more things that can be connected with your own personality, or interpreted in the light of your own case.

My love to your wife, and believe me,
Yours always, V. Paget

* 'In this *Modern Utopia* I made a suggestion for a temperamental classification of citizens as citizens. For the purposes of the state I proposed a division into four types of character, the poietic, the kinetic, the dull and the base. A primary problem of government was to vest all the executive and administrative work in the kinetic class; while leaving the poietic an adequate share in suggestion, criticism and legislation, controlling the base and giving the dull an incentive to kinetic effort.' *Experiment in Autobiography.*

P.S. If you have a book dealing with *love*, etc. ready, hold it back till it can be read for what it is. People will forget if you don't remind them.

The 'such sickening discussions of *Ann Veronica*' to which Vernon Lee referred disfigured the columns of the *Spectator*. The reviews had pretty generally expressed disapproval of Ann Veronica's character – not her unladylike behaviour in declaring her love, which could be forgiven in a tempestuous nature, but the insistence upon the physical side of sex, the illicit holiday together in Switzerland described as a honeymoon, and finally the birth of the baby and marriage justifying all things, with Mr Stanley, Ann Veronica's father, adamant before for virtue, now being judicious about the port. The end of the novel is in fact the weak part of the book; it bears too much the aspect of a patch hastily applied. But the moral issues involved are lost on readers of this generation. With a start we read the terms employed by the *Spectator* reviewer to denounce this 'poisonous book', one which is 'capable of poisoning the minds of those who read it'.

It is not that the language is coarse, nor are the 'suggestive passages' open to any very severe criticism. To our surprise we find that in 1909 the novel which was assumed to reflect life was expected to uplift morally, or at least not to debase. That this was not just the narrow view of a weekly widely read by clerics and prosperous paterfamilias, but what most critics expressed, can be seen from the summary of opinion in *H. G. Wells and His Critics*, but the *Spectator* went furthest in invective.

The loathing and indignation which the book inspires in us are due to the effect it is likely to have in undermining that sense of continence and self-control in the individual which is essential in a sound and healthy State. It teaches, in effect, that there is no such thing as woman's honour, or if there is, it is only to be a bulwark against a weak temptation. When the temptation is strong enough, not only is the tempted person justified in yielding but such yielding becomes not merely inevitable but something to be welcomed and glorified. If an animal yearning or lust is only sufficiently absorbing, it is to be obeyed. Self-sacrifice is a dream and self-restraint a delusion. such things have no place in the muddy world of Mr Wells's imaginings. His is a community of scuffling stoats and ferrets, unenlightened by a ray of duty or abnegation.

Capes is described as an erotic science lecturer who has broken his own marriage vows in circumstances of bestial depravity (these circumstances are imagined by the reviewer; they are not described in *Ann Veronica*); and Ann Veronica – 'while it is Christlike to pity and forgive, the great duties and prohibitions of life remain' – poor little Ann Veronica is condemned by quoting Dr Johnson's obliteration of Boswell's defence of the woman who betrayed her husband: 'My dear Sir, never accustom your mind to mingle virtue and vice. The woman's a whore, and there's an end on't.'

It was, Wells said ruefully, an illegitimate extension of the term to count Ann Veronica's single lapse as qualifying her for the profession. Such canting condemnation, passing for literary criticism, might have been dismissed as peculiar to the paper and the narrow-mindedness of its readers but for the circumstances that flowed from its publication.

The correspondence columns of the *Spectator* erupted into flame, and from the pulpits of the country echoed condemnation of this poisonous book. Smartly off the mark was the Reverend Herbert Bull, of Westgate-on-Sea, with a plan for setting up a Watch Committee to read all books, pounce on those likely to bring a blush to the maiden cheek, and launch a prosecution against them immediately. For this a 'Fighting Fund' would be needed, and the amount asked for by Mr Bull for 'the preservation of our English homes from needless contamination' was £1,000. Within a month he could report in the *Spectator* the receipt of £720 18s. od. and announce that contributions were still coming in.

Letters of support poured in, though most of the correspondents were writing from prejudiced positions. The

President of the Girls' Friendly Society wrote to express her 'great satisfaction' at the line the *Spectator* was taking with regard to poisonous literature, and to proclaim the hearty support of her organization for the Reverend Mr Bull's plan for prosecuting any further lapses. The Central Council of the Mothers' Union, representing over 300,000 members, and the President of the Y.W.C.A. weighed in with expressions of satisfaction with and support for all that had been said, and the editor of the *Spectator*, St Loe Strachey, encouraged by this evidence, proceeded on 4 December in a leader to rebuke the publishers of this kind of book and to declare with horrid unction his refusal to publish in his columns advertisements of any books of the *Ann Veronica* kind.

In all this excitement, with echoes coming from pulpits and platforms and provincial librarians, the original aim of defending the purity of the home against the assaults of the modern novel broadened out to express a middle-aged implacable hostility to a whole host of liberalizing notions. Wells was selected as the target because *Ann Veronica* was there to hand, her sin of adultery going unpunished in her final triumph as wife and mother-to-be, not to mention her original outrageous disobedience to her parent. Wells was a socialist, and the state of mind of the *Spectator*'s readers had for a long time been uneasy about socialism; it was uneasy over the threat of women's suffrage, and suspicious of Utopias, which had a disturbing influence on the young, involving suggestions, if not something more than that, of free love. They wanted to cry out that there were such essentials as abnegation and duty of which less and less notice appeared to be taken. It was time to eradicate the rot.

Most indefensible of all were the attitudes of the librarians anxious publicly to dissociate themselves from circulating books of this character. The circulating libraries – very popular at that time, and responsible for most of the sale of fiction – banded themselves together and made public announcement that they were setting up their own Watch

Committee to protect their readers, and would henceforth censor all novels before circulating them. 'A Public Librarian' reported in a letter to the *Spectator*:

It has been my duty on several occasions to report certain works of fiction by living authors as unfit for circulation, and as a rule they have, after examination, been condemned to be burnt. In the case of *Ann Veronica* the author's name and reputation would be sufficient to secure the introduction of the book into many public libraries without question; and the thanks of the nation are therefore all the more due to you for your very welcome article on the subject. The question is, and it is a difficult one to solve, how are we to hinder all this literary filth passing into the hands and minds of the public, and thereby polluting the moral atmosphere of our home life?

Nobody rushed in publicly to defend Wells, although Shaw expressed sympathy in a private letter to him. Touched by this unexpectedly generous gesture from his old rival, Wells wrote in reply that 'you sometimes do not simply rise to a situation, you soar above it', and told him where Amber Reeves was living with her child, and urged him and Mrs Shaw to call upon her. But of public support there was little. Gosse wrote a fine letter to *The Times* condemning the action of lending libraries in setting themselves up as censors. In such a way, he proclaimed, we might miss a Darwin's *Origin of Species*. To which the librarians replied: 'We are only going to censor fiction.'

Frederick Macmillan had correctly judged the public response to the book. Its sale was brisk, as generally happens when books are extensively discussed. In this case, Wells was a successful writer anyway, he was dealing here with the most important question of the hour, the right of a young woman to lead an independent life, and his sole offence was that he had affronted the social convention of the time by showing Ann Veronica as a nice genuine healthy-minded girl engaging first – with no sense of remorse at all – in unhealthy-minded thoughts, and getting finally what she craved for. Macmillan was no moralist himself – in fact, he was more of a man of the world than most of his fellow publishers. But he was also a good tradesman, and in saying that while *Ann Veronica* was a very well-written book, the plot developed on lines that would be distasteful to the public which bought the books that his firm published, he was correctly anticipating the reaction of his most profitable customers. Nevertheless something in Wells plainly fascinated him, and something in him fascinated Wells. It may have been that a born publisher could not help but respond to an author of genius, however much he might disapprove of the author's views; it may have been that the harassed author, unable to keep out of trouble, saw in Macmillan's urbane aristocratic man-of-the-world air all that the crumpled, troubled little figure longed to be. Their association as publisher and author lasted for ten years, and they corresponded for a good many more after that, but they remained on formal terms with each other, and, as far as I know, Macmillan never entertained Wells or introduced him to his home, as he was accustomed to do with other authors, for he was a man who liked the genial side of his business and he and his wife were very hospitable. Something kept them apart socially, but something plainly fascinated each in the other, and although *Ann Veronica* had taken Wells away, and Nelson were to publish the very successful *History of Mr Polly*, against which not a breath of criticism would be made, when Wells had his next big novel, *The New Machiavelli*, in view, he turned first to Macmillan again.

12

The New Machiavelli

Ann Veronica was published by Fisher Unwin on 3 October 1909, and the storm it was to evoke had not yet broken when on the day following publication Wells wrote to Macmillan about the political novel which he had mentioned in earlier correspondence as the third of a series of which *Tono-Bungay* was the first and *Ann Veronica* the second.

Dear Mr Macmillan,

I have in hand a long novel for the autumn of '10. It is a sort of companion piece to *Tono-Bungay*, as large and outspoken, but this time it is a picture of political life. Our agreement, of course, cannot be restored, but I think it only fair to advise you of the existence of the book, and all things being equal, I should like you to publish it.

Nelson's, by the bye, tell me that they have sold 43,000 of *Kipps*, which isn't bad for a book left for dead.

Yours very sincerely,
H. G. Wells

This last was a dig which Wells could not resist giving. Two years earlier, before all this trouble arose, Macmillan had reported sales of only 180 copies of *Kipps*, bringing Wells in no more than £13 10s. od. Nelson had offered to do the book in their sevenpenny library, a form of cloth-bound reprint just then coming into vogue in which Nelson were pioneers. Macmillan had protested to Wells that this was merely a lure on Nelson's part to get a successful author away, and had told Wells rather huffily that he was perfectly willing to relinquish his books if he wanted to go. Wells had responded soothingly, saying that he liked the Macmillan firm in many ways – he thought it unadventurous, but on the other hand it was safe and solid and sane. In the end he had persuaded Macmillan to agree to the experiment with Nelson, from which Macmillan would get half the royalty, and he could not resist now rubbing in the results.

Macmillan ignored this reminder, but to the suggestion that they should take up their relationship again where it had broken off over *Ann Veronica* he responded with enthusiasm. Ignoring the hint implicit in Wells's letter that he would want more money, he proposed the same terms for the new book as for *Tono-Bungay*, an advance of £500. But after the £1,500 from Fisher Unwin for *Ann Veronica*, Wells was in a confident mood. 'I'm afraid we can't deal this time. I shall want a much bigger advance', he replied loftily. Macmillan hastily wrote to say that he would guarantee the royalty on a sale of 10,000 copies, and he urged a meeting at which an agreement might be signed. Perhaps he had already heard that Wells had quickly followed up *Ann Veronica* with another novel, *The History of Mr Polly*, which he had given to Nelson to publish, and which was rumoured to be another *Kipps*. Perhaps *Ann Veronica* had been only a daring venture of which Wells now repented. Whatever the reason, he was now anxious to have Wells back on his list. The calls at the office had always been at Wells's initiative, but now Mr Macmillan was doing the pressing and it was Wells who was being evasive.

For the moment Wells did not even acknowledge this letter. The storm was beginning to brew over Ann Veronica, and he had more immediate preoccupations. He was almost certainly in need of money. Gone were the days of simple living when he could not help but save money because he and Jane did not know how to spend it. The Wellses now entertained largely if not lavishly, and lunching and dining at his clubs, with the Coefficients and other societies made life much more expensive than it had been when they were living at Spade House. His amatory adventures also were costly, and now at the end of the year the child of his love affair was expected.

Not only was necessity driving him, but the switch of

publishers for *Ann Veronica* had persuaded him that his work was being undervalued. Wells was always conscious of money, but never mean about it. It was not greed but the need for reassurance that now started him on the path of exacting larger and larger advances from his publishers. He was confident that *The New Machiavelli* was the best novel he had written, and he was in no mood to accept for it the sort of terms that had been good enough for *The Food of the Gods* five years before. On the other hand, the increasing complexity of his affairs – not only the scandal and its expenses, but his determination, now that he was done with the futility of the Fabians, to throw himself into novelwriting – made him long more than ever to have behind him a solid world-wide firm like Macmillans, the publisher of Hardy and Kipling, whose organization would help his work find the largest public.

Eager though he was to have Wells back on his list, Macmillan wanted to get from him an undertaking that the yet unnamed novel, however political its background, would not include any of the distressful elements that had made it impossible for the firm to publish *Ann Veronica*. He therefore pressed for a meeting at which this point might be clarified, and perhaps he was being urged to this by his less worldly brother and cousin. A hint that this may have been the case is to be found in a letter which Frederick wrote to his brother Maurice from Cannes in February 1912 about *The Passionate Friends:* 'I should certainly like to see the MS. of Wells's novel, and I hope we may not be obliged to refuse it. I don't want to publish indecent books, but if we are to deal in literature at all it will not do for us to be bound by the prejudices of the Rev. Mr Bull and St Loe Strachey.'

But this was six years later, and a lot of growing-up had been done in the interval. In 1909 he needed to have from Wells a direct assurance on this matter before he signed for the novel sight unseen. Finally, on 3 November Wells called at the office, and a long and private conversation took place between the two men. What was said at that meeting was not recorded, but Macmillan believed that Wells had given him the assurance he wanted, and an agreement was made on the terms Wells had asked.

The *Spectator* row was by this time raging furiously. Those readers who were becoming increasingly alarmed by Mr Wells's uninhibited heroines were making themselves vocal, and literary London was beginning to buzz with gossip over his affairs. The atmosphere at Church Row must have been extremely strained, though Jane put a brave face on it and entertaining went on at the usual pace.

On 28 February 1910 Jane Wells sent in the first part of *The New Machiavelli*. In March she advised Macmillan that the *English Review* would start serialization in May and complete it in November, and that Macmillan would be free to publish any time after 30 September.

Meanwhile in April *Mr Polly* made his bow under Nelson's imprint, and the critics were in raptures. The cries of alarm which had been sounding steadily in the *Spectator* all winter died away. This was Wells in his happiest mood. Sandwiched between *Ann Veronica* and *The New Machiavelli*, it shines out as pure comedy, and its appearance just at that moment seemed to confirm Mr Macmillan's hope, shared by many others, that this outstanding writer was going to come down on the right side of the fence. Actually Wells had recanted nothing, as the monthly serial parts of *The New Machiavelli* were to reveal in the *English Review*, starting in the next month. *The New Machiavelli* was almost finished. Mr Polly's radiance only reflected the joy that had been uplifting Wells's own spirits when he had written it right after *Ann Veronica*, before his love affair had been discovered.

The clouds were not long in gathering. The proofs of the book reached Macmillan from the printer some time at the end of May.

It may seem extraordinary that with so unpredictable an author, especially one with whom they had had such recent experience of trouble, the partners should have sent *The*

New Machiavelli to the printer before reading it themselves or taking the opinion of one of their trusted advisers. They were accustomed to do this with their reliable best-selling authors, for corrections to type were cheap to make in those days of ill-paid skilled labour, but while Wells qualified for such treatment by his sales, *Ann Veronica* had been merely the most outrageous example of Wells's regrettable tendency to be 'advanced' and 'daring' in his love stories. As the ensuing correspondence reveals, Macmillan was resting on the undertaking which he believed himself to have extracted from Wells; and Wells was busily denying that he had given any such undertaking.

On 21 June Macmillan wrote to Wells:

Dear Mr Wells,

As the manuscript of the final chapters of *The New Machiavelli* only reached the printers last week, we have not until now had the opportunity of reading the complete book. I much regret to say that in spite of the fact that it contains a great deal that is brilliant – parts of it seem to me to be better than anything you have done hitherto – the whole book is a great disappointment to us.

You will remember that at the interview which took place here when the terms of the agreement were discussed, I said that it would have to be distinctly understood that the novel (which was then unwritten) should not contain any of the elements which led us to refuse *Ann Veronica*, and that you agreed to this saying that the novel was to be a political one. Now this it cannot be called. It is true that it deals incidentally with politics, that the hero goes into the House of Commons, and that some of the most amusing parts of the book are the sketches of political life and persons, but in its essence *The New Machiavelli* is a novel dealing with social questions, and particularly with the question of sex.

It is unnecessary for me to particularize, but I feel sure you will agree that the kind of thing we objected to in *Ann Veronica* is here intensified, and that if we had good reason for rejecting *Ann Veronica*, there is twice as much reason why we should not publish *The New Machiavelli*.

My partners and I have discussed the matter very carefully,

and have decided that the step which we now take with much regret is one that must be taken at any cost.

We regret it because we are sorry not to be associated with a writer whom we regard as one of the ablest of the day, also as I am sure you will believe because we are sorry to do what may put you to some inconvenience.

I say nothing about breaking a contract, because in view of the proviso as to its contents which was made before the book was written I do not consider that the breach of contract is on our side. Fortunately the book has never been announced in any of our lists.

I am

Yours sincerely,

Frederick Macmillan

Wells's reply is undated but its tone suggests that it was answered the same day:

Dear Sir Frederick,*

I cannot of course allow you to break our contract in this fashion. I have a very clear recollection of our conversation about the subject of *The New Machiavelli* and I am quite sure there was no such exclusion of sexual interest as you now suggest. Every novel *must* have a sexual interest. I quite perceive however that there are strong practical objections to forcing a publisher who has changed his mind about a book to go on with its publication and if you are prepared with any proposals for the transfer of the book to some other firm or for any arrangement that will not inflict grave pecuniary injury upon me I shall be ready to consider it. I rejected an offer of Methuens (of £1000 down and 25%) in order to accept yours but I cannot of course go to him now, and indeed the whole position becomes impossible for me and leaves me no alternative but litigation unless you are prepared for a much more careful consideration of my difficulties in the matter than you appear to have given them so far. I don't want litigation if it can possibly be helped, our relations have hitherto been fair and frank and satisfactory and I suggest therefore we have a conference before carrying the matter to our solicitors.

Very sincerely yours,

H. G. Wells

* Frederick Macmillan had received a knighthood in the New Year's Honours List.

Each of these letters has the ring of absolute truth in it;
the defence in each case is that of the good man deceived.
It is not possible to believe that a publisher of Macmillan's
reputation and experience would have imagined that he had
been given this assurance, and the note of honest indignation in which he wrote to Wells when he had read the
proofs is understandable.

But Wells's angry response is equally understandable. *Ann
Veronica* glorified sexual freedom. In *The New Machiavelli*
sexual indiscretion brings highly moral disaster. What did
the fellow want? One can imagine him blowing with exasperation like Edward Ponderevo. He had thrown off *Ann
Veronica* in a few months; it was a *jeu d'esprit*, written
while passionate love was warming his soul, chilled by the
pettiness of the Fabian dispute. He had not stopped to
weigh its implications. What he had done was to sound the
trumpets for the young as against the old, glorying in their
rebellion. *Tono-Bungay*, planned as a social panorama in
the vein of Balzac, had been designed to show the disaster
which could ensue in an unplanned world subject to the
jungle laws of commerce. The moral lesson stood out a mile
here as it did there. The unbridled pursuit of money could
bring disaster; the ungoverned yielding to physical passion
could ruin a career. Sex was the biggest issue of all. It now
gripped his creative imagination fully; this relationship –
in every degree, mental and physical – between man and
woman was at the core of life; and that a study of this kind
should be objected to as not 'clean', that papers like the
Spectator and the *Westminster Gazette* should seek to suppress him, that Macmillan should abandon him, filled him
with rage as well as anxiety for his own future, and stopped
him altogether from getting on with his work. He had
always been two books ahead of his publisher, for serial
rights in monthly parts provided a good part of a book's
income, and a book had to be finished long before it saw
the light of day. Now he felt frustrated. He was being assailed on every side, by worry about the child which was

coming, and by the loss to another man of the girl he loved. He had been prepared to leave Jane and marry her. It was she who left him. Assailed too by the advice and sympathy of well-wishers like Vernon Lee and Bernard Shaw, who could not possibly imagine the furies that drove a man into his position, and by friends like Arnold Bennett, who thought they could. He confesses in his autobiography that for the second and last time in his life he almost made a bolt for it. But his aggressive spirit anchored him to the London battlefield. He was not a man to turn away from a fight.

The idea of litigation was dropped, and Frederick Macmillan undertook to try to find another publisher willing to publish the book and, in any event, to guarantee Wells against loss. But before that step should be taken, Wells, anxious to make peace, suggested some revisions in the last part of the story and took away the proofs to work on them. One does not know what was said at their interviews, but later correspondence makes it plain that Macmillan had made up his mind that he would not publish the book in any circumstances. Perhaps there was a lack of frankness at this stage, or Wells would not have thought of amending the end – notable for the frank exchange of views about sex between the abandoned wife and the absconding husband. As he worked, Wells evidently regretted what had happened, and wrote what was for him rather pleadingly:

I've been working very closely since I saw you and I am sure I can make the end far stronger, finer and better than it is, and also much more in accordance with your views. If I *can* induce you to stick to the book, I would like you to do so. It's possible it may induce a strain – not a very heavy strain, I think, but I think in the long run you won't be sorry for standing by me. The next book I'm planning [*Marriage*] won't cause any of this trouble – I'm passing out of a necessary phase in handling my medium. Sex *must* be handled, and few writers escape the gawky phase.

Sir Frederick replied:

We will, of course, re-read the whole book in revise but I must frankly say that I see very little chance of being able to publish it.

On 7 July Wells sent in the revised proofs:

You will see that there has been a very thorough revision and I do not really think there is much left of your objection. I do hope it will be possible for you to publish the amended book. Whatever was ambiguous in the time of the concluding episode is quite cleared up and it is now, as I have always intended it to be, the breaking off – and the quite disastrous breaking off – of the political career which is *the* book.

But Macmillan replied:

I am sorry to say that our ruling as to the publication of the book by our house is in no degree modified. We are in communication with Mr Heinemann, and I doubt not that satisfactory arrangements can be made to issue the book through him.

Macmillan would have been well aware of the identity of the Baileys in *The New Machiavelli*. They were only too clearly living portraits of Beatrice and Sidney Webb. The 'prigs at play' were plainly the Fabians, and the Pentagram Circle nothing else than the Coefficients Club. Balfour was to be recognized in Evesham; Sir Edward Grey, Henry Newbolt, L. S. Amery, Haldane and Milner were all identifiable; there could only be one original for Neal, the wild Irish journalist – J. L. Garvin, who was then very much to the fore, and whose articles were being widely discussed. These caricatures did not bother Macmillan, but Isabel Rivers did. Macmillan was a great frequenter of the Athenaeum, which has the Reform, Wells's club, next door to it. Along Pall Mall all the clubs were abuzz with gossip over this affair, and it was only too plain that Ann Veronica lived on in *The New Machiavelli* as Isabel Rivers. Her identity was now widely known. She had been at the very centre and flame of Wells's thoughts in the winter of 1909–10, when after his undertaking to Macmillan in November he had been writing *The New Machiavelli*. This was no more a political novel than *Tono-Bungay* was a book about a shop-chemist engaging in high finance. The political framework existed merely to allow the author to disagree with all parties and advocate in place of their programmes, amongst other intemperate notions, ideas about endowed motherhood and woman's place in society which were nonsense, not dangerous nonsense but trouble-making for all that. This was a novel about sex; and it as good as named names. Wells could say what he liked politically, but he could not, with Macmillan as publisher, extol adultery, and that, in Macmillan's view, was what *The New Machiavelli* did. It is possible to share Macmillan's exasperation, as a business man tricked into laying out £1,000 on a novel which was merely a fresh serving-up of one which he had already declined, and to find himself committed to publishing something just as much in advance of what was acceptable to the public who bought his books as *Ann Veronica* had been; or worse, rather, because for all the savagery of its portraiture of recognizable people, and for all the silliness of its political ideas, this was the work of a man of genius.

Yet the bare outline of the story Wells had projected to Macmillan in his letter of the year before was still discernible. It was a political novel in the sense that Remington was a politician, though fictionally not a very convincing one. But the novel which he had outlined as being 'big and various in the same way as *Tono-Bungay* is, and to give Westminster, a big north country election, a country house party, and at the same time a lot of the subordinate life, Socialist meetings, etc.' was very different when it was delivered as *The New Machiavelli* and the partners were made aware of what they had trustingly sent to the printer.

The first third of the book is a magnificent re-creation of Wells's own boyhood in Bromley, done with the power of a first-rate novelist. This sets the subject of the novel – waste;

the confusion and waste and planlessness of human life, as Richard Remington recalls his upbringing in an area of London which has been scarred and defiled by the back-wash of an unplanned get-rich-quick, every-man-for-himself industrial age. Remington tells how this affected him, and how he came to devote his life to the cause of enlightened statesmanship through which this giant selfish muddle might be remedied, and how he failed because he was be-trayed by a deep-seated instinct – 'the red blaze of sex', more powerful than the instinct of reform.

George Ponderevo had seen life from the servants' hall; Richard Remington sees it as the son of an ill-equipped, ill-trained, spasmodically energetic father who is a poorly paid science teacher in a suburb of London, the father and his desolate background both being presented as waste products of the Victorian age. Remington's father is a beautifully observed portrait of Joe Wells, a man who dreamt fine dreams but, with his insufficient education, could not battle against the disorder of the modern world. Remington's mother is Mrs Wells, the one unretouched portrait of her that exists, in which his dislike of his mother for her ignorant unfeeling ways is quickly demonstrated and then the curtain is drawn again. These opening chapters, so beautifully observed, so emotionally felt, are among the best of Wells's writing, justifying the comparison of him with Dickens and Hardy.

Remington goes to Cambridge, comes down and goes into politics. This second part is the story of his marriage to Margaret, a very contrived piece of storytelling, but sig-nificant because of the brilliantly drawn, savage portraiture of leading personalities in the Fabian movement, notably Sidney and Beatrice Webb as Oscar and Altiora Bailey.

The third part, called 'The Besetting of Sex', tells the story of his love affair with Isabel, a young Cambridge blue-stocking who works for him politically, and of the way in which they make a common wreck of their lives. It is the Ann Veronica story told again at greater length, more

passionately; it is a cry of anger against the oppressive conventions of society, and it makes very plain that not only
had Wells not forgiven the Fabians for rejecting his
dreams; he had been bruised by the rebuff, and had declared unceasing war on those who obstructed his way.

He was used by this time to fluttering the dovecotes, and
the outcry that arose as *The New Machiavelli* was unfolded
in the monthly issues of the *English Review* did not catch
him unprepared. In *Ann Veronica* he had been consciously
showing what it was that these young people flocking into
the Fabian Society were looking for – love and life as well
as the benefits to humanity that would follow on a more
equitable distribution of wealth, a fairer division of the
taxes, and better administration of the London County
Council. In *The New Machiavelli*, instead of showing love,
which he does only incidentally, he is showing his detesta-
tion for the oppressive, authoritarian establishment which
allows progress only in the directions it thinks seemly and
wise, is jealous, narrow-minded, unimaginative, self-centred:
dull people making beautiful life dull. When you write
about love, even illicit love, you betray only a secret.
The details may be shocking, the rupture of an established
relationship as a result of forming a new one may be painful and reprehensible. But everyone envies love, and cuckol-
ded husbands and deprived fathers are really figures of fun.
  Revenge is therefore the motive of *The New Machiavelli*.
Wells was getting his own back, and in order to demonstrate how narrow-minded and wrong-headed the Fabian
Old Gang were, he had to show how beautiful and noble
and free the alternative way of life could be. Here he was
led into an exaggeration that was fatal to the success of the
theme so impressively introduced. He set the story at a
national level. England was betrayed by these men, not the
few hundred Fabian middle-class socialists. In forcing
Remington out of public life because he would not give up
his mistress, a national leader is lost. The parallel was plain.

In combining to defeat Wells, the Fabian Society had lost its chance to become the active party in establishing socialism as the great viable force in English political life. Middle-class morality had done Wells down in that dusty conflict, not – as Shaw had tried to prove – the impracticability of his programme. The same fate condemns Remington to exile.

It was plain that Ann Veronica was not dead. Here was her story again, but the picture of a rebellious daughter fulfilling her natural destiny to love and be loved is now magnified to the tragic drama of a great career smashed by the world's little envy.

Remington has risen so far in the Conservative party that the highest office of all seems within his grasp. But for that he must forgo the girl with whom he is passionately in love, and remain with his wife, whose money and whose whole-hearted devotion to making a successful career for him have brought him as far as he has come. In the desperate struggle between ambition and passion which ensues, passion wins, and Remington abandons his career near the summit, going off like Machiavelli, out of favour with his Prince, to ponder what it is that makes the great state.

It was an overweening comparison, and Remington's political activities and subsequent speculations seem jejune in comparison with the subtle ones which Machiavelli recommends to his Prince. What makes this novel of particular interest in looking at Wells's work is that it is the high-water mark of his achievement as a purposive novelist. In *Kipps* and *Tono-Bungay* and *Mr Polly*, the central character is so firmly and skilfully established in our sympathies that the disordered background of life, responsible though it is for the hardships the characters suffer, is to us merely the entertaining setting against which 'our chap' – Kipps or young Ponderevo or henpecked Mr Polly, with his intuitive flashes of beauty elsewhere – struggles to survive. But in *The New Machiavelli* the background is the story. It is the explanation of Remington's career, if not of his moral lapse. With enormous natural skill as a writer, Wells was able to hold the reader's interest while the message was dispensed and inculcated.

If we leave out *Ann Veronica* as a hasty attempt to sketch the freshness and vitality of the young generation seeking to throw off Victorianism, *The New Machiavelli* is the first middle-class novel which Wells attempted. Here he did not have to assist him the echoes of the racy speech of the crowded lower-class world of his youth, the wall of comic repartee they put up as a sort of lean-to, meant to shut off the winds of adversity. There never was before, and never will be again, a class quite like the industrial poor who clustered in burrows round the smoky cities of the first industrial era and fortified themselves against the terrible burden of life with, of all things, humour. Wells, with his sensitive ear and clever head, had caught it perfectly, and rendered it marvellously when he began to write.

Amongst the middle class he moved as a stranger, never sure of what could be said and what not, what could be done, what couldn't. In *The New Machiavelli*, Remington comes from the same smoky, grimy world young Wells had known, and the memorable part of the book is the description of what life was like down there amongst the detritus. Remington's aim is to recondition the society that allows such things. The purpose becomes stronger than character or story. It is true that Wells did not go as far as Remington in preferring exile to existence without his mistress. But as we have already pointed out, Wells was prepared at this time to make a bolt for it, and was stopped, not by any scruples, but by the sacrifice made by the girl in the case. Except for this, Wells was telling here the story of his own love-affair, and this, in spite of his public denials, was recognized by the close London literary world.

It is this autobiographical content, reflecting so clearly what had happened to Wells since 1902, which gives *The New Machiavelli* a special interest. In all his books the narrator is always Wells, sometimes aggressively and demonstrably so, sometimes merely a man with his background who knows something of science. It was impossible to mistake Remington for anybody except H. G. Wells. Remington's political career reflected Wells's rise and fall in the Fabian Society; the identifiable figures make that all as plain as day.

One clear glimpse of the reflection of Wells's own story is given in the letter which Margaret sends Remington as he is leaving England.

I've always hidden my tears from you – and what was in my heart. It's my nature to hide – and you, you want things brought to you to see. You are so curious as to be almost cruel. You don't understand reserves. You have no mercy with restraints and reservations. You are not really a *civilized* man at all. You hate pretences – and not only pretences but decent coverings.

My dear, my dear, you can't think of the desolation of things … I shall never go back to that house we furnished together, that was to have been the laboratory (do you remember calling it a laboratory?) in which you were to forge so much of the new order …

But if the opinions are Wells's, and if the main figures in the domestic triangle in Remington's life are very like those in Wells's own unhappy situation, at the point of crisis Remington and Wells behave very differently. Remington yields to the passionate urge beating in his blood, and abandons wife, career and country for love in exile. Remington's creator did not, although we know that this was not through unwillingness on his part to 'make a bolt for it'. The last part of *The New Machiavelli*, in fact, like the last chapter of Ann Veronica, is fictionalized, a strange charge to bring against a novel, but justified by the close accord up to that point of everything in the Wells–Remington story. Margaret is a prettification of Jane – a portrait with the patina of remorse over it.

The mixture of sensual man and reformer which was the basis of Wells's character is fully reflected for the first time in Remington in *The New Machiavelli*. There had been indications enough before. In *The Sea Lady* Chatteris had abandoned his career for the delights of sensuality. In *In the Days of the Comet* Leadford had looked back with longing to the sensual thrills of the old disordered world before the Great Change had come. The growing chorus of criticism that met Wells's books was based not on their literary deficiencies but on the growing tendency to justify and excuse the actions of the sensual man. He was using the novel to portray actual living characters caught in the sensual trap which, if we were not on guard, might catch us all. The shock to middle-class decorum was severe. In a sense he blundered into the attack. But having done so, he did not withdraw. He insisted that the novel must be true to life.

The despair of the sensual man betrayed in his high aims by the tide in his blood had flickered momentarily in Wells's imagination from the beginning; it had been subdued at first in the intense effort and excitement of getting on. Now that he had succeeded as a writer and had time to speculate – and fail – his bitterness was intense. 'Why do I care for these things', Wells in the image of Remington cries, 'when I can do so little? Why am I set apart from the jolly thoughtless fighting life of men? These dreams fade to nothing and leave me bare.'

This was the moment of self-revelation in Wells's life as a writer. Many years later, intervening in a brisk exchange of scintillating hostile views then occurring between Wells and Shaw over the famous Wells–Stalin interviews, Maynard Keynes brilliantly put his finger on the defects in Wells's intellectual situation in its relation to his times:

Wells's peculiar gift of the imagination lies in his creative grasp of the possibilities and ultimate implication of the data with which contemporary scientists furnish him. At the same time he is a social and political dreamer – or has grown so as he becomes older – much more than a technical and mathematical dreamer; of the old school of Plato, not of Pythagoras or Archimedes. Wells's misfortune has been to belong to a generation to whom their economists have offered nothing new. They have given him no platform from which his imagination can leap. But he is fully conscious all the same, and justly so, that his own mind dwells with the future, and Shaw's and Stalin's with the past.

Remington despairs of humanity, as Wells was to do all through the events of that trying year:

'Hadn't I always known that science and philosophy elaborate themselves, in spite of all the passions and narrowness of men, in spite of the vanities and weakness of their servants, in spite of all the heated disorder of contemporary things? Wasn't it my own phrase to speak of "that greater mind in men, in which we are but moments and transitorily lit cells"? Hadn't I known that the spirit of man still speaks like a thing that struggles out of mud and slime, and that the mere effort to speak means choking and disaster? Hadn't I known that we who think without fear and speak without discretion will not come into our own for the next two thousand years?'

In hours black enough with personal unhappiness it was maddening to hear from Macmillan that he proposed to cancel the agreement to publish because in his view *The New Machiavelli* was only incidentally political – 'in its essence *The New Machiavelli* is a novel dealing with social questions, and particularly with the question of sex'. With one dismissive phrase, all those dreams for humanity swept aside! It is easy to sympathize with Wells's growing exasperation at being misunderstood, while at the same time making allowance for Macmillan's exasperation at being misled. Macmillan could see that politically this novel made no appeal to the imagination. It would be laughed at on that score. Wells had not the necessary knowledge; he had in fact an expressed distaste for party politics and intrigue. It was what had made him so irritated with the Fabians. This is a perfectly natural attitude for an artist. But he had the writer's curiosity about personality; he loved wining and dining with men of affairs, and he had kept up very actively his membership in the Coefficients Club which dined monthly to discuss the future of the Empire, where he rubbed shoulders with people like Lord Haldane and Sir Edward Grey, Bertrand Russell, Balfour, Garvin, Lord Milner and others. 'These talks played an important part in my education', he wrote in his autobiography.

They brought me closer than I had ever come hitherto to many processes in contemporary English politics, and they gave me juster ideas of the mental atmosphere in which such affairs were managed.

But if *The New Machiavelli* reflects what he learnt, these meetings gave him only a confused idea of the delicately balanced process by which political action is achieved through the political parties in England. It does not require much imagination to picture the scene of these dinners: a private dining-room in a club; men in evening dress, a little flushed and self-important on such masculine occasions; the mixture of gossip and information fed into the pool of the candle-lit table, the fumes of wine and cigars, thoughts swelling under the pressure of good-fellowship and the immense seriousness of that particular hour of life, the ship of state riding on, and one so near the helm. A positive longing to touch it and – for a moment at least – to direct this mighty enterprise. The mood would have been enlivening enough for the others there, all of whom were 'in the game'. How much more so for the observing little Wells, the novelist who, only ten years before, had been sharing a front-floor pair of rooms with one of his students whom he had run off with, and in those days putting his imagination to work on fantasy in order to earn guineas. And now to be at the very heart of things – and just at that moment when he was sore from the rebuff his visions had had at the hands of the tough realists, the Webbs and Bernard Shaw, in the Fabian Society. One can see why he planned *The New Machiavelli* as a political novel.

What had introduced him to this company was not the fame that came to him with the great success of *The Time Machine, The Island of Dr Moreau, The Invisible Man* and *The First Men in the Moon.* It was *Anticipations* and real-life adumbrations of the future that had excited at first the Webbs and then the membership of the Fabian Society. People, important people, had listened to what he had to say, and in the Coefficients they must also have listened, for he was a marvellously persuasive and stimulating talker, inept only when he had to rise to his feet and make a speech. And perhaps the Coefficients' dinner table was the right place for spinning such dreams. Stimulated by the wine, elevated by the grand company, free of responsibility, its members could plot and plan anything. They were, for those moments at least, all fantasists. Their proceedings were not written up and published. For the more serious members, it was a sifting-ground for possible schemes; for the less serious, it was entertainment. But for Wells it was the Samurai, plotting the course the ship of state was to take.

What is missing from this scene is H.G.'s customary scepticism. He made too much of the club's influence: it was only one of a score of such dining-clubs representing different shades of political interest. Among its prominent members was Pember Reeves, the father of the girl with whom in 1909 and 1910 H.G.'s name had been linked. She had appeared as Ann Veronica. Now she reappeared as Isabel, and the whole of that affair was blown up into a love story meant to rank with the Parnell tragedy. Only H.G. would have written *Ann Veronica* while he was still technically a member of the Fabian Executive. Only H.G. could have written *The New Machiavelli* while his scandal was raging and expect it to be accepted as a serious political novel.

With so much open to so many people, it is not surprising that Sir Frederick should have declared that 'it is unnecessary for me to particularize' in saying that 'if we had reason for rejecting *Ann Veronica*, there is twice as much reason why we should not publish *The New Machiavelli*'. There might be no more sex in this book than there had been in *Tono-Bungay*, but the scene was crowded with living portraits, and Sir Frederick would have none of it.

It was, of course, useless to deny that *The New Machiavelli* had a sexual base. The sexual relations between men and women had come to dominate Wells's mind, and no censure was going to divert him from this study. It was going to be part and parcel of all his books, whatever the subject, and so he was going to declare in a lecture on the Contemporary Novel which, in these troublesome, suspenseful months while *The New Machiavelli* was being hawked round the London publishers, he used some of his time to prepare.

For this interest was a part of Wells's nature. It had been there from the beginning. All young men have sexual imaginings, but this young man had the gift of words, a creative imagination, and a very narrow experience of life on which to let these imaginings feed. They came to dominate his mind, as perhaps they would not so compulsively have done if he had had a broader experience of life, a wider education instead of the intensive one he had submitted himself to, and if his first writings had not coincided with a time when the older, ampler novel of Victorian times was dying away as Hardy and Meredith ceased to write and it was plain that the new writers of fiction like Conan Doyle, Robert Louis Stevenson, J. M. Barrie, Anthony Hope, Hall Caine and Mrs Humphry Ward, for all their ability and popularity, could not make themselves heard by everyone. A new vigorous generation was thrusting up which resented and mocked the pretentiousness of the old. From the beginning Wells seemed to know that he echoed its aspirations, and he put into writing its needs and desires, the seriousness with which it was dedicating itself to the task of living, and its growing awareness of the power of the sexual instinct – and along with it, the notion, abhorrent to individuals whose upbringing had been rooted in the Victorian age, that sex was as powerful and demanding in women as in men.

At first circumspectly and tentatively he had advanced these bold ideas. *Love and Mr Lewisham*, written at the beginning of this decade, and *The New Machiavelli*, written at the end of it, are both about the same thing: how the red blaze of sex can burst out of a man and destroy his career. In the early book Lewisham's surrender of his ambitions to love is treated humorously and tenderly, while Remington's surrender to the same urge is raw with emotion and pain. In between these two books lay all Wells's own emotional development.

It was in order to deal with these burning matters that he had turned from the profitable field of scientific romances to become a serious novelist. In every one of his books from then on, sex becomes the dominating factor in the tension that makes the story, if it is a novel, or illuminates the argument, if it is a prophetic book like *Anticipations* or an imaginative design for better living like *A Modern Utopia*. And more and more, because of this, the constructive anticipations of what life might be like if we would only will it so become more like novels until in *In the Days of the Comet* the two forms are nearly fused and we have *Anticipations* fictionalized with fictional characters acting out very convincingly against an idealized world those urgent needs and desires which in this imperfect world drive every man and woman to private hells or delights.

With his growing fame and popularity, especially with the young, who are always difficult to control, but were never more so than in this post-Victorian age, the opposition to these liberal ideas began to express itself. Wells had had to threaten legal action to suppress the charge that *In the Days of the Comet* advocated free love. With *Tono-Bungay* he had had to complain to Macmillan about the attempt being made in the *British Weekly* to involve the firm as well as himself in the charge of purveying indecency. None of these attacks had been very serious, but they did represent a growing opposition to Wells's increasing daring. It was a new experience for him to be on the defensive.

It is true that *Tono-Bungay* contains at least one lady quite as uninhibited as Ann Veronica, whose determination to get her man had caused all the fuss over that book and had set off the campaign against Wells in the *Spectator*. And it is difficult to see how Macmillan could have accepted *Tono-Bungay* but jibbed at *Ann Veronica* and *The New Machiavelli*, the last refusal reiterated by every publisher to whom it was submitted, except Lane. The danger of libel, of course, was there, but a thorough revision of the book could have lessened that danger, and libel is a risk a publisher is accustomed to take. It is plain that other factors besides Wells's 'outspokenness' on the subject of sex motivated everyone's behaviour in this crisis. Antagonisms between classes, between generations, even between the sexes, were expressing themselves in strikes and lockouts, in lack of sympathy between social classes, in women's struggle for emancipation, in political uncertainties. A new order was evolving, making the young impatient to inherit their destiny, and the old grimly reluctant to yield up authority. If Wells was fortunate in the time of his beginnings as a writer, his luck did not hold. He was unlucky in coming to his full powers at a time when these antagonisms were at their fiercest, and when the sexual scandal in which he was involved cast doubts on the sincerity of his motives in harping on this dangerous subject.

Vernon Lee had stood amazed before the duality of Wells's nature which could preach such ennobling and uplifting things while displaying such callous and unfeeling behaviour towards his wife and the girl he had seduced. Wells lived as he wrote, and he wrote as he talked. His novels were extensions of this bubbling talk, as unstudied, uncontrived, as the constant outpouring of stimulating radical ideas which had amazed his friend Arnold Bennett, who noted in his diary that it was a waste that such good

talk should not be written down. But it *was* written down in
the stream of books that flowed from him in these highly
productive years, and more and more the assertive account
was tinged with autobiography. One sees why: it was to
come nearer to life. Like all people of a highly sensitive,
highly sexual temperament, he was an egoist. The passion
to dominate is instinctive in this temperament: it is the
whole rationale of sex. The duality in his nature is explic-
able in these terms. He wanted to dominate the reader with
his ideas; he was not powerless against the surge of sex so
much as seeking it, like Machiavelli, as a sensual release to
a mind overburdened by thought, and in seduction was
domination. He wanted thought like a sword, and desire
like a flame, and he saw no contradiction in these ideas.
He saw himself, without false modesty, as an originative
advanced thinker, using the novel as a scientific worker uses
his instruments and the laboratory bench to get the prime
necessities of life under control as an essential preliminary
to the reconditioning of it, which it was the bold task of
all creative thinkers, whether philosophers, statesmen,
artists or imaginative writers, to bring about. Thus it was
maddening to him that Remington's political aims should
not even be discussed by the critics, and Remington's moral
lapse be considered the whole story.

The delusion persisted with him that he had been misunderstood, whereas the truth was that he had failed to
make himself understood. Years later, when he came to
write that essay in self-analysis which is his autobiography,
he thought that the perplexities that had beset his life were
common to all creative writers:

We are like early amphibians, so to speak, struggling out of
the waters that have covered our kind, into the air, seeking to
breathe in a new fashion and emancipate ourselves from long-
unquestioned necessities. At last it becomes for us a case of air
or nothing. But the new land has not yet definitely emerged
from the waters, and we swim distressfully in an element we
wish to abandon.

Beautifully said, like so much that came from Wells, but reiterating a fault he constantly makes in his own diagnosis. He saw himself as an analyst, whereas he was in fact a visionary. His mind was essentially creative, but he flattered himself it was scientific, detached and philosophical. He was denying his own considerable gifts and claiming others which he did not possess, as Ford Madox Ford had pointed out to him long ago, and as Henry James was kindly and patiently reiterating in the carefully studied letters he wrote to Wells as book after book of this younger writer, before whom he had once declared himself 'prostrate with admiration', showed a deepening and widening chasm between art and doctrine. Wells could not see that what was to him a vision of a better world might seem to others a plea for licence.

During the few months that followed Macmillan's rejection, the book must have been read and its publication carefully advised against by the leading critics in London, all of whom had connections with different publishing houses. Amongst all those busy gossips, every one a clubman imbibing his share of the common tale every day, the originals of the central figures in the story would have been recognized. This was Wells's own story. The other leading figures were equally real, and threats of action to be taken if the book were to be published must have been freely circulated. News of this reached Wells when, after three months of fruitless negotiations on Sir Frederick's part, he stumbled on to the fact that it was not Remington's radical political ideas or the adultery which these publishers objected to, but the legal actions which might be taken against them by the originals of the figures in his story if they published.

Macmillan had to report failure. Heinemann and Chapman & Hall had both read it, he wrote on 13 August, 'but neither of them will touch it'. He was still trying other publishers without success when some time in September (like many of Wells's letters, this one is not dated) Wells wrote a revealing letter and one which showed the state of desperation he had reached. This was the first time in his long and hard career that he had threatened to give up writing.

Dear Sir Frederick,

The more I think over and go into this confounded business, the more unjustifiable the whole of this objection to *The New Machiavelli* appears. Apparently there is an enormous campaign of scandal going on about the character Isabel, who is supposed to be the portrait of a particular friend of mine. Well, that person has read the story in proof and her husband also and they not only don't object to the work but they don't see where they come in. A huge proportion of all this bother arises from the scarcely sane accusations of a near relative of the lady who seems almost as anxious to ruin her as he is to ruin me. The points of resemblance are amazingly flimsy at the best and if this thing is forced into an open and public row – and that is what it must come to if I can't get the book decently published without it – I shall win. To back down now will not only injure me but it will fix for good the ugliest imputations upon the alleged original of Isabel.

I wish extraordinarily you could have put the real objection to me in June before I went to Germany. Practically it has given all these subterranean people a free hand for three months. Naturally all the people immediately concerned in the accusations that make the nucleus of all the fuss have been silent – and they are the last to hear what it all comes to. Now the book is being mobbed.

I've given up the idea I had of handling the book myself. It's a big book and a good one and unless it can be published properly I see very little use in going on writing. I am forced to make a fight of it.

> Very sincerely yours,
> H. G. Wells

The suspense continued throughout October. The book could not come out now, if a publisher could be found to issue it, before the spring of 1911. He could not get on with another book while this uncertainty hung over him. Heinemann was now reconsidering the revised version, but said

that as there was a good chance of it being boycotted, he
might not be able to pay any advance on it. Wells was
becoming strapped for money. This had been an expensive
year. Macmillan offered to make an immediate advance of
£300 on one condition: that Wells should agree to give his
firm the first refusal of the novel (then called *Marjorie*,
which was to appear as *Marriage*) on which he was working.
Wells hesitated, on the grounds that Macmillan 'might
throw him over again'. 'There is no chance of our doing so',
replied Macmillan firmly, 'if the book is as you say it is – a
clean one.'

One can sympathize with Macmillan, shopping round
amongst his fellow publishers to find one who would be
willing to publish under his imprint a book which Macmillan was not prepared to issue under his own. Macmillan
persevered in what must have been a very embarrassing
task, not out of sympathy for Wells, or to save himself
financial loss, I think, but out of a sense of conscience that
this book which he did not like, should be published. It
ought to see the light of day. But it is an indication of the
power of the circulating libraries at that time to 'kill' a book
of which they did not approve that for nearly six months
no one was to be found who would touch *The New
Machiavelli*, even though at the beginning there went with
publication an option on this important author's future
works. Finally, John Lane of *Yellow Book* fame agreed to
publish. He was the last publisher Wells would have desired.
Although Lane was by then publishing some very popular
and respectable authors such as W. J. Locke, a faint odour
that held over from the black period of the Nineties, a hint
of impropriety associated with the *Yellow Book* magazine,
still clung to the imprint. Wells had been a contributor to
the *Yellow Book*, and very proud of the achievement in his
younger days. But now he took himself seriously as a novelist of ideas, and it is plain from the letters exchanged with
Macmillan that, while the extended negotiations with reluctant publishers had been embarrassing to his own good

opinion of himself, he settled down very uncomfortably with Lane. He never mentions Lane's name in subsequent correspondence with Macmillan without some abusive epithet, and he thankfully escaped from him with his next book.

But the relief to both parties that these long and embarrassing negotiations were over is plain from the exchange of compliments. Macmillan wrote:

I take this opportunity of thanking you for the consideration you have shown during the protracted and somewhat disagreeable negotiations with regard to the transfer of *The New Machiavelli*. Unless the libraries boycott the book, I see no reason why it should not do well in Mr Lane's hands.

Wells replied:

This has been a very irritating and disappointing affair for both of us, we've had diametrically contrasted points of view which have remained contrasted to the end, but I close the incident with my liking for and confidence in Messrs Macmillan very considerably enhanced.

The libraries – or some of them – did ban the book, and few of the reviewers could find anything favourable to say about Remington, whose constructive ideas and sensual dreams were dismissed as pretentious. For a man who was putting his own thought and reflecting his own nature in the book, these were smarting checks and rebukes. But his admirers were ecstatic as always, and John Lane wrote a few weeks after publication to tell Sir Frederick Macmillan that the book was 'going strong' – 'we have sold 11,000 copies'. But he had to report one or two little 'rebuffs' – one author who had sent him a manuscript demanded it back when he read *The New Machiavelli*, the *Spectator* refused all Lane's advertisements with Wells's name appearing, and Mac-Niven and Wallace, the leading Edinburgh booksellers, had written to ask if they could return their copies 'as it is not a book we care to stock or sell'. The Birmingham City Council not only banned it but the Chairman of the Book

Sub-Committee, Mr J. B. Burnham, in an interview, had some very uncomplimentary things to say about Mr Wells, his intentions and his 'influence'. A clipping was sent to Wells by a Birmingham admirer. Wells replied:

I do not see that I have any grounds for complaint if the Birmingham ratepayers choose to have their fiction filtered through the mind of Mr Burnham, and allow him to reject anything that he finds difficult or uncongenial. If Mr Burnham, under the stimulus of the interviewer, adds a trifle of insult to my exclusion, and claims that I make my books 'suggestive' in order to cover my literary deficiencies, it is really not my affair ... The best way to attack an author you don't like is to abuse his style, and Mr Burnham goes only a little further in imputing base motives.

Wells forgot his avowal when recounting these events in *Experiment in Autobiography* a quarter of a century later.

The New Machiavelli was first printed as a serial in Ford Madox Hueffer's *English Review* and persistent rumours that no publisher would consent to issue it led to a considerable sale of the back numbers of that periodical at enhanced prices – with the usual disappointment for the purchasers. 'What is all the fuss about?' the poor dears demanded. 'There is nothing in it!' There was indeed furtive work with the publishers on the part of what are called influential people, but I neither know nor care who were those influential people, and I do not know what was said and done. The respectable firm of Macmillan was already under contract to publish and could not legally or honourably back out, but it presently appealed to me in a state of great embarrassment, for permission to publish, in this particular case under the imprint of John Lane, who was less squeamish about his reputation for decorum. I consented to that, and so the gentility of Macmillan, or whatever else was threatened by those influential people, was preserved.

The letters quoted show that there was no embarrassment on Macmillan's part, and the records prove that, although certain of his legal position, he went to very considerable efforts to help Wells find a publisher for the book. That

Wells appreciated this is proved by his acknowledgement at the time that his liking and confidence in the firm had been enhanced, and by the fact that he came back to it with his next and subsequent books. There can be little doubt that the contemporary record is more correct than the memory recalled twenty-five years later.

When book publication was at last arranged, he asked Ralph Straus, John Lane's chief reader, for what would be called today a press conference in which he might be given an opportunity of answering some of the innuendos which had been circulating, and a copy of this, 'A Select Conversation', went out with each review copy of the book. In the course of it, Wells denies the imputation that the book is an erotic one.

There is not a single passage that offends against decency or against the established code of morals. Judged by the standards of Maurice Hewlett or Mrs Humphry Ward, the work is coldly chaste. ... It is, I have no hesitation in saying, part of a campaign of personal malice, and the people who make it know, as well as you and I know, that I would sooner cut off my right hand than write deliberately to excite sexual passion. They make it none the less. It invades my private life in the form of personal insults and anonymous letters ...

And with a cheek that only Wells could show, he went on, when asked by Straus about the identification of Remington with himself:

I no more care to pillory myself in a work of fiction than anyone else. And then, my dear fellow, just think what Remington does!

The reviews were on the whole favourable, though few of them failed to comment on the autobiographical element. John Lane, whom Wells detested, could continue to report through Macmillan that the book was selling very well. From Henry James came the customary letter of felicitation with which the older man greeted each of Wells's books, though this time one laced with more than the usual amount of criticism. James wrote from Boston, where he had remained on an extended visit with his sister-in-law following his beloved brother's death, that he thought it a mistake to have used the autobiographical form, 'which puts a premium on the loose, the improvised, the cheap and easy', and in a telling postscript he ruminated:

I think the exhibition of 'Love' as 'Love' – functional Love – always suffers from a certain inevitable and insurmountable flat-footedness (for the reader's nerves, etc.) which is only to be counter-plotted by round-about arts – as by tracing it through indirectness and tortuosities of application and effect – to keep it somehow interesting and productive (though I don't mean reproductive!).

This last mild witticism was meant to take the sting out of the stricture which Henry James felt himself bound to make. He frequented the same clubs, he was a great letter-writer, and only his intense observance of the code of manners put him above gossip and the exchange of scandal. But he must have known that this was Wells's own story, and his inner sense of delicacy and refinement, of what was done and was not done, must have quivered with shock at this outrage of the proprieties.

Wells's artistic instinct was just as deeply rooted as his sexual one, and that he winced under James's criticism is evident from the tone of his reply. He took a month to answer, and then he replied:

My dear James,

I've been putting off answering your letter because I wanted to answer it properly and here at last comes the meagre apology for a response to the most illuminating of comments. So far as it is loving chastisement I think I wholly agree and kiss the rod. You put your sense of the turbid confusion, the strain and violence of my book so beautifully that almost they seem merits. But oh! some day when I'm settled-er if ever, I will do better. I agree about the 'first-person'. The only artistic 'first-person' is the onlooker speculative 'first-person', and God helping me, this shall be the last of my gushing Hari-Karis. But the guts and guts and guts and guts I've poured out all over the blessed libraries and J. A. Spender and everybody! I run against all sorts of people festooned with the apparently unlimited stuff ...

No! It shall be an end of it.

I wish you were over here. I rarely go to the Reform without a strange wild hope of seeing you. In June I am going with all my household to a home in France and I shall return to London in October. Thenabouts perhaps you'll be out.

Very sincerely yours,
H. G. Wells

During this month he was preparing the lecture on *The Scope of the Novel*, which was delivered to subscribers to the Times Book Club just before he left for France. The lecture was not, as the title implies, a survey of the contemporary scene in fiction, but a plea that in an age of swiftly changing standards the novelist should be allowed to grapple with subjects that were in the forefront of everyone's mind, particularly the relation between the sexes.

What is the good of pretending to write about love, and the loyalties and treacheries and quarrels of men and women if one must not glance at those varieties of physical temperament and organic quality, those deeply passionate moods and distresses from which half the storms of life are brewed?

In those same troubled months when he could not get on with *Marriage*, he was feeding his resentment in another way. He was setting out in an extended essay that becomes almost a novel, to which he gave the title 'The Mind of the Race', his faith in the holiness of the writer's task, and his contempt for all the leading critics. The character who indulges in what is largely a lengthy monologue has at first the outward lineaments of Henry James, but gradually becomes a self-portrait of Herbert George Wells. Four years were to pass before the various sketches that make up *Boon* were assembled for publication, and the character of Reginald Bliss, someone not unlike Wells's friend Arnold Bennett, was introduced to edit the posthumous literary remains of George Boon.

The book consists of four pieces: 'Boon' is an introductory memoir penned by the admiring Bliss, in which Wells's irony has mischievous play. 'The Mind of the Race', the main part of the book, is a parody of the literary establishment, in which names are named and the ironic note shrills into effective satire as Henry James is singled out for Boon's invective – 'You see', says Boon, in extenuation of his attack, 'you can't now talk of literature without going through Henry James. James is unavoidable. James is to literature what Immanuel Kant is to Philosophy – a partially comprehensible essential, an inevitable introduction. ...' Two admirable sketches that are parables follow, and each, 'The Wild Asses of the Devil' and 'The Last Trump', carries the same message: The need for honesty, however painful it may be to come to that state.

Bliss closes his account when Boon's death has left him desolate; and one hears the authentic voice of Wells's mood after *The New Machiavelli*:

I know I must go on with my work under difficult and novel conditions (and now well into the routines of middle age) as if there were no such thing as loss and disappointment. I am, I learned long ago, an uncreative, unimportant man. And yet, I suppose, I do something; I count; it is better that I should help than not in the great task of literature, the great task of becoming the thought and the expressed intention of the race, the task of taming violence, organizing the aimless, destroying error, the task of waylaying the Wild Asses of the Devil and sending them back to Hell. It does not matter how individually feeble we writers and disseminators are; we have to hunt the Wild Asses. As the feeblest puppy has to bark at cats and burglars. And we have to do it because we know, in spite of the darkness, the wickedness, the haste and hate, we know in our hearts, though no momentary trumpeting has shown it to us, that judgement is all about us and God stands close at hand.

But four years were to pass before these concluding words were written to a book which Wells himself was to describe as the most self-revealing of all his works. When it was published, the Great War had been going on for a year, the circumstances of his life had changed, the Edwardian age was over, and a mood of deep despondency gripped him. He was to add the final bitter sketch, 'Of Life, of Literature, of Henry James' to the book and close, or seem to close, his connections with literature, to dissociate himself from the false writing of his time and turn for comfort to the larger theme of the universality of the human adventure in its blind thrusting towards the future. At this moment in 1911, when the hours were full of grief and not a day passed without its barb of pain prompted by some misunderstanding review or the pompous utterance of some librarian or other announcing the removal of Wells's books from his library shelves, he thrust away in a drawer these papers about Boon and went off to France for the summer, restless, unhappy, at odds with his world, to complete *Marriage*.

13

The Prig Novels

WE get a glimpse of him during that summer through Arnold Bennett, who went to stay with him at Pont de l'Arche. They had seen each other frequently in the few months of crisis that had attended the publication of *The New Machiavelli*. Bennett had been prominently present at Wells's lecture on the novel at the Times Book Club in May. But they had been parted for two months when in July Bennett paid his visit to Pont de l'Arche, and Wells had been isolated in work. A pleasant sketch of Bennett's survives, made during this visit and reproduced in his journal, showing the garden of the villa the Wellses occupied. One can imagine these two by now middle-aged writers sitting in the shade of this garden, or walking about the little town, talking 'shop' and girls, the two subjects that seem always to have fascinated them both.

Bennett had nothing to complain of in his own advancement; he was doing very nicely indeed after a slow start. He was not burdened as Wells was by any mission in life except that of Getting On. But he had the immense curiosity of the particular kind of novelist he was to become. The animosity which Wells had worked up against individual figures of the literary establishment, which had had to be suppressed in the lecture, comes out in 'The Mind of the Race', now composed and put aside, and there would have been much in Wells's flow of talk to hold Bennett's absorbed attention.

Much as these two men were in each other's confidence, one gets the impression that from about this time on their paths started to diverge. Only a few years ago they had been united by the unspoken awareness that they were outsiders trying to break in. In all sorts of ways they were complementary to one another. Bennett was a much more careful writer than Wells, he had a better ear and was more painstaking, yet just as industrious as Wells. Wells had incomparably the finer creative imagination and nourished the dream, from which he would not be shaken, that the world could be made a better place. The streak of the reformer which ran down to bedrock in him was wholly missing from Bennett's make-up.

In the early days they had given one another confidence. They had the same way of looking at things, the same lower-class derisory humour, and they had much pleasure from each other's jokes. Also Bennett liked Jane, and Jane liked Bennett, and that made it easier for the men to be friends. Frigid in temperament, uncertain of herself, yet an admirable hostess, this tiny, pretty fair-haired woman, whom Frank Swinnerton saw as an amusing mixture of terror and confidence, melted completely to Bennett. An added prod to the divergence now beginning was, perhaps, Bennett's equivocal position in the great love affair that was shortly to become the centre of H.G.'s life; he was to find himself with one foot in each camp. Something of the shallowness of Bennett's character – Wells describes him as having the quality of good crockery, hard, definite, shiny on the surface, nothing of value underneath – began to evince itself as Wells passionately pursued his ideas and his love-life, and Bennett first involved himself, then strove to extricate himself from his own timid encounters with sex, and meanwhile and as steadily pursued success.

The visit was soon over, and Wells got down to work again in his usual businesslike way. By October, when he was ready to return to London, he had completed *Marriage* and was already planning the book that was to follow it up. Quickly he healed his breach with Macmillan, who in any case had an option on *Marriage* on the strength of having advanced £300 to Wells while the publication of *The New Machiavelli* was still in doubt. Macmillan could have refused to take up his option, sacrificing his £300; Wells, if he had wished to be free, could have asked the sort of price that would have precluded Macmillan from closing the bargain. But both men were genuinely anxious to resume the hopeful relationship with which they had started off nine years before. Within a week of sending the manuscript to Macmillan, Wells had back a letter which read:

I am delighted with *Marriage*, and more grateful to you than ever for sticking to us after the bothers we had about *The New Machiavelli* last year. This new book seems to me not only very clever, but admirably suited to the large novel-reading public; I shall be disappointed if we do not sell twenty thousand copies.

To which Wells replied:

Many thanks for your letter. Now let us try to settle down and have no more crises.

This was the tone of one who had been sorely tried rather than that of the penitent. Macmillan's enthusiasm for what he must have known was not a very good novel was almost certainly prompted more by relief in finding that it did not contain any of the dangerous elements that had produced such storms between them than by the conviction that a masterpiece had been delivered into his hands. Also, he would have had a natural keenness to get back some of his money he had invested in Wells. A slip of paper in the file, drawn up presumably by the accounts department at the partner's request, still remains to show that after the firm had published five of Wells's most successful novels, the debit balance on the whole enterprise at this time was over £500. With each book Wells had asked for a larger advance, and for *Marriage* he was to get 1500 guineas. At six shillings, a lot of copies had to be sold to cover that guarantee, but Wells was selling more and more, if not writing better and better, and with this irreproachable discussion of what could threaten a marriage – an extravagant wife – Macmillan could hope to recover his loss, something he could not do if Wells went elsewhere. Macmillan printed twenty thousand, but although the book sold well, it took until 1939 to sell out that edition. Soon they were bickering again. Wells was one of those authors sent to try publishers' souls.

With *Marriage* he was entering on the period of what he was later to call his 'prig' novels, he himself defining a prig as someone elected by himself to lead the world. The six novels he was to write before the war which brought about a dramatic change in his frame of mind included *Bealby*, a return to the manner of *Kipps* (but *Bealby* he described to Macmillan as 'a bye-blow, an illegitimate child; it came accidentally'), and *The World Set Free*, a return to the form in which he had established himself as absolute master, the scientific suspense story, this time fortified by a strong element of immediate prophecy. But it was the other four – *Marriage, The Passionate Friends, The Wife of Sir Isaac Harman* and *The Research Magnificent* – which made up the prig novels, and they received much more attention at the time than those 'bye-blows' of an unquenchable creative imagination. In them it is plain that he was putting into practice what he had preached in his lecture on *The Scope of the Novel*, the characters being subordinated to the particular problems with which their lives are involved. Sex plays a leading part. The blind frustrations of sex bring about the centre of interest in each novel; discussion follows, too much of it, before the solution is reached. One is left with the sense of having been argued with rather than moved deeply.

It was plain that Wells had meant all too seriously what he said about the novel's value as a sifting-ground for ideas, and it was equally apparent that the novel could not bear this weight and still remain a picture of life. Nobody knew better than this storytelling genius what was required to hold the attention of the reader, the importance of establishing character, the need for action, the necessity of suspense, the essentiality of echoing life. Talk about ideas made a poor substitute. There are, of course, flashes of humour and brilliant bits of characterization. But the jokes are the privileged inside jokes of the schoolmaster, and the characterization is expected, not surprising; it does not awaken interest. Worse still, a creative lack is apparent. Even the titles lack spontaneity. They do not have the liveliness and bounce of *Kipps*, *Tono-Bungay* and *The History of Mr Polly*. The sparkle has gone out.

Matching the depressed state of his literary output at this time, his amours were lacking in zest, and the spice of adventure was missing. He was making an exhibition of himself with a woman who seems, on the evidence of those who witnessed his discomfiture on occasions, to have enjoyed displaying her command over this well-known literary Casanova. Elizabeth von Arnim, whose *Elizabeth and Her German Garden* had attracted great attention when it was published in 1898 just as Wells was beginning as an author, and who was now between marriages – she was later to marry Bertrand Russell's brother – was an attractive woman with a sharp wit and a very wide circle of friends in the literary and social worlds. She had taken a house in London, and here she entertained a great deal, flirted furiously, wrote busily, and was the centre of a little maelstrom of activity.

Wells fell under her spell, and one sees why. She represented the aristocratic disdain – which can be melted, and then what fire! – discernible in Beatrice in *Tono-Bungay* and the girl on the wall who captivated Mr Polly's imagination; as a type, she reappears under one name or another in many of the novels he was to write long after the painful episode of his experiences in 1912. He was to have his revenge on Elizabeth von Arnim in the part she was given to play in *Mr Britling Sees It Through*, where she appears as Mrs Harrowdean.

In this frustrating year of 1912 she was an excitement that became an irritant. He bombarded her with letters, telegrams and protestations of love; she seems to have enjoyed humiliating him in front of others and using him for her own convenience, even to sending her son, the small Count von Arnim, to stay with Wells's family at Easton Glebe. In her memoirs, published in the thirties, she speaks rather offhandedly of Wells, but by then the passion was long dead, and he bore this final slight uncomplainingly.

It was in the quarrelsome and sharply aggressive mood that dominated him in this year that he took delight in squashing a move by Gosse and James to have him elected to the Academic Committee of the Royal Society of Literature, an accolade which, since the Committee in question already included such well-known figures as Barrie, Bridges, Conrad, Galsworthy, Hardy, Henry James, Gilbert Murray, Shaw and Yeats, might have been appreciated by anyone else as a signal mark of honour. But not by H.G. in his present mood. His rejection of the proposal, put to him by Gosse, was flat and curt and left very little room for persuading him to change his mind. He had slammed the door on the aesthetes fiddling away with their artful ploys; he was dealing with life, and academic committees were just what should not stand between the writer's subject and his audience. But dear Henry James, whose affection for this touchy, perverse little artist had never wavered, felt strongly that Wells should be in the Committee, not out; and he undertook to Gosse to try his persuasions. In one of his most circumlocutary and flattering letters, he put the case to Wells for agreeing to his election, urging it upon him with all the truth and feeling at his command. 'You would do something for us that we lack, and don't want to lack – and we would do for *you* that you would find yourself *within* still more moved than without to that critical, that ironic, that even exasperated (if I may call it) play or reaction! – which is the mark, or one of the marks, of your genius.'

But Wells was adamant. He used the excuse that the literary creative world is best anarchic, least good when it combines to establish fixed standards and controls. Better, in his view, the wild rush of Boomster and the Quack than 'the cold politeness of the established thing', and he declares that he would rather be outside the Committee with Hall Caine than in it with Gosse and Gilbert Murray and Shaw. Not even a further and more passionate attempt on James's part to persuade him could move him. He was Ishmael; his hand was against the literary establishment which had tried to make him conform, had tried to lecture him into writing the sort of novel it could approve, which made literature an artefact rather than art, an adornment to life rather than the vital fire that leaps from generation to generation. Reporting the failure of his mission to Gosse the next day, Henry James defended the absolute sincerity with which Wells held his objections, but 'he has cut loose from literature clearly – practically altogether; he will still do a lot of writing probably, but it won't be *that*'. But that this difference of opinion did not signify a lessening of James's affection for 'this very swagger performer indeed', or of Wells's genuine admiration for James as man and artist, there is ample evidence in the correspondence that continued to flow between them right up to the moment that Wells published *Boon*, which, under cover of lampooning the literary establishment, picked out James as the figure which typified its follies and pretensions.

Once again Wells had confused an issue about which he felt deeply with the figure on the other side he most admired and envied: Macmillan amongst publishers, James amongst authors, Shaw amongst the Fabians. Because they would not come over to him, their very sureness lighted up his own misgivings, and for him, to be uncertain was to be assertive and dogmatic, working himself into a self-justifying rage before breaking the bond he treasured. He continued to publish with Macmillan, he continued to exchange visits and letters with James, before in a fit of rage he told Macmillan in the war to 'use your paper to better purpose' and before he committed the final offence of *Boon*. A similar rage was to shake him at his sad end. *Mind at the End of Its Tether* was *Boon* repeated, with the accusations now hurled against humanity which had refused to let him save it. This paranoidal tendency to feel himself persecuted and misunderstood had been present in him always, but in this year or two before the war came to distract attention, it intensified and was responsible for much of his difficulties of temper and his swings between wild optimism and despair.

What makes Wells so interesting a figure is his restless energy, his constant questioning, his sceptical attitude to all accepted dogma. The more or less placid life of the successful novelist was uncongenial to his hasty reforming temper. He wanted to alter things, and this disposition, growing more daring with self-confidence and success, can be traced in the transition from the bustling figure, bursting with energy, ideas, and entertainment, who took London by storm with books like *Kipps, A Modern Utopia, Tono-Bungay* and *Mr Polly*, to the serious reformer turning from stories about the human situation to ideas about humanity, and becoming argumentative and discursive in the process. One has to remember in his defence how swift the rise had been from the dullest of all social ranks to the one where he was meeting his intellectual peers, and how easy it was in such circumstances, with such a disposition, to turn his back on the success he had so effortlessly achieved as a novelist, and try to be taken for a Thinker.

But there is one additional factor which gives this period of his life a highly dramatic colour. He fell in love. He had been doing that with great regularity, as we have seen, ever since he had acknowledged to himself that his second marriage was, on physical grounds only, not the ideal of which he had dreamed, and that sexual love was essential to his life; to everyone's life, he believed, though the degree of intensity varied with the individual temperament. None of these adventures had proved perfect, but they had proved a lot of other things: the rampant hypocrisy which surrounded this subject and prevented an open discussion of it, the old-fashioned domination of the man in the marriage contract, and the unrecognized – and unadmitted when it was recognized – part that physical relations between man and woman could play in making life worthwhile or ruining it.

It was to the airing of this subject that he now devoted

himself, and it was in the course of pursuing this that he encountered a girl whose brain was the equal of his own, and who combined with her high intelligence a striking dark beauty and a daring courage equal to his own in speaking out on these matters on which there was general obstinate silence. Chance brought Rebecca West and H. G. Wells together in 1912. In the narrow literary society of that time they would have been bound to meet before long. But the accident that found them both free, both full of reforming zeal, and each immediately attracted to the other, was to have lasting consequences for his life and work.

We catch glimpses at this stage from various angles of this energetic, argumentative, much talked of writer who was dividing families against themselves. What the critics thought of him and his work; what his anxious publisher thought of a difficult and unpredictable author, always demanding bigger advances than even his steadily increasing sales justified. What most readers thought may be seen in his rising sales figures, but that the public was beginning to divide into Wellsites and an equally emphatic if not so numerous anti-Wells faction may be glimpsed in the attitude of some booksellers and librarians, responding to pressures from quarters that did not like all this talk about free love and this questioning of the matrimonial contract. Impatience with a talent misdirected marks many of the literary judgements. That of the *Times Literary Supplement* reviewer on *The Passionate Friends* may be taken as typical of this view. Lady Justin, who is presented by Wells in a highly sympathetic light as a woman who cannot get from her husband or the world the intellectual response her own brain entitles her to, is carrying on an adulterous relationship under her husband's roof, and it was this fact which prompted the *Times Literary Supplement*'s reproof.

People do these sort of things under circumstances that are more or less painful to themselves and everyone else around them, because they are a little sordid, but we can't accept people who thus act as tragedy Queens.

On the other hand, there were the ardent admirers, and how ardent they were, making pilgrimages to Easton Glebe* by the bus load and tramping across the park to pay their respects to the Master, as Frank Swinnerton pictures for us in his memories of a week-end at the Wellses'. These were the young and the hopeful, who found in *Marriage* and *The Passionate Friends* and *The Wife of Sir Isaac Harman* and *The Research Magnificent* a discussion of problems which they thought of urgent concern: how to break out of the repressive restrictions which an older generation endeavoured to maintain, how to make one's life worthwhile in purpose, how to find that companionship in love which was essential even in the pursuit of high aims. The issue was made clear by Wells in book after book. We are all caught up in the toils of an unregulated life. Man has reached a point when a new life opens before him for which his mind is unprepared; he is leaving the ancestral shelters and going out upon the greatest adventure that ever was in space and time. What Benham yearns for in *The Research Magnificent* sums it up:

Behind the dingy face of this world, the earthy stubbornness, the baseness and dullness of himself and all of us, lurked the living jewels of heaven, the light of glory, things unspeakable. At first it seemed to him one had only to hammer and will; and at the end, after a life of hammering and willing, he was still convinced there was something, something in the nature of an Open Sesame, perhaps a little more intricate than one had supposed at first, a little more difficult to secure, but still in that nature, which would suddenly roll open for mankind the magic cave of the universe, that precious cave at the heart of all things, in which one must believe . . .
And then Life – life and the wonder it just so perplexingly isn't.

* In 1912 Wells had taken The Old Rectory on Lady Warwick's estate near Dunmow in Essex, primarily as a holiday home for his children. Soon afterwards he had given up the Church Row house in London, and The Old Rectory, renamed Easton Glebe, became the family's permanent home.

But these stories were not of space and time. Lost to sight now was the endearing little narrator of the early short stories and the scientific romances. Vanished into the mists, too, was the reporter of lives like those of Kipps and George Ponderevo, who had caught so perfectly the echoes of that narrow crowded world of the common man. The lives of the prosperous, educated middle class, and particularly those of the intellectual and political circles to which the Fabians and his own success introduced him, were shaped by very different anxieties and needs. The action of the series of novels which begins with *Marriage* is not with the fundamental issues of life for the human race in a world enlarged by science, but with the oppressions and limitations and restrictions that hampered the freedom of the gifted, if they were men, the beautiful, if they were women, to be personally adventurous in their own lives. He was saying that this was life, and this is how men and woman should conduct themselves. But it was not as most lives had to be lived. From such isolated cases there was no general lesson to be drawn. The leading figures become more and more set apart from the roughcast of ordinary humanity, more and more aristocratic, not only in pride of spirit and superiority of mind but, alas, in station of life too.

He was never fully to recover the first fresh outpouring of his genius. He could no more recapture that than he could have recaptured his innocence. He was now a man of the world, and in the tubby, middle-aged figure, ruddy-complexioned, well-dressed, socially experienced, only the shadow of the lean, consumptive, handsome, vital and crude young Wells was to be detected. Then he had been struggling for recognition; now he was famous the world over, and the self-assurance of his manner, reflected in the more careless craftsmanship, was nothing like so pleasing as the impertinent boldness of his younger self, which had hidden such an agony of shyness and uncertainty.

The moment was ripe for him to be recalled to a sense of purpose, and by chance an opportunity was provided when a

clear young voice assailed him, in a review of *Marriage* in
an intelligent feminist weekly of small circulation called
the *Freewoman*, for the falsity of his values, the faults of
his literary style and the fetish of his sex obsession. Wells
would certainly have remained impervious to this, as he
did, or tried to do, to all hostile reviews in even more important papers, if it had not been for the wit and pungency
with which this particular criticism was expressed. Too
often the word 'sordid' or expressions of shock baited him
into an angry war of words and strengthened his determination to persist in his course. That tone was missing from
this reproof, which said sharply and clearly everything that
Henry James said in sentences that were balancing feats of
suspended meaning about form. This reviewer was not
shocked by the sex element so much as bored by the emphasis given to it, and she had her own very clear notions
as to how the problem which *Marriage* set out to discuss
could be shortly and effectively solved, by thrusting this extravagant charming Marjorie out into the world to stand
on her own. Make women equal, then there would be no
sex problem, and, the inference was, Mr Wells could return
to his proper occupation of writing novels instead of discursive tracts disguised as novels.

In *Marriage*, Marjorie Pope has married Trafford, a scientific researcher, who has been forced to give up a promising
career in the laboratory and enter the commercial world in
order to maintain his wife in her extravagances. This is Mr
Lewisham's problem at a higher economic and social level.
Lewisham had surrendered mutely to forces within him too
strong to be withstood. Trafford is of sterner stuff, is full of
ideas, is as talkative as Wells. When a crisis comes in his relationship with his wife, they go off to Labrador together to
talk things over. Here a few adventures provided by hostile
nature occur in intervals of longish areas of talk, in the
course of which it is agreed between the parties that man
is superior to woman. 'We can't do things; we don't bring
them off', wails Marjorie, 'whereas you, you monster, you

dream you want to stick your hand out of all that is and make something that won't begin to be.'

This detestable submission to masculine complacency maddened the reviewer, but not more so than Mr Wells's fatuous suggestion for endowed motherhood as a solution for women's difficulties, especially if that was going to allow helpless parasites like Marjorie to breed. Miss Rebecca West, who went for him in this fashion, was dead against the suggestion that all women should be kept by the state: she had a much simpler solution – make women free! Then

the weaker sort of Marjorie would be sucked down to prostitution and death, the stronger sort of Marjorie would develop qualities of decency and courage and ferocity. It is worth trying. Not only because men ought to be protected from Our Lady of Loot, but because women ought to have a chance of being sifted clean through the sieve of work.

He would have known who Miss Rebecca West was, for her contributions to other papers of wider circulation than the *Freewoman* had in the past year begun to attract attention and comment. H.G. himself had contributed to the *Freewoman* at the editor's request, an invitation which came from a suggestion from Rebecca West, though he did not know that. He may already have met her at one of the many literary parties everyone in this literary world was always attending, and his roving eye might have been caught by her striking appearance, dark, slender, a wonderfully modelled face with beautiful bones and dark eyes under the mop of disregarded hair which was the sign manual of the blue-stocking.

He responded to the review by inviting her to come and stay at Easton Glebe, which was full every week-end with visitors; and from the diary of a governess to the Wells boys, later given to the world in her reminiscences of life in a famous writer's house, we get an impression of the first recorded appearance on the scene of someone who was to exercise a profound influence on Wells's life and work.

Sept. 27th, 1912.

Miss Rebecca West arrived today. She looks about 22 years of age, and is very vivacious. She writes in *The Freewoman* and has just reviewed Mr Wells's new novel, *Marriage*.

Enlarging on this note in her reminiscences many years later, Miss Meyer wrote:

I remember seeing one of Mr Wells's illustrations of Rebecca West in his book, *Boon*, published in 1915. He represented her as a pensive little girl holding in her small hand an enormous pen which stretches right across the page.

What Miss Meyer saw as vivaciousness was plainly a meeting of minds above her head. H.G. was meeting a mind as good as his own, one that was as yet inexperienced but equally direct, daring, unshockable, asking 'Why not?' as he had done at the beginning, but insisting on common-sense solutions. How stimulating he must have found discussion with her. The conversation at table, which H.G. was used to conducting as a lively monologue, must have merged into a duologue, with the others silent. Did Jane see in this intellectual girl, with her dark, striking looks, her ability to stand up to H.G. in argument, someone who threatened her domestic peace, this time more fundamentally than ever before? Nobody will ever know what Jane thought. As Frank Swinnerton says, she was discreet. But it is plain that what she feared most was not the physical attraction of someone else, but a mind as good as his own that might draw him away.

Rebecca West had been born Cicily Fairfield, the youngest of the three daughters of a gifted Irishman who had begun life as a professional soldier and ended as a writer on social and political subjects, being an individualist of the school of Herbert Spencer. His brother, Edward Fairfield, had played a sad but honourable minor part in history; he was a senior civil servant in the Colonial Office, and had been chosen as scapegoat for the Jameson Raid by Joseph

Chamberlain, on which he had had a stroke and died.
Charles Fairfield also died when his daughters were still of
school age, and they had been brought up on the tiny remains
of his family inheritance by their mother, a brilliant Scots-
woman who was a fine pianist, a remarkable linguist and a
connoisseur of art and architecture. A reflection of her may
be recognized in the character of the mother in *The Foun-
tain Overflows*, which her daughter was to write many years
later. When Cicily Fairfield was at school in Edinburgh, she
acted in a charity performance which was seen by Rosina
Filippi, the famous dramatic teacher, who was on the staff
of the Royal Academy of Dramatic Art. Miss Filippi promised the girl that if she came to R.A.D.A., she herself
would see that Cicily had a chance to realize her promise.
This was a message as from an angel, for a year or two
earlier all the three Fairfield sisters had had brief attacks of
tuberculosis, and it had seemed for a time as if Cicily was
fated to live in a clinic. But the disease had passed, leaving
her with a disposition to haemorrhages from the mouth
that was to recur throughout her life. This encounter with
Miss Filippi seemed the beginning of better things.

A year later the girl went up to London and was accepted
by R.A.D.A., but found that Miss Filippi had left the staff.
She expressed her disappointment, and did not realize for
some time that this had earned her the undying ill-will of
various important members of the staff. Confident of her
ability, she tried to 'stick it out', and for a year she endured
continuous discouragement and derision. Her fellow students
knew that authority was against her, and joined in the fun.
She felt that she might get a good part when she got into
the fourth and final term and there was a public show. But
when the fourth term came, she, alone of all her group, was
not promoted to the final school but was kept in the third
term. So she went away, tried to get engagements on her
own, and might or might not have proved her point that
she was a good actress, had it not been that another career
suddenly adopted her as its own.

All the Fairfield family wrote, as they ate or slept. It occurred to Cicily Fairfield to send in an article on Mrs Humphry Ward, who was an anti-suffragist, to a new feminist weekly called *The Freewoman*. To her pleasure but not really to her surprise, for it was taken for granted in her home that one wrote articles and they were accepted, she got a letter from the editor, not only accepting it but saying that it would be put on the billboards the following week. As Mrs Fairfield greatly disapproved of the *Freewoman*, Cicily rapidly chose a pseudonym and hit (to her regret, for it sounded to her afterwards as a hard and unfriendly name) on the name 'Rebecca West', a role she had once played in an empty theatre to a manager who was delighted but immediately went out of business. From then on she had more work than she could handle. She became a writer, and nothing could alter her state, or turn her back into an actress. Her failure to establish herself on the stage, and the humiliations she suffered at R.A.D.A., left a wound that was never quite healed. If she had to pass the R.A.D.A. building in Gower Street, decades afterwards, tears came into her eyes.

The *Freewoman* was coming to the end of its brief existence when she was given H. G. Wells's *Marriage* for review, but by then she had already made arrangements to join Robert Blatchford's *The Clarion*, a socialist weekly of much greater influence and circulation. Here she was to find not only a wider platform, but the inspiration which comes from working under an editor who encourages his writers to originality and adventure. Blatchford himself was a man of limited education but great humanity whose robust honesty made his views widely respected. He had perfected a style of simple short sentences, marked with humorous observation, which gave a sort of bluff, genuine wholeheartedness to the socialist message and appealed to all classes. It was typical of him that he should welcome to his staff a young blue-stocking, give her her head, let her say what she liked, and back her up with editorials when she was attacked for the outrageousness of her views.

Given her head, it was not long before she was assailing the establishment, which included the Pankhursts as well as bishops – anyone who was guilty of pretentiousness, false values, hypocrisy, whether it wore gaiters or bloomers or the costume of propriety and prosperity, silk hat and frock coat. Miss West not only attacked Bishop Weldon, who was rash enough in a paper read at a church congress to bring Christ in as an inviolable argument against allowing women the vote, on the grounds that Jesus had instituted the chivalresque ideal and that he alone could place the relations of woman and man 'on a firm, pure and sacred foundation'; she also attacked Miss Christabel Pankhurst for some intemperate utterances that that nearly hallowed figure had seen fit to make in an article in the *Suffragette* headed 'The Dangers of Marriage', from which it appeared that men were wicked and frequented prostitutes and, as a result, could pass on syphilis to their wives. 'Dear Lady', wrote Rebecca West,

behind whom I have been proud to walk in processions, this is rather a partial view. The strange uses to which we put our liberty! There was a long and desperate struggle before it became possible for women to write candidly on subjects such as this. That this power should be used to express views that would be old-fashioned and uncharitable in the Pastor of a Little Bethel is a matter for scalding tears.

The girl who was expressing these views so boldly was only twenty, not the twenty-two which Miss Meyer had guessed. The attraction between H.G. and her was mutual. H.G. could be wonderful company when his interest was aroused, witty, inventive, a born raconteur, and at this stage of his life a man of the world in the true sense: sophisticated, knowledgeable about affairs, an agreeable, lively, stimulating companion. He was irritable only with fools. Creatively he might appear to be passing through a slack period, but the ideas were so urgent and pressing that there was no time to build character as there had been when he was reaching into his own past. What made him temporarily less of an artist made him the more interesting as a man. The more one got to know him, the more one realized how his books belied him. He was a dreamer for the world. He saw more clearly than any of his contemporaries the way the world was going and what was necessary for its salvation. When you knew him, he disarmed your criticism. In 1912 he was the most stimulating company in the world to be with.

One sees it from his point of view. A girl, beautiful and well-bred, who spoke her mind and had a mind worth listening to. All his life he had been seeking somebody like this, who combined immense physical attraction with a mind as quick as his. That had been Remington's dream too – desire like a flame and thought as quick as a sword. Here at last was the Venus Urania for whom he had been restlessly seeking.

For the first time he had somebody who stirred his admiration with qualities other than her beauty and youth. She was a writer whom he could respect. She had the gift of evoking for him an entirely new view of something he had never questioned before. 'She was the only woman', he was to say later in life, 'who ever made me stop and wonder when she said "Look".' Her company was a constant joy to him. Her mind was in many respects superior to his; all that he half envied, half scorned in the intellectual artist's method of creation sounded much more justifiable when the rules were stated by her and not by Henry James.

By the beginning of 1913 they were seen everywhere together. The association which developed was accepted by all his friends; they were asked out together and they entertained together in return. Throughout 1913 she continued to work on the *Clarion*, although she now wrote for the dailies as well and her trenchant, witty, outspoken articles were attracting increasing attention. During this time Wells was writing *The Wife of Sir Isaac Harman, The World*

Set Free and *Bealby*. It is too much to say that Rebecca
West's appearance in his life restored to his work the
humour and liveliness that had been notably absent in
Marriage and *The Passionate Friends*, but the strongest
feature of his work, the vein of comedy that had been missing since Mr Polly had made his glorious appearance in
1910, returned with Lady Harman's middle-aged lover,
Mr Brumley, and was apparent, if not altogether successful, in *Bealby*. Lady Harman is also a much more sympathetically presented heroine than Marjorie Pope in *Marriage* or Lady Justin in *The Passionate Friends*. Lady Harman is a beautiful and intelligent creature – the girl on the
wall who comes down on the side of life and feels her way
shyly and tremulously towards it. The gleam of real life
shines through the argument, which is the by now familiar
one of dissatisfaction with the existing sexual code, and of
one woman's attempt to break the bond into which matrimony has delivered her – 'the uniform standardized implacable marriage of contemporary civilization, concentrated not upon children and the future, but upon a household and contemporary stability', as Wells charged in the
preface to the volume containing this novel in his collected
works.

At the end of 1913 Rebecca West disappeared from the
pages of the *Clarion*, and an outcry from disappointed
readers followed. Blatchford found it necessary to insert a
notice in the paper which said: 'Miss Rebecca West remains very ill in a nursing home, and we cannot tell when
she will return.'

She was never to return. Walking across Hampstead
Heath one afternoon towards the close of 1913, she experienced a particularly violent haemorrhage, of the kind
that had been attacking her at intervals since she was fifteen. This time she was borne off to a hospital. Her career,
life itself, promised to be brief. But she was only at the
beginning, not the end, of her life as a writer. When she
began to write again in 1916, it was as a critic, then as a

novelist, and her work was to show a depth of understanding and an intellectual quality for which these two exciting years of journalism had been only a preparation.

In January 1914 Wells paid his first visit to Russia, in the enlivening company of Maurice Baring. It was an experience that he was never to forget. He was by this time a well-known figure in Russia, for all his books had been published in Russia in a collected edition in 1909. On this visit he met Maxim Gorki again; the last time he had seen him had been in New York in 1906, when Gorki, who had arrived there in a blaze of glory and renown to appeal for funds to help the victims of Czarist oppression, was in the process of being evicted from his hotel upon the discovery that the woman accompanying him was not his wife, but an actress. Maria Andreyeva was in fact his common-law wife, a woman of education and versatile gifts who was a close friend of Lenin's, and who was destined to play an important part in organizing the Bolshevik Revolution. Gorki was greatly in love with her, although he remained on the most affectionate terms still with Mme Gorki and the children. But this situation was too much for the American mores of the time. It was assumed that since she was not his wife, she must be a common prostitute. Although Gorki had been received with adulation on his arrival, he and Mme Andreyeva were hastily thrown out of their hotel, and could find no other in New York to receive them. A public dinner to honour Gorki at which Mark Twain and other notables were to speak was abandoned, and within days of their arrival for what was to have been a nation-wide tour, Gorki and Mme Andreyeva found themselves at Ellis Island awaiting deportation from the land of liberty. From this absurd position they were rescued by a generous and, fortunately, influential as well as rich American, who took them into his house in upper New York State, and there Gorki spent several months in complete and happy isolation, writing as he had never written before.

This had happened during Wells's American tour, and

naturally a situation like this had aroused all his excitement and ardour. 'At one moment Gorki was in immense sunshine, at the next he was literally being pelted through the streets. ... To me it was astonishing, it was terrifying. I wanted to talk to Gorki about it, to find out the hidden springs of the amazing change.'

A friendship had been established then which was renewed and strengthened on this visit. Fame had come to Gorki as well as Wells since that first meeting. They were very much the same kind of writer, the new kind coming in, the socialist with a message which he spreads through his fables. Their conversation had to be conducted through an interpreter, but it was lively and stimulating.

When he returned to London from Russia, excited by all that he had seen and by his talks with Gorki, some of the problems he had put aside in those glowing weeks returned to plague him. Sir Frederick Macmillan, to whom he had sent half of *Bealby* before he left, was ready to publish it, but wanted to reduce the advance. With the necessity Wells was now under of providing for two homes, money was important. He quickly found Methuen ready to meet his terms.

His position as a novelist could least afford further attack at this juncture, and by an unhappy chance Henry James chose this moment to deliver himself of a judgement on the way the modern novel was going, in the course of which Wells's work, though treated respectfully, even admiringly, for qualities that were not literary, was treated dismissively as the work of one lost to the higher art of the novel. In the *Times Literary Supplement* in March and April, Henry James set out in two formidable front-page articles to examine the younger generation of English novelists, and to indicate what their work 'signified'. Naming Wells and Bennett as the two chief exemplars of the new novel, and a number of younger men – Compton Mackenzie, Hugh Walpole, D. H. Lawrence, Gilbert Cannan, whose work was influenced by them – as the most influential practitioners of the new form, James made the point that the novel had been allowed to develop free of the higher criticism to which all other art was subject, and that as a result of this freedom it had become formless, overwritten, undisciplined. His charge was that these new writers made atmosphere take the place of story: in a memorable Jamesian phrase, 'they squeeze out to the utmost the plump and more or less juicy orange of a particular acquainted state, and let this affirmation of energy ... constitute for them the treatment of the theme'. Since the work of these new novelists, widely read as it was, represented what people thought, and helped people to think the way they did, James saw this looseness as a danger in a democratic age, and he rebuked it as inartistic, damaging and perverse.

It was a reasonable judgement, but it was not likely to be appreciated by James's fellow critics. The desire of the public at the moment was for fiction to be as close to reality as possible. Popular newspapers inclined the popular mind to the persuasion that just outside their humdrum lives drama impended. The new novel, whatever its artistic faults might be, gave the impression of reflecting actual life. The restlessness of the age, changing social patterns, freedoms and possibilities open to all who could read, whatever their class, no matter, now, what their sex, gave an air of adventure to the immediate future and excited curiosity in *how* other people lived. The ample, leisurely paced study of character was as dead in these circumstances as the Victorian newspaper was dead in this time of Northcliffe and the *Daily Mail*. What Henry James frowned upon as bad art was what the new public panted for.

When the author of *Clayhanger* has put down on the table, in dense unconfused array, every fact required to make the life of the Five Towns press upon us and to make our sense of it, so full fed, content us, we may very well go on for a time in the captive condition, the beguiled and bemused condition the acknowledgement of which is in general our highest tribute to the temporary master of our sensibility ...

Yes, yes, but is this all? These are the circumstances of the interest – we see, we see; but where is the interest itself, where and what is its centre and how are we to measure it in relation to that?

James said nothing in these articles that he had not repeatedly and with growing emphasis affirmed in his successive rapturous outbursts over each new novel that Wells published. Even here he was ready to grant that Wells was a special case before whose work all criticism of the 'composition' falls away:

before the large assurance and incorrigible levity with which this adventurer carries his lapses, far more of an adventurer is he than any other of the company. The composition, as we have called it, heaven save the mark! is simply at any and every moment 'about' Mr Wells's own most general adventure; which is quite enough while it preserves, as we trust it will long continue to do, its present robust pitch.

There was nothing here that could really irritate Wells and Bennett except the implication that the high tide of their endeavour had been passed, and that the work of their younger successors and imitators was important. The magisterial judgements of Henry James had from the beginning amused as much as they impressed him. James cut such a Grand Figure in the world of letters that the irrepressible Cockney in Wells found the temptation to be cheeky almost irresistible. He was still in 1914 some way from committing the outrage of *Boon*, but only a few months before these articles appeared, he had acknowledged James's letter about *The Passionate Friends* with an impatience barely concealed beneath the mock penitence.

Sept. 22nd, 1913

My dear James,
   You are the soul of generosity to me. That book is *gawky*. It's legs and arms and misfitting clothes. It has spots like an ill grown young man. Its manners are sly and clumsy. It has been thrust into the world too soon. I shall now be an artist. (The image alters here.) My art is abortion – on the shelves of my

study stand a little vain-gloriously thirty-odd premature births. Many retain their gill slits. The most finished have still hare lips, cleft palates, open crania. These are my children! But it is when you write to me out of your secure and masterly *finish*, out of your golden globe of leisurely (yet not slow) and infinitely *easy* accomplishment that the sense of my unworthiness and rawness is most vivid. Then indeed I want to embrace your feet and bedew your knees with tears – of quite unfruitful penitence.

Yours ever,

H. G. Wells

It was not like Wells to nurse in secret a grievance when he felt one, and the fact that he made no public response to James's articles indicates that he felt at the time no more than a passing irritation with yet another example of the literary gang's attempt to classify him as an interesting but exasperating failure to be the sort of novelist they thought was important.

This springtime also saw the publication of a novel that is always cited as an example of his uncanny prophetic powers. *The World Set Free*, written on a holiday in Switzerland while the move from Church Row, Hampstead to Easton Glebe was in progress, was inspired, as its dedication acknowledges, by Professor Frederick Soddy's *Interpretation of Radium*. Fired by that book, he wrote to his friend A. T. Simmons, now editor of the *Times Educational Supplement*, to say that he had

suddenly broken out into one of the good old scientific romances again. . . . My idea is taken from Soddy. Men are supposed to find out how to set up atomic degeneration in the heavy elements just as they found out long ago how to set up burning in coal. Hence limitless energy. Will you do me the kindness to write under the enclosed just whatever books you think will give me tips for this?

There is indeed something uncanny in Wells's blind instinct for anticipating events. When this book was written in the spring of 1913 the scientists were very far from splitting

the atom. Everyone knew that a European war was inevitable, but nobody expected it for ten or twenty years.
Nor was anybody in authority really convinced that science
was going to play a decisive part in mankind's mass-killing
propensity in the future. Yet here was a famous writer
stopping in the midst of a series of novels dealing with
social and behavioural problems to picture a world war set
ahead in 1956, in which the Free Nations of the world
would be allied against the Central Powers, the desperate
struggle being brought to a conclusion only by the application to a bomb of a scientific discovery made twenty-odd
years earlier in 1933 (the actual year in which the Joliot-
Curies were to succeed in making a substance artificially
radioactive). This discovery was in 1956 to provide the
atomic bomb and nearly world-wide destruction, to be followed in his story by mankind's moral revulsion at the
effect of this terrible weapon, leading on at last to the
Wellsian formula, the Wellsian dream, a group of highly
educated and highly favoured leading and ruling men
voluntarily setting themselves to the task of reshaping the
world.

It was this last prospect that spurred H.G.'s imagination.
The literary invention of scientific detail was child's play to
him. It was a trick, an automatic response to the stimulus of
any scientific problem that caught his fancy. Where a scientist would pause and say 'This far we can come: at the
moment there is a gap in our knowledge, we can go no further', the imagination of Wells leapt to invent the missing
substance, give it a name, and then proceed to make use of
it to furnish the setting of his tale. So was cavorite, which
enabled men to overcome gravity and reach the moon; and
so carolinum, the bomb charge which anticipated the function of plutonium.

If Wells himself was impatient of these details, hastening
on to deal lovingly with the establishment of a World State,
the public did not share this taste. Wells was a masterly
describer of large-scale dramatic action, and his skill in this

regard makes the opening chapters of *The World Set Free* vivid and exciting, quite apart from the thrilling and horrifying reminder that we ourselves have since lived through the actuality of Hiroshima and Nagasaki and tremble still under the threat of what he here so vividly depicts. Not only the common man but scientists too have been excited and spurred on by Wells's powerful imagination, as we know from the tributes that have been paid to him by Sir Richard Gregory and other leaders in the scientific world. One who was to play a basic part in the development of atomic energy and the bomb, the late famous scientist Leo Szilard, acknowledged the debt he owed to Wells in a book that appeared in 1968.* It was not until 1932 in Berlin that Szilard read in a German translation *The World Set Free*. In London the following year, attending a British Association meeting, it suddenly came to him how a chain reaction could be set up, and in the spring of 1934 he applied for a patent to cover his invention. Szilard writes:

Knowing what this would mean – and I knew it because I had read H. G. Wells – I did not want this patent to become public. The only way to keep it from becoming public was to assign it to the Government. So I assigned the patent to the British Admiralty.

H..G would have been flattered if he had lived to read this acknowledgement, but he would have been pleased as well as flattered if the lesson of this book had been driven home, if men of all nations had proceeded after Hiroshima to acknowledge the horror of what they had done, and had devoted themselves to a world-wide effort of salvage and reconstruction. They haven't. The time has not yet come. But Karenin in *The World Set Free*, as he is dying, glimpses how it may come – through the window mankind will open one day upon space. Says Karenin:

'We can still keep our feet upon the earth that made us. But the air no longer imprisons us, this round planet is no longer chained to us like the ball of a galley-slave. . .

* Perspectives II, Harvard University Press.

In a little while men who will know how to bear the different gravitations, the altered pressures, the attenuated unfamiliar gases and all the fearful strangeness of space will be venturing out from this earth. This ball will be no longer enough for us; our spirit will reach out. ... Cannot you see how that little argosy will go glittering up into the sky, twinkling and glittering smaller and smaller until the blue swallows it up? They may succeed out there; they may perish, but other men will follow them. It is as if a great window opened', said Karenin.

This book was published in May 1914. But in that summer Wells had other things on his mind. For a month or two he forgot the world and its troubles, Henry James's convoluted flattery and rebuke, his continuing war with the critics and the librarians, while under a different name in a seaside town in Norfolk he lived idyllically, enjoying every minute of life until on 28 June the assassination at Sarajevo ominously sounded a warning of a possible European war. Event followed event rapidly in the unfolding of that huge drama. They were of a kind to seize the imagination of Wells. In the last weeks of July, as the European nations mobilized, it was plain that Armageddon was at hand, and we know that he was tense with excitement. By a painful coincidence, the drama in his private life was approaching its crisis at the same moment, aggravating his own domestic peace of mind.

On 4 August his and Rebecca West's son was born. He spent that strange Bank Holiday awaiting that event, and when the mother and child were safe and well, and it was plain that Germany was not going to respond to Britain's ultimatum and that Armageddon might indeed be at hand, he sat down late that night to write an article to which he gave the title that was to be taken up as a national catchword, 'The War That Will End War'.

In the shattering excitement of the hour, he forgot James's ponderous judgements. He abandoned novel-writing and flung himself into journalism with all the ardour of his nature, with all his pent-up ideas for making the world a better place suddenly apt to this moment when the old foundations were slipping. Also, perhaps, with some relief that his second scandal should be hidden under the general excitement of the hour.

14

Boon

QUICK off the mark as always, woken as from a happy dream in his love affair, Wells wrote in the course of the month following the outbreak of war ten articles notable more for their shrill aggressiveness than for their sagacity, though they did advance some far-seeing ideas to be implemented once the struggle was over, such as the neutralization of the seas and total international disarmament. First put forward in these articles also was the rough outline of a world organization for the maintenance of peace, to emerge later as the League of Nations.

But the prevailing note was jingoistic patriotism, and mixed up with the solid matter was a good deal of free abuse which earned him considerable hostility in some quarters. He deeply offended many of his old friends in the socialist party, for instance, who were not all by any means in favour of this capitalistic war; some, as convinced pacifists, were enduring difficulties of conscience enough as patriotic Englishmen who loved their country, and did not need Wells's public hectoring to remind them of their duty.

Shaw, who had retreated to the Hydro Hotel at Torquay, joined in with alacrity and wrote *Common Sense About the War*.* It was not long before he and Wells fell into public argument. One of Wells's articles in the *Daily Chronicle* evoked a reply from Shaw. The letters between them spattered like gunshot until Wells, as usual, lost his temper and let fly:

Mr Shaw objects to my calling him muddlehead. But I have always considered him muddleheaded. If I have not called him

---

* Published as a supplement to the *New Statesman*, it was subsequently issued as a pamphlet in November 1914.

that in public before, it is simply because I thought the thing too obvious to need pointing out.

If we see a man making an ass of himself, we indolent English accept him rather than face the boring task of pursuing him into the recesses of his unsoundness. We hump our backs. If we believe a man is systematically propagating some specific error we may take the trouble to study and combat him, but if we perceive that he is flinging himself about in a paroxysm of merely personal activity we leave him alone, or if we notice him, we notice him as we fling a hairbrush at a nocturnal cat, because the irritation has become intolerable.

And that is how things stand between Mr Shaw and myself. I have been quite exceptionally disposed to take him seriously, and find out what he amounts to, and this is what I find he amounts to. He is an activity, a restless passion for attention. Behind that is a kind of jackdaw's hoard of other people's notions; much from Samuel Butler, scraps of pseudo-philosophical phraseology such as that 'Life Force' phrase he got from Dr Guest, old Hammersmith economics, worn fragments of Herbert Spencer, some Nietzsche, conveyed no doubt from the convenient handbook of Mr Orage, shreds of theosophy, current superstitions, as for example his idea that fear 'poisons' meat, or that wool is a more 'natural' and hygienic clothing than cotton, sweepings of all sorts of 'advanced' rubbish, but nothing anywhere of which one can say 'Here is the thought of a man.' And it is just this incoherent emptiness, combined with an amazing knack of fluent inexactitude which gives him his advantage in irresponsible attack, and which from his early repute as the Terror of the Fabian Society has spread his vague and unsubstantial fame about the globe far beyond the range to which even his confusedly entertaining intellectual forces would have taken it.

Mr Shaw is one of those perpetual children who live in a dream of make-believe, and the make-believe of Mr Shaw is that he is a person of incredible wisdom and subtlety running the world. He is an elderly adolescent still at play. To understand that is to have the clue to all Shavianism.

It is almost as if there was nothing happening in Flanders. It is almost as if there was no pain in all the world. It is under the inspiration of such delightful dreams that Mr Shaw now flings himself upon his typewriter and rattles out his broadsides.

And nothing will stop him. All through the war we shall have this Shavian accompaniment going on, like an idiot child screaming in a hospital, distorting, discrediting, confusing ... He is at present ... an almost unendurable nuisance.*

His love affair had been absorbing his attention. This time it involved domestic stresses that were more than usually trying, but these were momentarily forgotten in what appeared a heaven-sent opportunity for the establishment on earth of the New Republic of Mankind, about which he had dreamed and written for so long. He threw himself into the war with all the ardour of his nature and all the resources of his mind, and with his characteristic disposition to overlook inconvenient obstacles. With his visionary powers he saw this as a struggle of the people. He saw the powerful alliance that was being forged between a fast-developing technology and a vast population of men who had been taught to reason. The world-reconstructor was in his element. Ideas shot from him like sparks from a grinding-wheel.

As so often, he was right in his conclusions but wrong in his methods of reaching them, and characteristically – as he had done in his struggle for the soul of the Fabian Society – he suddenly tired of it all. The Old Gang again, obstructing his plans for a neat, quick solution. In the course of a couple of months he swung the full scale from high patriotism to gloomy despondency. The war was not a crusade, as he had so belligerently proclaimed in his early articles. It was a struggle for domination between the old national sovereignties. The coming to birth of the world order of mankind was being obstructed by the generals and statesman on both sides who were making a botch of it. As usual, he cried out in his lamentations like the psalmist:

How are we to gather together the wills and understanding of men for the tremendous necessities and opportunities of the time? ... There is work for every man who writes or talks, and has the slightest influence upon another creature. All the

* *Daily Chronicle*, 31 December 1914.

slaughter is only a darkness of the mind. It goes on only because we who are voices, who suggest, who might elucidate and inspire, are ourselves such little scattered creatures that, though we strain to the breaking point, we still have no strength that would turn on the light that would save us. There have been moments in the last three weeks when life has been a waking nightmare ...

That Wells could laugh at himself in this pose is shown by the short story 'The Wild Asses of the Devil', which, although written three years earlier, he was now preparing to include in *Boon*. There is obviously self-parody in the picture of the successful author who, out for his constitutional one rainy day, encounters a tramp, disguised appropriately as an out-of-work stoker, who has been despatched from hell to round up the Devil's Wild Asses, who have strayed into the world, where they are braying and kicking up their heels and upsetting everything. Taken home to the author's fire to dry out, the stoker pitches a tale of the hardships endured in such a quest in a world unwarmed by infernal fires. But the little author is appalled at the threat offered by this wild rampage, and is not in the least interested in the stoker's condition. He becomes excited, energetic, stimulating, uplifting, bending over the stoker, urging him to pull himself together: 'The confounded brutes may be doing all sorts of mischief. While you – shirk!' The author gives it to him hot and strong; and in the process gets himself all worked up, appoints himself leader of the mission to hunt down these beasts. 'We must work from some central place, London perhaps.' We are reminded of Wells's first attempts to wake up the Fabian Society by taking bigger offices, employing a paid secretariat, increasing membership.

It says something for the mental fire within him that he could detach himself sufficiently to laugh at his own excesses. Nevertheless, the abiding weakness was there. He could scoff, yet at the same time be impressed by his own powers. The articles stimulated an enormous correspondence, and he was not slow in communicating this evidence of public interest in his views to Sir Frederick. A postcard to Macmillan urges a renewal of advertising for *The World Set Free*. A letter to Macmillan reports the tons of correspondence his articles were bringing him, and repeats the affirmation he had made as a modest young author eleven years before: 'There is a considerable interest in what I have to say.' Only a month earlier he had readily agreed with Sir Frederick's recommendation that *The Wife of Sir Isaac Harman*, then on the point of publication, should be postponed. Sir Frederick had written: 'It will be useless to publish any books appealing to general readers while this unfortunate war goes on', and Wells had concurred. But now he writes:

I am convinced that both here and in America the public will presently read ferociously. There will be no games, no more cars, no young men to flirt with, invalids wanting books ...

But the very intensity of his efforts and the intemperance of the language produced its own counter-effect. In all this shouting an artist was being lost, and he must have had moments of revulsion from his own loudness. There is detectable even in some of these war articles an occasional paragraph which demonstrates the despondency that the artistic temperament feels when it tries to grapple with practical issues. As November drew on with its rains and mist and mud, and the huge armies became bogged down in Europe, and it became plain that the war was going to drag on, he became depressed, and this mood was intensified by the pressures of his private life. His restless search for the idealized love had succeeded in making his own life uncomfortable. Always there was before him the vision that perfection of beauty and mind together offered. The stretching out for it was exciting in itself, but the failure to grasp it was agonizing.

Jane represented for him a settled, well-ordered background. She not only managed his home, entertained his friends, made life run smoothly for him, she was secretary and nurse as well; she was solid common sense when he was driven to sudden madnesses by impatience, by boredom or desire. He knew how much he owed her; he acknowledged it at the same time that he resented it, for he knew too how much their marriage had really failed, and at the heart of it what hollowness there was.

This marriage was now to be put to the supreme test. The long-suffering Jane had learnt to be patient with his affairs; it was the price they had agreed on for the survival of their adventure together. Jane had been younger then; and soon she had had children to occupy her attention, while her husband's growing wealth and fame offered her at least the consolation, which the evidence of a few contemporaries suggests that she enjoyed, of becoming mistress of a beautiful home where intellectuals and men and women famous in the world of the time were entertained in the extravagant mode of the Edwardian era. Wells enjoyed this himself, but it did not engage, as it did hers, the whole of his mind.

The affair with Amber Reeves must have been a painful shock to her, and it says much for her loyalty, and perhaps a little for her vanity, that she should have stood by him unswervingly and continued to entertain largely and put a brave face to the world.

When this happened a second time in 1914, the shock was greater, but she was an older, more experienced woman. By then, too, it is possible that she knew her own strength – and his weakness. Perhaps she knew that her marriage was not really threatened. In this again, all one's sympathy is for the girl, who was put in an impossible position by an understanding arrived at between husband and wife. Jane continued to be the bright and vivacious hostess of Easton Glebe, where entertaining went on apace, while H.G., blown like a feather in the wind by the opposing gusts of conscience and desire, maintained two homes, appearing suddenly with suitcases at either, and leaving as suddenly again.

His depression at the turn the war was taking in the winter

of 1914 was intensified by these domestic complications, and in this mood he found himself unable to get on with *The Research Magnificent*. That novel, so far as it had gone, had been carefully written; it contained the summation of the philosophy he had been working towards ever since he had first excited the young Fabians, and indeed himself, in 1908 with his declaration of personal faith in *First and Last Things*. What he was founding in the New Republic he then described was a quasi-religious cult, and the enthusiastic response he got just at the moment when his disagreement with the Old Guard of the Society had broken into open revolt led him to adopt this as the central dogma of his life and thought. Continually he was giving expression to it, always most intensely when his own emotional nature, particlarly the sexual side, led him into open scandal, or he found himself blocked by the ranks of the respected, the orthodox, and the established in his attempts to storm positions fortified by tradition and authority.

The Research Magnificent sets out at considerable length Benham's search for the New Jerusalem of this cult, a pilgrimage which takes him round the world. But Wells's despondency, as winter set in, and perhaps a lively sense of the inappropriateness of Benham's pursuit of the aristocratic spirit, particularly his hardening himself to danger, when every day hundreds of thousands of young men were facing worse perils, not for self-improvement but for love of their countries, disinclined him to go on with it at this moment. The truth is that, being Wells, and being frustrated in his aim of winning the war within a month or two, he wanted to have a blazing row with someone, and he wanted to restate his faith without the obliquity which fiction demands, believing that it was as important to this crisis as *First and Last Things* had been important at the moment when he was abandoning the Fabian Society.

The means lay temptingly at hand in the essays, parodies and stories which he had accumulated at intervals over the years, all centering around George Boon, a highly successful popular novelist who is compelled by public demand to continue to write the romances his large public expects from him, but who broods continually upon the grand literary designs he means one day to undertake. The original sketch of Boon had been written at the time in 1901 when he had turned his back on the scientific romances by which he had made his name and was devoting himself to becoming a serious novelist. *Love and Mr Lewisham* was then being concluded, he was building Spade House, and he was making his first visits to Henry James at Rye and engaging in high-level conversations with the Master about the art of the novel. When he returned from these excursions to report them to Jane, the derisive note became uppermost and 'Boon' was born, a private caricature, like the 'picshuas' he drew for her amusement, of what little Wells was expected to become if he was to amount to anything as an artist.

'Boon', then, was born of his contact with Henry James. How this original sketch grew over the years into a full-length portrait, how it became both defensive of Wells and harshly and cruelly offensive against Henry James, has been fascinatingly traced in *Henry James and H. G. Wells: A Record of Their Friendship, Their Debate on the Art of Fiction, and Their Quarrel*, by Leon Edel and Gordon N. Ray. It is the editors' opinion that as Wells's conversations with James proceeded over the next few years and as Wells became more confident with success, he enlarged the portrait to invest Boon with some very affirmative ideas and a philosophy that was unmistakeably Wellsian, and that in the process Boon becomes not merely a popular novelist who longs to write more elevating books than his public are prepared to read, but someone who holds passionate views about the holiness of the task of those who create through writing. Boon becomes not merely the figure of fun sketched in the opening pages, but the champion of literature, determined to rescue the ark of the covenant from the hands of the wicked and corrupt priests who have seized it. What

George Boon is recorded as saying is what young H. G. Wells, his squeaky voice rising to shrillness in excitement, might have been overheard saying in the library at Lamb House all those years ago. Or something like it. What he is saying is that art is not a collection of priceless artefacts to be kept from the vulgar touch behind glass, verified as genuine works from the hands of masters only, but the finest thoughts in religion, philosophy, literature, science, in every field of the self-conscious in which the mind of man has meditated, and from which has come a contribution to his growing life.

Here in growing volume, in this comprehensive literature of ours [says George Boon at one point], preserved, selected, criticized, restated, continually rather more fined, continually rather more clarified, we have the mind not of a mortal but of an immortal adventurer. ... This wonder that we celebrate, this literature, is the dawn of human divinity.

It is possible to note, as 'Boon' develops, the changes in Wells's attitude to his subject, from the more or less gentle caricature at the beginning, of a successful author dwelling in a house not unlike Spade House in Sandgate and dictating his immensely successful novels to his secretary, Miss Bathwick, who is not unlike Jane; through the period when the concept of the collective mind of the world seizes Boon's imagination, and grows into the conception of the mind of the race, which at this stage is a typical Wellsian idea, of the wholesale illumination of the public mind by bringing it into contact with the greatness of the past. The passionate urge to simplify, to convert, can be detected here. The humour is still retained, there is still an ironic detachment, for Boon and his companion Bliss (in whom he confides these immense conceptions) see the need of demonstrating what is wrong with public thought, and invent someone very like H. G. Wells to sound the alarm:

'This man of ours ... will see that the faith has gone, the habits no longer hold, the traditions lie lax like cut string –

there is nothing to replace these things. People do this and that dispersedly; there is democracy in beliefs even, and any notion is as good as another. And there is America. Like a burst haggis. Intellectually. The Mind is confused, the Race in the violent ferment of new ideas, in the explosive development of its own contrivances, has lost its head. It isn't thinking any more; it's stupefied one moment and the next it's diving about ...

'It will be as clear as day to him that a great effort of intellectual self-control must come if the Race is to be saved from utter confusion and dementia. And nobody seems to see it but he. He will go about wringing his hands, so to speak. I fancy him at last at a writing-desk, nervous white fingers clutched in his black hair. "How can I put it so that they *must* attend and see?"'

The tension mounts, the language sharpens in tone, until we reach the last stage, when Wilkins (hard-headed, down-to-earth Wells) gets the better of the argument with Boon (idealistic, dreaming Wells), the war has come, humanity is beyond saving, and Boon dies, leaving behind his literary executor, Bliss, to put together his scribblings and musings, for they have not, in spite of their great pretensions and noble purpose, ever amounted to more than some scattered ideas bolstered by a good deal of talk from Boon of a booming, impractical kind, which the alert Wilkins has not found it difficult to puncture.

Beginning with an engaging parody, mounting to intense invective, dying away in despair, the changing mood of *Boon* accurately reflected the state of Wells's mind at the various stages of its composition. Glowing with vitality and humour in 1901, angry and hurt in 1908 when he went back to it in the period following the outburst over *Ann Veronica*, bitter and sharp with invective following a second quarrel with the literary establishment at the time of the publication of *The New Machiavelli*. It was then that he had claimed new liberty for the novelist in his lecture 'The Scope of the Novel', retitled *The Contemporary Novel* when published. And ending in despair when, after three months of total war, humanity seemed to be turning its back on the high prospect all his work and thought had been urging it towards ever since he had quarreled with the Fabian Society and decided to 'go it alone'. Although he barely mentions *Boon* in his autobiography – one of the several curious silences in that illuminating book – *Boon* remains an *apologia pro vita sua.* And what prompted the publication at this moment, when for so long it had been kept hidden in a drawer, taken out only at moments of intense irritation when its function was that of a scratching-post, was not only the shock of the war but also perhaps the close companionship of a mind, Rebecca West's, which stimulated him to examine himself honestly, and the agonized feeling that he had not made proper use of his talents.

Both men – James and Wells – were artists talking about the same thing, art: what makes it, what distinguishes it from rubbish. The finely trained Henry James, whose life from childhood had been a dedication to art, saw its highest observance in the discipline it called for. The humbly born and self-educated Wells, every bit as much of an artist, saw this strange and beautiful thing which invaded his life and mind as something to be worshipped, not a discipline but an ecstasy – the immortal reflection of mortal man's finest hours.

This is what Wells, and Boon, meant by the mind of the race. Typically Wellsian in its broad visionary sweep, its inspirational quality and its persuasive mingling of science and sensibility, it offered the consolations of religion without the disciplines and rules. Man is himself, and is at the same time a member of the species. Man dies and becomes dust – but not what man does. His thinking, his art, his consciousness – these, when personality ceases, are absorbed by a process of continual synthesis into the Unconscious Being, the mystical deity, who harbours the mind of the race.

How he came to use this phrase he explains in the preface to the 1914 edition of *Anticipations.*

I saw then [after the quarrel with the Fabians] what I had hitherto merely felt – that there was in the affairs of mankind something unorganized which is greater than any organization. This unorganized power is the ultimate sovereign in the world. It is a thing of the intellectual life, and it is also a thing of Will. It is something transcending persons just as physical or biological science or mathematics transcends persons. It is a racial purpose to which our reason in the measure of its strength submits us. It is what was intended when people used to talk about an Age of Reason. It was vaguely apprehended when people talked of Public Opinion. I called it The Mind of the Race.

It is this that *Boon* is about. It took him only two months to write. The original amusing sketch of the successful author dreaming of the really great books he means to compose one day is retained. Soon the narrative deepens into 'The Mind of the Race', the chapters which describe Boon's plans for a summer congress in the house by the sea, plainly Sandgate, which is to go into the state of the republic of letters, the profound decadence of which is deeply troubling Boon. The description of the arrival there of the leading figures of the literary establishment – figures like Gosse (the official British man of letters), Hueffer, James, Yeats, Shaw – is in the best tradition of parody, and serves to remind us what English comedy lost when Wells turned serious. But while the conference does assemble, nobody remains to hear what is said. One by one, the eminent persons steal away while the President is making his opening speech, and Boon is left alone with a few cronies to confide in them what would have been said if the conference had really got down to the discussion it was convened for.

The cronies were few in number. Wilkins the novelist is very obviously H. G. Wells, the business-like author who turns out a novel a year, is sardonic, destructive, iconoclastic, pessimistic to the last degree, and plainly no fool. Wilkins the novelist makes sudden appearances in several of Wells's novels, always the down-to-earth realist, impatient of any highfalutin nonsense. He is to be Boon's antagonist in the argument that follows.

Also present is Dodd, a leading member of the Rationalist Press Association, and a militant agnostic, described by the author as 'one of those middle Victorians who go about with a preoccupied, caulking air, as though having been at great pains to banish God from the Universe, they were resolved not to permit Him back on any terms whatever'. Boon used to declare that every night Dodd looked under his bed for the Deity, and slept with a large revolver under his pillow for fear of a revelation. Dodd was based on no original, or rather on a thousand originals – the mind released into agnosticism by the revelation of the laws of the universe which science had made plain, and deeply suspicious of mysticism of any kind.

And there was Reginald Bliss, author of *The Cousins of Charlotte Brontë, A Child's History of the Crystal Palace, Firelight Rambles, Edible Fungi, Whales in Captivity* and other works: the non-creative hanger-on of literature, the recorder of this argument.

It can be seen in what a spirit of parody Wells approached this declaration of faith. As though the whole thing were a joke. But it was not. The circumstances of his life made this one of the most serious moments of his career, comparable with that Sunday talk with his mother in the woods of Up Park, and in the housekeeper's parlour after, when he had threatened suicide if she did not allow him to break his apprenticeship, or with that moment when he had turned his back on the profitable scientific fantasies to become a serious novelist. Boon was Wells, and Wilkins was Wells. Boon was he who Wells longed to be, a sage, a thinker with a rigorously intellectual basis. But Wilkins was Wells as he really was, a creative writer, a dreamer, a myth-maker, who did not know what intellectual rigour was, and who was inherently incapable of clear rational thinking. It is a weird sensation to see a brilliant mind dissecting itself, and in the process uncovering that characteristic which was the distinguishing mark of his genius, the savage contempt for humanity, while reserving all his eloquence for that figure he longed to be, the Social Planner and Saviour of mankind. Wilkins, rather than Boon with his booming hopes, has the last word just before Boon expires. Comparing men to a hutch of rabbits living within sound of a battery of artillery who look up only momentarily when the guns go off:

Men will go on in their ways though one rose from the dead to tell them the Kingdom of Heaven was at hand, though the Kingdom itself and all its glory became visible, blinding their eyes. For men and their ways are one ... men are human beings and creatures of habit and custom and prejudice; and what has made them, what will judge them, what will destroy them – they may turn their eyes to it at times as the rabbits will glance at the concussion of the guns, but it will never draw them away from eating their lettuce and sniffing after their does.

Wells himself called *Boon* the most revealing book he ever wrote. In the preface to the volume containing it in his Collected Edition, he makes no mention of the fury aroused at the time by his attack on James, especially amongst those already disposed to regard him as a trouble-maker because of his attack on the Webbs in *The New Machiavelli* and his exposure of the details of his amours in that book and in *Ann Veronica*. Wells merely says that it is his weakness to be his own *enfant terrible*, and that these chapters of *Boon* represent an outbreak of naughtiness! But there was something more to it than that.

The English had a conscience about Henry James. His person was admired, but his works had been neglected, and now in the last year of his life, as it happened to be, instead of retreating to neutral America, James was demonstrating his love for his adopted country by wholly associating himself with her cause. His work as a writer had had not the slightest effect on the social revolution which had changed England utterly; he was a late Victorian who had survived into the Edwardian age, and who brought to the art of fiction a fine abundant brain, but the old-fashioned, leisurely gestures and pedantic speech of an earlier time. He was the very antithesis of Wells, the common Englishman of the early twentieth century. But it is fair to remember that he was also the antithesis of Galsworthy's money-grubbing Forsytes, though their social rank more nearly equated with his. One gets the impression of an immense and aching shyness hidden embarrassingly behind a self-deprecating, involved verbosity which would have made him an immense bore if his devotion to the art of letters had not been so genuine and his devotion to the English so thoroughgoing. In the end he was to abandon his American citizenship and become a British subject, in order to associate himself even more closely with England in her hour of peril. Having failed to read his books, England awarded him the Order of Merit, and a month later he died to the organ music of full-length obituaries.

These events – becoming a British subject, being awarded the Order of Merit – occurred in the six months before his death in February 1916. It was just at that moment, when he was suffering from heart disease and nearly blind, when, in Rebecca West's words, he had enlisted in the English cause as a spiritual soldier and his generous acts were drawing great tides of affection towards him, that the wretched Wells chose to publish his vindictive parody of the man and his style. The wrath that fell upon him nearly drowned him; would have done so but for his unsinkable quality. A certain satisfaction is taken by those who still resent Wells's behaviour in the fact that, although he was to go on writing for another thirty years and was to know even greater success than before as encyclopedist, historian and novelist, he did not write a novel after this that is remembered today, while the novels of Henry James have survived from generation to generation and seem likely to outlast anything Wells wrote except two or three of the scientific fantasies and a handful of the early social comedies.

Literary history rightly remembers such things by their endurability, not by their effect on their generation. But the truth is that people did read Wells, they did not read James. To gauge something of Wells's influence, you have to think of what television and radio do in our age to mould our opinions, and reflect that the novel before 1914, as it had done in the seventy years since the great days of the Victorian masters, helped to form opinion. Even James continually acknowledged Wells's mastery in conveying impressions, though he frequently criticized the arrangement, the 'art' of the thing. But the general effect was beyond all praise.

I only want to say that the thing is irresistible (and indescribable) in its subjective assurance and its rare objective vividness and colour. You must at moments make dear old Dickens turn – for envy of the eye and the ear and the nose and the mouth of you – in his grave.

He was writing here of *Ann Veronica*, where in the principal character he found some want of clearness. But of the general effect, nothing could be said except that '... the total result lives and kicks and throbs and flushes and glares – I mean, hangs there in the very air we breathe; and that you are a very swagger performer indeed and that I am your very gaping and grateful HENRY JAMES'.

We know that Henry James longed for the recognition of public interest that only sales can testify to. He was never to experience it. We know that Wells longed to be accepted as a thinker. He was careless of the great creative gift that he had, partly because he undervalued what came to him so easily, partly because he was prepared to use the novel as a means to an end, rather than an end in itself. He used it as a means of explaining the mystery of life, as an illumination of the darkness still surrounding us, as an interpretation of what might bring us nearer to God. It was a holy task, and he was impatient with those who obstructed him, the critics particularly, who praised or condemned his novels as they fitted or failed to conform to critical standards set up long ago when the issues of life which his novels discussed were not bothering people. He resented the laws of fiction, inherited from an age when novels had been written for a small educated society protected by wealth from the harsh imperatives of the struggle for existence. He saw rightly that public opinion was changing, and that the old-fashioned novel no longer appealed. The mind of the race, the collective consciousness of humanity, Boon optimistically believed, reached restlessly towards other things. Boon thought towards higher things. Boon optimistically was confident of the steady and inevitable growth of human wisdom. But there have always been pessimists to undermine confidence, and Wilkins was one of them, and the Wilkins side of his nature, the essence of the spirit of his genius as a writer, Wells was always at pains to suppress. It bursts out in *Boon*, and that is why, in an unguarded prefatorial comment, he was to acknowledge it as the most revealing book he ever wrote.

Wilkins doubts whether the product of writers sitting in their studies creating literature can really (and rightfully) be described as the mind of the race. The Wilkins side of Wells asserts that the history of mankind does not show now, and it never has shown, any consecutive relation to human thinking. Thought is nothing in the world until it begins to operate in will and act. Wilkins sees the real mind of the race as something not literary at all, not consecutive, but like the inconsecutive incoherences of an idiot. 'No,' said Boon, 'of a child.'

Wilkins instances wars, great waves of religious excitement, patriotic and imperial delusions, economic disasters, to show the intermittent and non-consecutive character of human progress, and to demonstrate that humanity as a whole is a mere creature of chance and instinct.

But Boon stoutly maintains that the mind of the race is getting out of the study into the market place, that reason and sanity grow steadily. He does not prove it. He states it.

'And that is where I want to take you up', said Wilkins. 'I want to suggest that the Mind of the Race may be just a gleam of conscious realization that passes from darkness to darkness.'

'No', said Boon.

'Why not?'

'Because I will not have it so', said Boon.

Wilkins presses home his point. There is no proof of a broad progressive movement of humanity; there are too many signs to the contrary.

'The Mind of the Race', said Wilkins, 'seems at times to me much more like a scared child cowering in the corner of a cageful of apes.'

'It will grow up', asserts Boon.

'If the apes let it', said Wilkins.

Wilkins and Boon, Boon and Wilkins: two sides of the same nature, now elevating this genius to prophetic dreams, now plunging him into despair. He could never entirely overcome his contempt for humanity nor resist his impulse to make it better than it was. Conrad had put his finger on the trouble when he wrote to Wells: 'The difference between us, Wells, is fundamental. You don't care for humanity but think they are to be improved. I love humanity but know that they are not.'[*]

It irritated him beyond endurance that while he was try-ing to save humanity, to lift it out of the mess in which through sheer ignorance it was wallowing, prissy people should judge his work by outworn standards which in these active stirring new times no longer had any real validity. The standards of Henry James, for instance, suitable enough for the well-bred and the well-to-do living sealed off from brutal life in their parks and gardens and great houses while the great mass of humanity seethed and tumbled outside. And if one turned one's back on the intellectuals and looked amongst common men, what ignorance and blindness and stupidity there!

[*] Quoted in Jocelyn Baines, *Joseph Conrad*, Weidenfeld & Nicol-son, 1960, p. 232.

What was there to say, then? In the face of such circumstances, one just had to keep on. With faith. Once could not prove it, one just had to believe, and at the last all Boon can do, when Wilkins has out-manoeuvred him on every one of his arguments, is to cry out that this mind of the race does exist, that it will merge with the God-mind. He has no proof but faith! He confides to his biographer, Reginald Bliss:

'If all the world went frantic; if presently some horrible thing, some monstrous war, smashed all books and thinking and civilization, still the mind would be there. It would immediately go on again and presently it would pick up all that had been done before – just as a philosopher would presently go on reading again after the servant-girl had fallen downstairs with the crockery . . .

'It is the Mind of the Race. Most of the race is out of touch with it, lost to it. Much of the race is talking and doing nonsense and cruelty; astray, absurd. That does not matter to the truth, Bliss. It matters to Literature. It matters because Literature, the clearing of minds, the release of minds, the food and guidance of minds, is the way, Literature is illumination, the salvation of ourselves, and every one from isolations.'

And that is what *Boon* is, the confession of faith of a tired, troubled and depressed mind, maintaining dispiritedly, against his own questioning, the certainties to which he has clung for so long. The attack on Henry James came out of jealousy. It was the spark that lit the fuse that made of these scattered papers about Boon a continuous book. *Boon* has a short section on this very subject of jealousy, which Boon calls the defensive instinct of the individuality, at war always with the great de-individualizing things, with Faith, Science, Truth, Beauty.

We have already noted that the war had caught Wells at a most inconvenient time in his private affairs, and it did not help him to discover that in her forced retirement Rebecca West had started to write a critical and biographical study of Henry James. It was strange that just when his own loud bellicosity had died away and he was perhaps a little ashamed of himself for his overstatement, he should be reminded in this personal way of a life that had been wholly dedicated to literature, and of how far he had betrayed his own high pretensions in his eagerness to have a platform and to hold an audience.

At the same time, he could justify his part. The modern English novel was being born. People were asking, 'What shall we do with our lives?' and the novel, not in Wells's hands only, but most noticeably in his, was offering guidelines. These aims seem a little quaint, a little elevated and pretentious to our later taste. But at least that generation were not hedonistic materialists, as we may later be judged to have been. They had been torn suddenly from ancient faiths and beliefs, and the rupture had left them raw. They had to snuggle up to something they could believe in, and the discussion novels, which we find the least interesting of all Wells's work, were, in spite of the reservations of the critics, lapped up by an eager public. But there was something missing, that sudden awareness that one has stepped outside one's own individuality and is looking at life, which is the power that great enduring novels have over us, no matter how many times we submit to their thrall. Wells was aware that some of his later novels had been written too hastily, and that the dialogue about ideas was too loose and ample. *The Research Magnificent*, when the war came to interrupt its writing, was being most carefully written; it was to express all that life could mean – when suddenly life became something else. Humanity turned to self-destruction. After the first wild inflated hopes that this might mean the overthrow of the old order, despair overcame him, and, unable to get on with *The Research Magnificent*, he turned again to *Boon* and persuaded himself that the moment was right to publish it. As he saw it now, it had one argument only. Humanity betrays itself by its own addiction to old passions. God waits, but man hangs back, hating to leave his earth. Men are contemptible slaves, shackled by their own passions to wallow in the mess of their own making. For the moment he was irritated with his world, not minded to save it. And yet. ... How much better to turn one's back on the false literary values of the time and associate oneself with the larger theme of the human adventure. In the end that decision won out.

There was little to add to *Boon*. Only to extend that part of 'The Mind of the Race' which deals with literature as part of the God-mind. Discussing it with Rebecca West must have reminded him of his days of discussion with Henry James. Jealousy, that most potent force – the defensive instinct of the individual – came to sharpen an antagonism he had never really felt all that fiercely, being much too fond of the older man, as his letters to him attest, and too admiring of his great talent. But at a moment like this, when his feelings were deeply involved and jealousy was rampant, the Palladian features of those formalized novels of James's seemed more than ever out of place in the landscape, out of touch with contemporary life. They seemed so valiantly trying to be art that in the process they became artless.

What perhaps made his views more emphatic, just as one tends to shout when one is in the wrong, was the knowledge that here beside him was Rebecca West's very capable and intelligent brain setting out to extol James as an artist. He knew that her critical judgement was sure, and he knew that she did not spare from criticism some of the Master's undeniable faults. But, nevertheless, she was conclusively proving him to be a great novelist whose works would endure when the hurried tumultuous outpourings of the new men had trickled away to dry up in the sand.

From Rebecca West's small book the portrait of a warm and very great man emerges. At first there is something slightly ridiculous in the intensity with which the young Henry James devotes himself to art. Then one begins to see the character he was, pedantic perhaps, but not pompous, a figure at once ludicrous and dedicated, and in the end wholly lovable, a quality which radiated a glow into his work, which did not penetrate to the multitude or help sell his books, yet acted powerfully on those who knew him.

In her study, the different stages of his long career are analysed dispassionately, the faults, where they obtrude, never glossed over, the over-elaboration of style and image vividly pinpointed in memorable similes, as when she remarks of *The Tragic Muse*, which had come into the bookshops by chance in the same year in which H. G. Wells's *Anticipations* had become the best-seller of the day, that 'with sentences as vast as the granite blocks of the Pyramids and a scene that would have made a site for a Capital, he sets about constructing a story the size of a hen-house'.

She makes us aware of the influences coming from James's heredity and upbringing which made him choose for his novels and stories such subjects as he did. We see where the elaboration of his style was engendered, and we are made aware all the time that an artist is at work, 'for the state of genius consists of an utter surrender of the mind to the subject. The artist at the moment of creation must be like the saint awaiting the embrace of God, scourging appetite out of him, shrinking from sensation as though it were a sin, deleting self, lifting his consciousness like an empty cup to receive the heavenly draft ...'

The image is almost the same that Wells puts into the mouth of George Boon to describe the writer's attitude to his art:

And all reading that is reading with the mind, all conscious subjugation of outer attention to expressed beauty or expressed truth is sacramental, is communion with the immortal being. We lift up our thoughts out of the little festering pit of desire and vanity which is one's individual self into the greater self.

They were together during all the time Rebecca West's book was being written, and while *Boon* was being shaped for publication, with the addition now of the part describing the proposed conference by the sea on the state of the republic of letters, and the sharp and open attack on the art of Henry James in the section called 'Of Art, of Literature, of Mr Henry James'. There is a curious antiphony here. How could two lovers, sharing a home, both so highly intelligent, hold such diametrically opposed views of the same subject and publish them to the world? It was not a question of differing critical evaluations. Wells was trying to justify himself to himself, and the art of self-defence with him was always to attack venomously. He wanted in his usual way to dominate the mind and person of this critic who meant so much to him. But the mind was exceptional, and more powerful than his; it resisted domination.

It is easy enough to see that Wells resented what Henry James represented rather than the man himself. What he distrusted and wished to make fun of was that cosy sure world of accepted values to which he himself was a stranger. It was typical of him that he never knew when he offended until the outraged cries reached him. In the world from which he came, the instincts that preserved the more delicate persons of the upper classes from knocking into and hurting each other were not available. One can imagine him now fixed by that piercing and beautiful eye, and that mind which always stopped him with some unexpected aspect when it said, 'Look!' And avoiding it, when it came to the question of publishing these unkind things. This was a moment when anything could be said. One can imagine him pleased with the humour of the parody, skating lightly over the hurt that parody always generates. When it came to the decision to publish, the thrustful Wells was again in command. He always was at critical moments; otherwise the world-famous author who was about to publish a stinging attack on the most distinguishing, if not most successful, author of the day would still be in a drapery shop, bowing over the counter and murmuring, 'Yes, Modom'.

The conference by the sea represented feelings of quite strong resentment against the critics for imagined offences Wells thought he had received from them, but the parody, to begin with, is good-tempered: Henry James and George Moore, for instance, pictured returning from a stroll, both in full and simultaneous conversational spate, George Moore describing in loving detail a little sexual adventure he happened to have in the South of France, while James, reverberating immensely in an endlessly qualified and hesitant sentence, is explaining to his unlistening friend just why he has come to this conference. Some of the unforgettable comic scenes of *Lewisham* and *Kipps, Tono-Bungay* and *Mr Polly* are equalled here, with literary figures like Bernard Shaw, Edmund Gosse, George Moore, Hugh Walpole and others in place of Chaffery, Coote, Uncle Ponderevo and Mr Polly himself.

But in the turn of a page the mood changes, and Henry James comes under Boon's attack as the obstacle to progress in contemporary literature. In bitter, barbed phrases he goes on to ridicule the straining after effect, caricaturing James as a man who 'seems to regard the whole seething brew of life as a vat from which you skim with slow dignified gestures, works of art. Works of art whose only claim is their art.' He charges him with having no penetration; he sees him as the culmination of superficial type, 'spinning about like the most tremendous boatmen – you know those insects? – kept up by surface tension. As if, when once he pierced the surface, he would drown'.

As he went on, he argued again for his own conception of literature,

something that pierces always down towards the core of things, something that carries and changes all the activities of the race. ... The thought of a community is the life of that community, and if the collective thought of a community is disconnected and fragmentary, then the community is collectively vain and weak.

To him literature should be a part of life, should be alive with passion and will, not a stillness from which works of art can be elaborately drawn. If the novel is to follow life, it must be various and discursive; it cannot be selective, as

James would have it be, excluding those elements which do not contribute towards the picture effect he is aiming at. Life, says Boon, is diversity and entertainment, not completeness and satisfaction. James sets himself to pick the straws out of the hair of life before he paints her, but without the straws she is no longer the mad woman we love.

The phrase Henry James had used in his *Times Literary Supplement* articles of April 1914 about 'saturation' came back to Wells now in the bleak December of that year, and he argues again with him as he had done in the library at Lamb House all those years ago. The man up from suburban Bromley, who had made good and was up-to-the-minute, resenting the calm authority of the highly educated gentleman from New England, spoofed his mannerisms but did not really get at what made Hanry James at the same time important but uninfluential (if he had, he could have made rich fun of that, but he was blind to it): the moral integrity of James's characters, real men and women confounded by real problems because they, and the limited audience who read about them, had been taught that life offers these quandaries which each individual must solve for himself, again and again, in generation after generation. It was not enough to submerge one's identity in the collective mind and will; that was a confession to having no background, and the only interest then was to penetrate to the core, since neither on the surface nor just beneath was there any comparison by which you could measure grief or pain or joy. Wells, as Boon, charges that James's characters never make lusty love, shout at an election, or perspire at poker; never in any way *date* . . . and he draws a picture of a Jamesian novel as

like a church lit, but without a congregation to distract you, and with every light and line focused on the high altar, and on the altar, very reverently placed, intensely there, is a dead kitten, an eggshell, a bit of string. . . . Having first made sure that he has scarcely anything left to express, he then sets to work to express it, with an industry, a wealth of intellectual stuff that dwarfs Newton. He spares no resources in the telling of his dead inventions. He brings up every device of language to state and define. Bare verbs he rarely tolerates. He splits his infinitives and fills them up with adverbial stuffing. He presses the passing colloquialism into his service. His vast paragraphs sweat and struggle; they could not sweat and elbow and struggle more if God Himself was the processional meaning to which they sought to come. And all for tales of nothingness. ... It is Leviathan retrieving pebbles. It is a magnificent but painful hippopotamus resolved at any cost, even at the cost of its dignity, upon picking up a pea which has got into a corner of its den.

Boon was published in June 1915, by which time Wells was deep in *Mr Britling Sees It Through*, which required an altogether different mood, equally self-revelatory of the bustling, bubbling, pushing Wells. That he had a conscience about what he had done is evident from the fact that *Boon* was published under the name of George Bliss, 'with an ambiguous introduction by H. G. Wells' in which he begs readers and reviewers not to jump to what may seem an easy identification: 'Bliss is Bliss and Wells is Wells. And Bliss can write all sorts of things that Wells could not do.' Still he was uneasy, and he demonstrated his uneasiness by leaving a copy of the book, without a letter, addressed to Henry James at his club.

By this time James was ill and going blind. He had just renounced his American citizenship, a step for him fraught with the deepest significance, and was on the point of becoming a naturalized British subject when he picked up *Boon* at his club and, reading it, found there the cruel portrait of himself and his work.

Another man might have counter-attacked vigorously or consulted his lawyers. One remembers Hugh Walpole dressing for dinner and skimming through Somerset Maugham's *Cakes and Ale* as he dressed, finding in Alroy Kear the cruel portrait of himself, and sitting back on his bed, bursting into tears of self-pity. There were these several ways of reacting, but none of them was James's. Even if he had not been old and tired and overwhelmed by a sense of failure, it is certain that he would not have been abusive. It was not in his nature or his training. He kept his pride. In the letter in which he acknowledged the book was only a cry of pain at being so cruelly treated, the sense of utter loss at the sudden and unlooked-for collapse of a bridge of understanding that he imagined to have existed between them; and then a wonderfully moving and sincere reaffirmation of his faith in the perfectibility of art, the means by which its beauty may be most exquisitely produced.

It is difficult, of course, for a writer to place himself fully in the place of another writer who finds him extraordinarily futile and void and who is moved to publish that to the world. ... The fact that a mind as brilliant as yours can resolve me into such an unmitigated mistake, cannot enjoy me in anything like the degree in which I like to think I may be enjoyed, making me greatly want to fix myself, for as long as my nerves will stand it, with such a pair of eyes.

'In the end', said James,

one has to fall back on one's sense of one's good parts – one's own sense, and I at least should have to do that, even if your picture were painted with a more searching brush. For I should otherwise seem to forget what my poetic and my appeal to experience rest upon. They rest upon my measure of fulness, fulness of life and the projection of it, which seems to you such an emptiness of both ... I hold that interest may be, *must* be, exquisitely made and created, and that if we don't make it, we who undertake to, nobody and nothing will make it for us.

Wells, in his reply, sought to excuse his conduct by blaming it on other pressures:

Your view was, I felt, altogether too dominant in the world of criticism, and I assailed it in terms of harsh antagonism. Writing that stuff about you was the first escape I had from the obsession of this war. *Boon* is just a wastepaper basket.

James's answer to this meagre and grudging apology said that he did not think it made out any sort of case for the bad manners of *Boon,* and that the comparison to a waste-basket was infelicitous in that what one throws into that is exactly what one doesn't publish.

Bewildered by the savagery of the attack made on him by a younger man whose work he had always admired, the half-blind sage could only repeat his belief:

It is art that makes life, makes interest, makes importance for our consideration and application of these things, and I know of no substitute whatever for the force and beauty of its progress. If I were Boon, I would say that any pretence of such a substitute is helpless and hopeless humbug; but I wouldn't be Boon for the world, and am only yours faithfully,

Henry James

The excuses Wells made for his attack – that he was worn out and depressed by the war, and had long felt that these things needed saying – sound insincere in comparison with the immensely dignified tone of James's reply. The long and interesting preface to Professor Leon Edel's and Gordon Ray's book which traces the association between James and Wells from its beginning lays stress on the difference in their origin and background, and their different attitudes to the art of the novel, and shows that beneath the praise which James constantly lavished on his young friend were criticisms which had always needled Wells. Certainly Wells's letters to James in the last few years of their association show an increasing impatience with the old man's polite strictures. It is the editors' opinion that James would certainly have read Wells's lecture on the novel, and that the two articles on the novel which James contributed to the *Times Literary Supplement* were indirectly an answer to the demand for licence for the novelist put forward so vigorously by Wells in his 1911 lecture, *The Contemporary Novel.*

The editors believe that Wells was privately irritated by these articles, that it seemed to him a betrayal of friendship that James should have praised him so much in private correspondence but in public print should denigrate his work, and also that he was greatly upset by James's unqualified attack on the work of his friend Arnold Bennett, for whom James had reserved his heaviest fire, his least-restrained phrases; and that *Boon*, or that part of it called 'Of Life, of Literature, of Mr Henry James', was his answer six months later, when he would have been writing this section.

Yet that does not seem in the temper of Wells. He was a man given to sudden outbursts of rage, but they were over quickly, and he could forgive anyone except a perfect fool. For Henry James he had immense respect – and affection. Wells loved no man. He was held to some – Morley Davies, Richard Gregory, A. T. Simmons – by old ties of companionship, but it is noticeable that these were men who could be useful to him. His capacity for affection, unlike his capacity for physical love, was not unlimited. To make it last, some form of respect was necessary, an acknowledgement of some inferiority in himself, and that was very hard for Wells to make. The two men to whom he gave his unstinted affection were George Gissing and Henry James, and it is interesting that both these men should have been conscious artists and gentlemen. They exasperated him by being too good for their own good, too attached to outworn usage – Gissing his classicism, James his Victorian mannerisms. But he had dropped everything at Christmas-time to go to Gissing's deathbed, and he would have done anything in the world for James.

But on one point he was excessively sensitive: the justification for his work, the belief that it was not being done in vain. Except for the early science fantasies, every novel that he had written had had a purpose, had aimed at something. It was not just romance; it was meant to play its part in shaping the moral outlook of the times. He knew that he had sometimes written too hastily, but he did make his readers feel that he was discussing matters of vital importance to them, and the interest and excitement aroused by his books, especially among the intelligent young, showed that they readily forgave what made Henry James wince, his 'sacrifice to the casual' in the motivation of his stories.

How the characters in his books got where they did was of little importance; what they saw, what they said, what they felt when they had arrived – that was the heart of the matter.

But in his overriding attempt to win the reader's assent to his convictions, dialogue – the talk about ideas – had begun to assume a larger and larger place in his work, and he justified it to himself on the grounds that this *was* life, these *were* the ideas that generated human conduct, and if they could not be glazed and polished into something perfect and beautiful, it was because life was neither perfect nor beautiful – yet. It might become so when the last shreds of doubt and ignorance had been torn away.

He profoundly believed that the novel was an instrument of education; that it enlarged the mind and understanding. What he overlooked was that few people submit to education, they have to be enticed or forced into it; and the novel has to succeed first as a novel before it can undertake additional functions. It is only partly odd that so clever a man should miss so obvious a fact. Clever men often tend to be myopic in fields outside the immediate range of their vision. The mythological cast of Wells's imagination had always swept along an arc to the future. His was an imagination that could generate visions of some majesty, as he had proved time after time. But it failed when it came to practical steps; it equally failed when it came to moral judgements. Mixed up with his strongly expressed dislike of the critics, and of those who disagreed with him, was his uneasiness over his own behaviour.

There is no blinking the fact: Wells, with all his wonderful charm and wit, his brilliant intellect, his stimulating ideas, was a man without moral balance. The irregularity of his sexual life was a manifestation of that rather than the central fact of it. Morality is more than adherence to rules; it is gentleness, and a consideration for the feelings of others; it is a reluctance to inflict pain. It is a discipline of self, just as art is a discipline of matter.

He was not prepared to submit to these disciplines, and this was not only because of his irritable, impatient temperament. Built into him, as ineradicable as a birthmark, was the lower-class resentment which not all these years of moving amongst intellectuals had been sufficient to suppress. Always he was to see the whole human condition in terms of the kind of resentment engendered by the background from which he came. This was a handicap to a social novelist. There had been novels about the English working class before, but there had not been an English working-class novelist of Wells's stature, bringing to the judgement of the morality of solid middle-class bourgeois England a brilliant intellect and persuasive style, but one stained with the spiteful and envious spots which the ugly, ignorant crowded world of his upbringing had left on him. The picture of that world he gives in *The New Machiavelli* and *Experiment in Autobiography* could not be bettered. This environment, mental and physical, withheld some vital essence, the more noticeable in a clever boy like Wells than it would be in another. His cleverness made him aware of his loss, and he was seeking substitutes: free love instead of married love; literature as an expression of the mind of the race rather than the art of individual human minds expressing beauty; a satisfactory organized classless society which would be essentially an expanded middle class. He wasted no sympathy on the class from which he had emerged. There had to be a lower stratum – and 'I have never believed in the superiority of the "inferior".'

'I would not be Boon for all the world.' But Wells literally could not help it. It was in his very nature; he was powerless in the grip of Boonism. That hated ugly background of his beginning had left its mark on him. The dreaming boy playing in the dust-bin in the back-yard of Atlas House had grown into the man who wanted desperately to make the New Republic. Although Boon dies, and Wilkins really has the last word in 'The Last Triumph', Boonism is not dead, only momentarily down. From time to time Wilkins was to raise his head to shout realities, but the spirit of Boonism was to be in control hereafter until nearly the end. It was Boonism that brought God into *Mr Britling*, the cheerful, pugnacious chronicle that followed, and that allowed God the Commanding Officer's privileges through the books that followed until, at the war's end, God was discharged and education promoted in his place. But education was Boonism too, and Wells the artist, who had begun with such miraculous promise and had seemed to draw a whole world after him into the light of common day, failed when Boon took possession of him.

15

Mr Britling and the
Captain of Mankind

IF *Boon* drew down on him the hostility of the literary
world, on the public at large the book made hardly any
impression at all. It had been published as the work of
George Bliss, but if the reviewers were not taken in by this
flimsy attempt at disguise, the public was. It remained indifferent to Bliss's work, and Fisher Unwin, who had printed
a modest five thousand, was continually pleading to be
allowed to withdraw it and reissue it under Wells's name.
But Wells refused. He continued publicly to maintain that
the true authorship lay with another; the most he would admit was that the book was of 'blended' origin.*

When *Boon* appeared, the second battle of Ypres was just
over, poison gas had been used on the western front for
the first time, trench warfare had taken the place of the
swift movements, promising early victory, which had
marked the first stages, and almost daily there were heavy
attacks on both sides which were repulsed with heavy losses.
Flanders had become a killing-ground, and the eyes of the
world were on it. Literary quarrels left the public un-
moved, and the Race Life was of minimal interest compared
with the threat to the life-threads of millions of young
men.

The Research Magnificent, completed immediately after
Boon and published in November 1915, failed also to strike a
satisfactory response. It had taken too long to write, it had
been taken up and put down so often, it bore so palpably on
every page the marks of pre-war planning and thinking,
that Wells was not surprised when it fell fairly flat.

*Letter to the *Daily News*, March 1916.

Everything that he touched seemed destined to arouse frothing hostility, but he was at work on a novel in the winter of 1915 which was to turn out to be one of his greatest triumphs. Witty, evocative, reflecting beautifully the English character and scene at a crisis in history, yet at the same time justifying itself as a discussion novel, *Mr Britling Sees It Through* is thoroughly English, and Mr Britling is unmistakably H. G. Wells as, purged now of his rage against the critics, he turned back to his task of reconstructing society, displaying in the process the engaging Mr Polly side of his character.

For in spite of his denials, this is demonstrably the most autobiographical of all his novels. It is a curious fact that Wells's greatest successes as a novelist always followed some set-back in his private affairs, as though his indignation at unendurable conditions forced him to take the case of himself, where he could speak with the conviction of experience. *Kipps* and *Tono-Bungay* were protests against the existing social order as seen from below by young Wells; *Ann Veronica* and *The New Machiavelli* blasts against the feeble efforts of the Fabians to remedy the state of affairs. They are all Wells's own story. When he invested imagined figures with the passionate feelings that raged in him, as he did in the novels of social reform which preceded *Mr Britling*, he failed to convince. They became prigs, and voluble prigs, isolated from the common world of men in their search for perfection.

The setting of *Mr Britling Sees It Through*, Matching's Easy, is plainly Easton Glebe. It was a home that he had loved and – one might say – lost, for the time being at any rate. It was a large rambling house on the edge of the Countess of Warwick's estate. It had a large garden, lawns and abundant fields where Wells could organize the strenuous ball games and the amateur theatricals in which he loved to involve his guests. Mr and Mrs Britling are plainly Mr and Mrs Wells, and even the neighbours and visitors can be identified. Mr Britling has his mistress established in a house twenty miles away, and some of the tensions aroused by this relationship – which reflects in its clash of temperaments the affair H. G. Wells had had with the Countess von Arnim two years earlier, an affair in which H.G.'s part was not dignified and the Countess's behaviour not very kind – are amusingly reflected in Mrs Harrowdean's torture of Mr Britling. On to this active scene comes Mr Derrick, an American, in the full flush of academic earnestness, to meet the famous author Mr Britling, express his admiration and issue an invitation to lecture in America. Mr Derrick proves to be the anvil on which are hammered out most of Mr Britling's commentary and constructive ideas.

The book opens in the summer of 1914, and we see the shadow of war creeping over this sunlit happy landscape, with Mr Britling doing a tremendous amount of talking about the possibility of war but not really believing that it will come. It is in his nature to get worked up about things; his very loquacity is our comfort, for he feels all our joys and experiences all our fears. Mr Britling thinks that the world is his egg.

He had a subconscious delusion that he had laid it. He had a subconscious suspicion that he had let it go cold and that it was addled. He had an urgency to incubate it. The variety and interest of his talk was largely due to that persuasion; it was a perpetual attempt to spread his mental feathers over the task before him ...

In the course of the year much happens. Mr Britling does not, as he has anticipated, see the war through to its conclusion. But he sees through to an understanding of himself and his place in the universe, and to an awareness of a figure who is a personification of the higher virtues, who is part of this battle between good and evil, and yet who is above it, and whose constant presence makes the terrible struggle meaningful.

The novel is a pure reflection of the changing moods which had chased one another across Wells's mind in the first full year of war. We have seen how he went into it, in a mood of aggressive patriotism, shouting abuse at the Germans and anyone on his own side who counselled restraint or consulted his conscience. This was succeeded swiftly by despondency, and Mr Britling reflects this changed mood. It is one in which Mr Britling no longer thinks of the rights and the wrongs of the conflict but of the underlying instincts in mankind that make war possible. He now thinks there is as much to be said for the Germans as for the British. Then comes a third stage in which deep pessimism has him in its grip, and he contemplates the possibility that the whole of life is evil, and once again we are back with the mood that crossed like clouds every now and then through the scientific romances. In the fourth stage, when Mr Britling is beginning to see it through, he contemplates the struggle as a dynastic and economic one out of which a new order will come, and at the end he is writing about the imperative necessity of some league of world government. He sees that the world can no longer be run by sovereign states or empires and that some overriding authority is necessary. He calls it, with prophetic instinct, the League of Free Nations.

But it cannot be left to the statesmen to manage, and Wells-inspired Mr Britling discovers a new road which calls for the subordination of the will of the self-seeking individual to the idea of racial well-being embodied in an organized state under God. Wells was entering on a new phase in which religion was to be the instrument he used to gain acceptance of his never-failing dream of a World State.

Its revelation is very exactly reflected in Mr Britling's troubled thoughts when, his own son having been killed, and having heard through a friend in Norway that the German boy who had been tutor to his sons has also been killed fighting with the German army, Mr Britling sits down to write to the father of the German boy a letter of comfort. He spends the whole night attempting to frame it;

trying, as he expresses it to himself, to find a way of working into the situation its only possible satisfactory solution,
the coming of the World State. Mr Britling explains to
himself that this is only England bereaved writing to Germany bereaved, but remnants of the old antagonism keep
coming in and attempt after attempt to express what is in
his mind is torn up. Until, as dawn breaks, a vision of what
the death of these two young men really means comes to
him.

For the first time clearly he felt a Presence, of which he had
thought very many times in the last few weeks, a Presence so
close to him that it was behind his eyes and in his brain and
hands.

The Presence is not only his dead son but the German boy:

It was all these and it was more. It was the Master, the Captain of Mankind, it was God, there present with him, and he
knew that it was God. It was as if he had been groping all this
time amidst rocks and pitfalls and pitiless things, and suddenly
a hand, a firm strong hand had touched his own. And a voice
with him bade him be of good courage . . .
There was no need of despair because he himself was one of
the feeble folk. God was with him indeed, and he was with God.
The King was coming to his own. Amidst the darkness and confusions, the nightmare cruelties and the hideous stupidities of the
Great War, God, Captain of the World Republic, fought His
way to Empire . . .
'I have thought too much of myself,' said Mr Britling, 'and
of what I would do by myself. I have forgotten *that which was
with me.*'

As he stands at the open window in the fresh dawn light,
hearing far away towards the church some early worker
whetting a scythe, he makes his resolution.

'Religion is the first thing and the last thing, and until a man
has found God, and been found by God, he begins at no beginning, he works to no end.'

He sees God fighting through men against blind forces and night and non-existence. 'He is the only King', says Mr Britling to himself. 'Of course, I must write all about Him. I must tell all my world of Him.'

Wells's God, summoned thus late to play a leading part in the grand design, at least had his entrance well-timed. In moments of extreme peril men instinctively turn towards a mystical Being, supreme above the dangers that beset them. Wells's conception of a finite God, mystical in the sense of being raised above humanity, but finite in the sense that he is simply the collective consciousness of mankind, the Captain at the head of his troop, who fights through man against Evil, answered the need of men and women who had ceased to believe unquestioningly in the conventional God of the Christian Faith, but who had not lost the longing in moments of stress for the strong shoulder of a comforter to lean against. What they wanted in 1916, above all, was some explanation of this holocaust, and the reassurance that their sacrifice was not in vain.

There is a fascination in tracing Wells's mental processes when he has been seized by an idea and is anxious to convert others to it. The procedure is always the same: an extended monologue, an incantation, and the first victim to fall for it is the author himself. We can follow this in Mr Britling's night watch. We witness Mr Britling's awareness of the Presence; it is conversion no less, a spiritual quiver in the veil between himself and the universe. It was something immensely lost in distance, some 'other thing' in Nature that assured him that all was not planless and inchoate; order emanated somewhere. His son and the German tutor and a million or more other lads had not died uselessly; their deaths contributed to some immense Will working through aeons to some solution.

All this Mr Britling felt as an emotional, personalized shiver. He had ceased for some time to be a novelist. All the characters in his story had left the bright stage except himself; even Britling was Britling no longer, really, but little Wells conducting an extended monologue, highly charged emotionally, in which he is making an effort to bring the external optimism which it had been his habit to shout, and which anyway was highly congenial to his sensuous active nature, into balance with the savagely pessimistic conviction he was never able to free himself from entirely, that the curse of evil was on mankind, and self-destruction its ultimate destiny. From the beginning, he had had to fight against this deeply rooted dark despair about humanity, hiding his hatred of its ugliness and stupidity and animality behind excessive activity in planning its betterment. This was what George Boon had meant when he shut his ears to Wilkins's suggestion that humanity could never grow up; it was a child cowering in a corner in a cageful of apes. 'No', said Boon. 'Why not?' 'Because I will not have it so.'

Who could brave the apes and encourage man to stand up and be freed from his captivity? There was no alternative in this last extremity but some force outside the world, something mystic but, as imagined by Wells, characteristically something managerial and practical. He could not, of course, accept the conventional God of the established Christian Church; he had to shape him to his own design, and a curious Wellsian, not unattractive figure emerges, young, radiating a spirit of courage, a finite Being who shares men's troubles, is not aloof from them.

The fantastic success of *Mr Britling Sees It Through* – there were thirteen printings in England between publication in October 1916 and Christmas of that year, while its success in America was legendary – did much to restore his fame and recruit his fortunes. But it also had the undesirable effect of prompting that dominating instinct which was always aroused in him when he saw that his ideas were being accepted. First the shy, stumbling suggestion tentatively advanced; when it arouses interest, a fully worked-out and documented plan is advanced firmly; when anyone questions that, a cry of outrage. 'Fools, knaves,' he seems to say, 'you are obstructing the coming of the glory!' It had been so in the Fabian Society; it had been so in his lecture on the novel. He had not been able to take over the socialist cause and mould it to his militant desire, so he abandoned it and abused the leaders for leading the flock astray. He had not been able to establish a new direction and set of standards for the English novel, so he had abused the critics and held poor old Henry James up to ridicule. He had to dominate, or he turned aside and reviled what he had formerly extolled.

All this sounds like bullying and bluster. But always he was right in his conclusions, wrong only in the methods he advocated for reaching them. The Fabians did have their ridiculous side, and were on the whole politically ineffective. The Edwardian novel, overshadowed still by the grandeur of the Victorian masters, was out of touch with the revolutionary note of the last Edwardian years. And in the great tragedy of the war there was a longing for the consolation that religion can offer the anguished spirit, which men and women were not finding in the conventional faiths. Wells was needed, or someone of his vision and his combative powers, to point to these needs, and to reshape a faith that had lapsed. Wells's God – the God of his presentation – was to bring comfort and inspiration to millions in the midst of a disaster that seemed to have passed beyond the power of man to stop.

The pattern was always the same, and Wells acknowledged it in the self-portrait he drew of himself in the person of Mr Britling. This characteristic is illuminated when we are made privy to Mr Britling's mental processes on an anguished wakeful night of self-examination at an earlier stage in the story when Mr Britling is remorseful over a motor-car accident for which he has been responsible. He passes by insensible gradations from sorrow for his carelessness and vanity, to a general remorse for his irregular sex-life, the consequences of which, like the motor accident, have been aggravated by his tendency to precipitate action; then to remorse for all the confusions in which the world finds itself; thence to plans for rescuing humanity from its predicament and setting it on the path to better things.

The blueprint had been laid down in *First and Last Things* to the young Fabians seven years before. In *God the Invisible King*, to which he turned immediately after *Mr Britling Sees It Through*, he attempted to gather up into the recognized form and terms of contemporary religions the beliefs and aspirations embodied in that original declaration. It was an attempt to redefine in modern terms the two God ideas, God-as-Nature or the Creator, and God as the Redeemer, which had prevailed in the world since men first began to think of a Power greater than themselves who controlled their lives. Christianity, with its Triune God, had been the first great attempt to fuse these two conceptions, combining the Outward God, ruling with justice rather than affection, aloof, awe-inspiring, with the Inmost God, the God of the human heart.

With typical confidence that his own assumptions are shared by everyone else, Wells takes it for granted that everyone in this time of stress is questioning the validity of Christian practice as established in the Church, that everywhere there grows in people's minds a new religion which will replace the old. The Christian practice of religion did indeed need redefinition after Darwin, and in dodging this necessity, in trying to shout the evolutionary theory down, the Church had done itself much harm for too long. The schoolmaster in Wells has a field day as, with that incomparable lucidity which always marked his style when he was explaining something, he puts into a well-ordered thesis thoughts and instincts that have been swirling about in people's minds without forming a definite pattern.

Wells states his own position, which was that of most of those who were products of Darwin's and Huxley's teaching: complete agnosticism in the matter of God the Creator, entire faith in the matter of God the Redeemer. It is the latter who is God the Invisible King. But he is a humanized, finite God, the intermediary between us and the

Veiled Being, beyond whom is the source of life, the Unknown, the Ultimate Being. The finite God, indeed, seems more like a senior N.C.O., able to commune with the Commanding Officer, but definitely representing the men, and not asked to sit down but only to stand at ease in the Presence.

Human analysis probing with philosophy and science towards the Veiled Being reveals nothing of God, reveals space and time only as necessary forms of consciousness, glimpses a dance of atoms, of whirls in the ether. ... Some day in the endless future there may be a knowledge. ... To that it may be our God, the Captain of Mankind, will take us.

How this finite God makes Himself known to us is very much as Mr Britling had experienced it.

Then suddenly in a little while [with the release of the mind from past superstitions which the new Religion gives], in His own time, God comes. This cardinal experience is an undoubting immediate sense of God. It is the attainment of an absolute certainty that one is not alone in oneself. ... 'Closer He is than breathing, and nearer than hands and feet.'

What God is not he clears out of the way before defining what God is. He is not Magic, not Providence, he does not punish and is not God the Avenger (relics here of Mrs Wells's continual threats of what God would do if little Bertie didn't obey his mother, and of his defiance while he was being confirmed). God is not sexual: the religious passion and insult and persecution upon the score of sexual things were a barbaric inheritance which had passed into Christianity.

God instead is Courage. He is a Person: this is the axis of the new religion. He exists in time, but not in matter or space. This does not prevent him having moods and aspects, as a man has, and a consistency that we can call his character. God is Youth, a contrast with the patriarchal aspect of old religions. And God is Love – not the love of man and woman with its climax and satiety, but the love a comrade gives to a comrade.

This compound Being is a finite intelligence of boundless courage and limitless possibilities of growth and victory, who has pitted himself against death, who stands close to our inmost beings ready to receive us and use us in his immortal adventure to establish the new kingdom.

The divine kingdom turns out to be very much the Wellsian Utopia. Mankind, on the way to salvation, led by the Invisible King, would abstain from insensate and self-destroying quarrels and concentrate upon certain divine ends – those, as it happened, which Wells had been tirelessly advocating since the days of *Anticipations*: the maintenance of the racial life, the exploration of the external being of nature, as it is and as it had been, i.e., history and science. To this should be added the exploration of inherent human possibility, which is art, and the clarification of thought and knowledge, which is philosophy, And, finally, the progressive enlargement and development of the racial life so that God may work through better minds, so that he and our race may increase for ever as we master the blind forces of matter throughout the deeps of space.

This transfiguration of the world into a theocracy may seem a merely fantastic idea to anyone who comes to it freshly without such general theological preparation as the preceding pages have made. But to anyone who has been at the pains to clear his mind even a little from the obsession of existing but transitory things, it ceases to be a mere suggestion and becomes more and more manifestly the real future of mankind. From the phase of 'so things should be', the mind will pass very rapidly to the realization that 'so things will be'. Towards this the directive wills among men have been drifting more and more steadily and perceptibly and with fewer eddyings and retardations, for many centuries. The purpose of mankind will not be always confused and fragmentary. This dissemination of will-power is a phase. The age of the warring tribes and kingdoms and empires that began a hundred centuries or so ago, draws to its close. The kingdom of God on earth is not a metaphor, not a mere spiritual state, not a dream, not an uncertain project; it is the thing before us, it is the close and inevitable destiny of mankind.

In a few score years the faith of the true God will be spreading about the world. The few halting confessions of God that one hears here and there today, like that little twittering of birds which comes before the dawn, will have swollen to a choral unanimity. In but a few centuries the whole world will be openly, confessedly, preparing for the kingdom. In but a few centuries God will have led us out of the dark forest of these present wars and confusions into the open brotherhood of his rule.

God the Invisible King raised considerable discussion. Mr Britling's conversion had provided the text for inspiring sermons from pulpits up and down the country, but *God the Invisible King* was another matter altogether. The clergy found themselves in the position of the Webbs, who woke from bliss at finding such a famous recruit to the knowledge that he was ready to take over the Fabian Society. In a time of stress and danger, theologians are flattered when the tormented soul turns to find comfort in their doctrine, even if the pilgrim misunderstands some of its finer points. But when with *God the Invisible King* Mr Wells, pursuing his new religion, set up in business, so to speak, with a detailed theology of his own, appropriating both God the Father and God the Son for his own purposes, and assigning them parts in the divine scheme which two thousand years of Christian scholars had not suggested, this was going too far. The clergy are likely to shudder when laymen use terms like the Veiled Being and the Life Force as synonymous with the divine power. They are also likely to look sideways when the assertion is made that God is a person who has moods and aspects as a man has, that he exists in time but not in matter or space. But most of all they were uneasy when it became plain that the God of Mr Wells's imagining was simply commandeered by Mr Wells in order to promote his New Republic.

Once again he had not been able to resist the temptation

to take command. The pattern is always the same. He comes into the movement, sits quietly for a little while, then makes suggestions with a view to increasing the efficiency of the body. When his suggestions are not received well by the Old Guard, he makes an impassioned plea for all to come away with him to this obsessional landscape which had gripped his imagination for so long, and was to grow in force and strength until his last despairing years.

The Undying Fire, one of his finest novels, followed *God the Invisible King*. It was written after Wells had been involved in considerable controversy over his theological speculations, and it is most revealing as showing how the mythological cast of his mind brought every debate in the end to the confrontation between ethical man and the animal instincts in humanity. 'Blind nature spews these people into being' says Jacob Huss, the elderly schoolmaster who is the central figure of *The Undying Fire*, 'and there is no light to guide their steps.' Education offers the only hope, but there must be a new approach to it. It is Huss's view that salvation may be reached through the teaching of history and science and philosophy instead of Latin and Greek.

'The end and substance of all real education is to teach men and women the Battle of God ... to show them how man has arisen through the long ages from amidst the beasts, and the nature of the struggle God wages through him to draw all men together out of themselves into one common life and effort with God.'

This is Boon at his most rhetorical, and little Wilkins would certainly have been as quick as at least one critic of *The Undying Fire* was to point out that knowledge in itself is not necessarily a guide to right action, that men are not made unselfish, modest and sincere by the use of globes.

Wells acknowledged that *The Undying Fire* was the sunset of his divinity. The short excursion had started when Mr Britling looked for a comforter at a time of great tribulation and found the God he had first adumbrated in *First and Last Things* rather than God in the image that our literature and our faith have fashioned for us; a God who personified courage, a very appealing figure for those anguished times.

When Wells sought in *God the Invisible King* to elaborate and codify this doctrine, he immediately drew to himself some effective criticism that this was heresy, not divinity, and he had to tack and turn more than a little to maintain a tricky position. As he acknowledged in his autobiography, he could not then, or afterwards, really distinguish between the genuineness of his theocratic beliefs and the political opportunity the adoption of these offered him to get over to the multitude the idea of the New Republic which otherwise they might have been reluctant to entertain.

What we see in these years is an artist revealing the fatal flaw that prevents him from taking his place among the great ones of his kind. Missing in Wells, disregarded in the new relationship he seeks to define between suffering humanity and a humane loving leader who is God, was something that is as essential to religion as it is to literature or any other form in which art expresses itself: a moral sense which had brought man along the path as far as he had come. What this brilliant mind of Wells's was blind to was the moral resources of humanity, which had enabled it to stagger on and continue to combat the blind forces of nature, gradually overcoming them by its own toughness and endurability. Novels were about this unending struggle, and once he had almost seemed aware of this when Kipps and Mr Polly and George Ponderevo stood up against the harshness of their environments, aware that somewhere there was light outside their darkness, and that man must not rest until he finds it. But it was only a gleam, flickering uncertainly, and Wilkins from time to time was conscious of what he missed, and grew sardonic and angry.

While all this was going on, Wells was engaged in great activity. The war was to prove one long train of quarrels for him. He quarrelled with the generals about their strategy, with the War Office over its refusal to take up a device which he had invented for sustaining duck-boards in the mud of France, with Lord Northcliffe about propaganda, and with Sir Frederick Macmillan about his books.

Yet all the time his busy fertile mind was proposing admirable ideas. In May 1916 he attended a gathering of members of the British Science Guild, summoned by Sir Ray Lankester to Burlington House to protest against the prevailing neglect of science in British education and industry. He became a member of the committee set up by the meeting to deal with this neglect. Under a pseudonym he addressed, in June and July that year, a series of six letters on the subject to *The Times* which aroused a great deal of correspondence and discussion. They were subsequently published in book form under the title *The Elements of Reconstruction*, Wells's authorship of them not being made known until the third edition of the book. It was a further sign of his growing concern with the question of education, more essential than ever now that the illimitable power which science had given man was being used to destroy him. Education was the whole subject of *The Undying Fire*, as it was of *Joan and Peter*, a novel which he wrote in 1918, not of much interest today. He was moving rapidly towards his work as an encyclopedist, but *The Outline of History*, the first great manifestation of the genius he had for teaching, was sparked off by his political experience in helping to launch the League of Nations.

Wells was not a patient man, and he had an explosive temper, so that when Mrs Wells sent to Macmillans, at her husband's direction, the first half of *Mr Britling Sees It Through*, and Sir Frederick wrote her saying that he had been 'very much struck with the way Mr Wells had made use of the material provided by the present war', adding that he would be very glad indeed to publish the book on the same royalties as before, but:

In the present disastrous state of the book market, it would not be prudent for us to make as large an advance as hitherto, and we should propose therefore that the advance payable on publication should be exactly the sum which has been earned by the previous book up to the date of publication, whenever that may be

Wells replied brusquely:

My wife has just shown me your letter of the 21st. I am afraid that if you are not disposed to publish *Mr Britling Sees It Through* on the terms of our old Agreement and understanding, there is nothing for it but to take it elsewhere.

So at last, after many trials, these two came to the parting of the ways. They had really never understood one another. Each of them respected in the other qualities with which he was anxious to ally himself. Wells wanted a safe, sane publisher who would gather all his books together, promote them collectively, back him up in the adventurous line he was taking, put him in the class with Kipling and Hardy (both of whom Macmillan also published), give him, in short, the security and status of a man of letters. Macmillan wanted Wells. He knew that Wells was a first-class storyteller. When Macmillan took him on, Wells was just beginning to make his name – and make it in a fresh new line of interest in which he had no competitors, and for which the public was hungry. The partnership of a famous firm and an author on his way to public fame should have worked perfectly. That it did not do so, that their relationship was always troubled and suspicious, and that it ended finally in a rupture that made them both the losers was due not only to their differences of temperament but to a failure of functions.

Wells was, of course, a very difficult man, and Sir Frederick Macmillan was a very grand one in his professional circle. In 1903 good business sense prompted the acquisition of a writer of Wells's promise, but he then remained aloof, and this was not at all what Wells expected or desired. He wanted to be made much of – not petted and flattered, but to have his work worried over and discussed;

he wanted desperately to feel himself a part of the firm's industry. He could not get over the lack of animation and activity shown as he delivered the successive children of his brain to this disciplined machine. His outburst over *Kipps* is typical of the undercurrent of resentment he was feeling against such unemotional acceptance of his works. In publishing as in his sex-life, his search for the perfect partner had ended in disappointment. The response was not what he had dreamed of. He attributed to disdain what was really only distraction with larger affairs. Wells carried on his shoulder the chip of resentment about his origins. Macmillan was used to having his own way, and he was the dominating figure in this family firm and had many authors to deal with.

That Sir Frederick was not altogether blind to this need was shown by the attempts he made from time to time to show enthusiasm, but the efforts were short lived. Branches were being founded in India and Australia and Canada, while the branch in New York was establishing itself as a distinguished American company. This large enterprise was wholly directed by three men of a family; no one else was allowed a position of responsibility. Alexander Macmillan had taken on George Lillie Craik and had made him a part-ner, but the experiment, although it had lasted for some time, had not been a success, and it had not been repeated by the younger generation when they came to power. There was in fact no one with the time and the talent and the res-ponsibility to play the part of editor to a writer so danger-ously new and temperamentally so sensitive as Wells. The ideal publishing relationship in which the publisher sub-merges himself, his scholarship and experience in the author's mind and invention, bringing to the author's work the objective judgement of the critic and the true under-standing of an affectionate friend, was missing here, and the loss to both author and publisher was incalculable. *Ann Veronica* might have been published and its daring upheld and the *Spectator* outfaced, and *The New Machiavelli* might have been a better book, if this understanding had existed. It was a task none could have envied except those who are born for such work, for Wells was a difficult and dominating man. But if such an understanding had existed, how different his subsequent work might have been.

Tempers were frayed in those difficult days. Paper was scarce, its quality was poor and its price was rocketing. Aflame now with his new missionary fervour, overworked and overwrought with the war, Wells was 'touchy' to a point where the implication of a guarded enthusiasm in Sir Frederick's suggestion of a reduced advance determined him not to argue but to turn his back on this man with whom he had had such a long and troubled relationship. He brooded on the fancied insult and a few days later wrote again:

Dear Sir Frederick,
I think that on the whole it is better that you should not publish any more editions of any of my books. It is good neither for author nor publisher to have these dispersals of interest, and so I will assume that you release these cheap edition rights as they fall in. So use your paper to better purpose.
Very sincerely yours,
H. G. Wells

But time changed this view. When the war had ended and he had completed *The Outline of History*, which he thought of as a book for schools, he turned again to Macmillan with an offer of the book rights. Surprisingly, Macmillan refused it. In spite of this, Wells wanted Macmillan to keep on with the old books.

Dear Sir Frederick,
I would rather you kept on with those editions of the books you have at 6/–. We've differed at times, and failed to hit things off together, but I've always had a friendly feeling for you and Macmillan's, and it will be pleasant for me to see you going on with those books you've had so long . . .
I'm rather sorry you wouldn't look at the book edition of *The Outline of History*, which I suggested to your people some time

ago. Newnes & Co. will publish it in about 20–25 parts. In an
abridged form it ought to be a schoolbook before many years
have passed.

Yours ever,
H. G. Wells

A pleasant postscript to this long and difficult relationship
might be brought in at this point. In the middle of the
Second Great War, when Macmillans were celebrating their
centenary in the modest way imposed by paper rationing,
with a short history of the firm by Charles Morgan, the part
concerning Wells was sent to him for his approval. 'Yes,' he
replied, 'publish all this. It is a correspondence equally
creditable to both you and me.'

From 1917 on he began to concern himself more and more
with the world that was going to emerge from the eventual
peace treaties. He has given us in his autobiography an
exact account of his own absorption with the League
of Nations idea and his own profound disappointment and
distress when from the Treaty of Versailles there emerged
a truncated League, from which Russia and Germany were
excluded, and which was without military power to enforce
any sanctions it might have to bring against aggression.
His plans for a League of Free Nations had been bold and
far-reaching. Britain would have had to give up her Empire
and her navy, and become a republic. Every nation in the
world would have been admitted, and the League would in
effect have controlled the world's armed forces, and would
have been public trustee for the world. His first biographer,
Geoffrey West, tells us that Wells put forward as early as
May 1917 suggestions along these lines in a letter he hoped
The Times would publish. But *The Times*, understandably
enough, declined the letter on the grounds that it was altogether too revolutionary, as the proposal to dissolve the
British Empire and the Royal Navy indeed was.

Wells was a persistent man, particularly on the subject of
the World State. He was not to be put off by *The Times*'s

refusal to publicize his views. Early in 1918 when Lord Northcliffe was made Minister of Propaganda, he invited Wells to assist him as Director of Propaganda against Germany. It was an unequal partnership, a brilliant newspaper proprietor, whose mind was showing the first signs of being unbalanced, to be allied with a restless genius capable of sparking off original and powerful ideas often of an impractical nature, and with a built-in inaptitude for working with anyone else. Wells did not suffer civil servants, with their strong reliance on precedent and protocol, gladly, and he must have been intolerable to them. The appointment lasted only for a few months. In mid July he quarrelled with Northcliffe over the virulent anti-German campaign which Northcliffe's newspapers were carrying on, undermining the work of the Propaganda Ministry, which aimed at inducing the Germans to surrender, not at hardening their resistance by insult. He told Northcliffe that he must control his own papers and stop this fooling. Northcliffe refused to interfere with the direction of his newspapers, and Wells slammed out of the Ministry.

In his various discussions and committee work throughout the war he had been struck to find that his colleagues working for world peace and world unity were generally ignorant of the history of any country except their own, and usually that knowledge was biased by the determination of historians to put the best possible construction on the part their own countries had played in these events. His own lack of education, or rather that which he had achieved by cramming, had given him a sense of history as being one subject just as chemistry is one, which must be told as a whole before it can be dealt with in part; his more elaborately educated colleagues, educated in depth rather than in a wide sweep, possessed no such sense. He saw that it was hopeless for world peace-makers or world-staters of any kind to embark wholeheartedly on their plans unless they first had a comprehensive knowledge of world history. And as no book of that kind existed, Wells with his usual precipitance – like Mr Britling, whose actions were taken before his resolutions were fully formed – set about single-handed to provide one.

A year of immense, of terrible but exciting labour followed. Before he could tell it, he had to learn it, summarize it, trace the relationship of one part to another, see where it tended, illustrate, in short, why the world was in the condition that it was, and show what steps must be taken if the human race was not to destroy itself. Amazingly, he accomplished this without any assistance, though he arranged to have the chapters checked by experts as he wrote them. But this work of nearly three-quarters of a million words, tracing the history of the world from before the coming of man to the end of the First World War, was accomplished by one man in the course of a year, and stands as a monument to Wells's genius for absorbing and synthesizing knowledge, and to his capacity for sustaining long hours of work.

He intended it, as his letter to Sir Frederick Macmillan shows, as an educational work aimed at the schools. He did not intend to make money out of it, and before undertaking it he had weighed up his financial resources – much depleted by the war, though supplemented a bit by the extraordinary success of *Mr Britling*. But he was convinced that life was a race between education and catastrophe, and before getting down again to novel-writing he determined to take a year off for this task, just as at the beginning of the century he had determined to write *Anticipations* before beginning to write his serious novels. Before he could portray individual life, he had had to study for himself the environment in which life had to be lived, 'to study and state for my own satisfaction the social process in which we swim as fish swim in a flood of water'.* And now, before taking up life again after the war, he had to show how the world had reached its present dangerous state, and what the future held for humanity.

* 'Mr. Wells Explains Himself', *T.P.'s Magazine*, December 1911.

The result was altogether different from what even he, accustomed to be enthusiastic about the prospects for success of anything that he wrote, had expected. The schools ignored it, but the public swallowed it whole. More than 100,000 copies of each of the twenty-five serial parts were sold in England, and when it appeared in book form two million copies were sold in England and America. It was translated into nearly every language in the civilized world.

It had seemed when the war began that Wells had done his best work, and had just failed to reach the top rank. He, who had seemed to promise to be for the twentieth century what Dickens had been for the nineteenth, a novelist who made the life of his times come alive, had wandered off to become an argumentative debater. *Boon* had revealed the tortured spirit that inhabited uncomfortably this power-house of ideas and emotions. The artist was too often subdued, either by the raptures of the mythmaker or the energy of the engineer. Under the strain of these forces, gaps and weaknesses appeared. The moral force which makes the great artist was missing, and something that passed for it, Boonism, was not at all the same thing. But what veins of ore there were in this rich mine. When one ran out, another could be tapped. Wells was still perhaps the most famous and successful writer in the world. But a new age was opening up, and although it shaped much as he had forecast and his one world was to come nearer to realization than it had ever done before, he was not to see it. The last unhappy years were about to begin just as he scored his greatest success.

16

The Outline of
History; Breakdown

If in 1901 *Anticipations* had not caught the imagination as it did, Wells might have remained at Sandgate and followed the career of a successful literary novelist to which he had dedicated himself when he built Spade House. Flattered by the Webbs into throwing in his lot with the Fabians, he had succumbed to the heady atmosphere of social and political discussion generated by his contact with his new Fabian friends, and speculative books took precedence over novels. *Kipps*, started in 1901, did not appear until the end of 1905, elbowed out of the way by *Mankind in the Making* and *A Modern Utopia*.

Similarly, if *The Outline of History*, begun as no more than an educational work to be issued in parts, and intended to seize the opportunity of the post-war reconstruction period to reconsider the teaching of history, had not had the outstanding success it did, he might have regained his position as the leading novelist of the age.

But what made *The Outline* a success with the public – its bold and brilliant generalizations, its wide sweep, its command of detail – were the very things that got it into trouble with the specialists and the traditionalists. Not surprisingly, in a work so large, offering such an extensive view of the history of mankind from his very beginnings on earth to the end of the Great War, there were bound to be gaps, misjudgements, and misproportions, which the specialists rushed in to point out and condemn; and with an author of such definite opinions as Wells, there were also bound to be here and there intolerant passages and Philistine assumptions which laid the great work open to attack in some of its particulars. No single man had ever attempted a history on this scale before, perhaps no one will ever do so again. Although he had had the help of many specialists in checking his materials, he had reserved the right to maintain his own judgements, and *The Outline of History* was pure Wells, prejudices and brilliant insights, superficial judgements and intellectual depths all mixed up by no hand other than his.

The most brilliant and lively of his critics was Hilaire Belloc, with whom he had been arguing, as he had with Shaw and Chesterton, these many years. Belloc's own work was prejudiced enough, but he was a master of debate, and in defending the Catholic Church against Wells's summary judgement of its history and influence, he was clearly in his element. And so, it may be said, was Wells. Their debate flowered into books: Belloc issued *A Companion to Mr Wells's Outline of History*, and Wells replied with *Mr Belloc Objects*. The controversy is amusing to re-read now – they were foemen worthy of each other's steel – but it gets nowhere, and illustrates not much more than the tenacity with which each of them held his views and the agility with which they danced round one another. It is of interest only because answering Belloc demanded more time and close attention than did the criticisms of some of his other adversaries, sustaining the point that the shattering, worldwide success of *The Ouline of History* distracted Wells from his proper task of writing novels just at the moment when new men were coming up and new voices were being listened to.

The novelist in Wells, in fact, went to sleep between *Mr Britling* in 1916 and *The World of William Clissold* in 1926. The novels that appeared between were mostly argumentative pieces done up as fiction, like *The Soul of a Bishop* (1917), reflecting the dying glow of his religious phase; *The Undying Fire* (1919), which, splendid piece of writing though it is, is not really a novel but, by his own admission, a dialogue; *The Secret Places of the Heart* (1922), the most boring novel he ever wrote and really only a travelogue of southern England, spattered with some well-worn intellectual ideas; _Men Like Gods_ (1923), a return to Utopia in which contemporary figures like Churchill, Balfour and others play recognizable parts; and _The Dream_ (1924), which also has a Utopian theme. The one other novel written in this period, _Christina Alberta's Father_ (1925), is by far the best of the batch, perhaps because it had living models for both Christina Alberta and her father, Mr Preemby, and perhaps because Christina Alberta is Ann Veronica brought up to date, and Mr Preemby, in his fight to maintain his individuality, is a relief after so many Wellsian heroes who were intent on losing theirs in self-surrender to some higher cause.

If _The Outline_ had not been the success it was, we might never have seen the other two great encyclopedias, _The Science of Life_ and _The Work, Wealth and Happiness of Mankind_. But we might have supported their loss if some novels over which he could have taken time had come in their place. As it was, the novels of this period were all Thinker's novels. Lytton Strachey is quoted by Michael Holroyd as saying: 'I ceased to think about Wells when he became a Thinker.' Wells might have replied that he was writing not for Strachey but for the new public emerging from the war who had missed some precious years of enlightenment and had to rebuild from a shattered world a new human order.

Some people _were_ thinking about the problems with which his novels dealt. But the prevailing public mood was one of relief that the dark years were over. The general belief was that there would never be another war; the common desire was to forget the past, to leave it to the statesmen to ensure that the old enemy and his threats were cut off from the chance of ever creating havoc again. The immediate anxieties were economic ones, the problem being to adapt oneself to life again; not how to order life, but how to come to terms with it. New voices were sounding, and they had a dry ironic note conspicuously absent from the robust humour and the rhetorical earnestness of the pre-war writers and world-builders of whom Wells had been the leader. A new public was coming up in 1920, as new to these times as the one to which Wells's early appeal had been addressed in 1895 had been to theirs. In the drawing-rooms and on the library shelves the books one saw opened now were those by young Aldous Huxley; the stories that held people were the thin, neat explicit ones by Somerset Maugham. Sex had got out of the pages of daring novels and into the bed of the common man, and woman's independence was taken for granted.

Yet, paradoxically, Wells's fame was greater than it had ever been. Until Gissing took him to Rome in 1898, he had not even crossed the English Channel. Until he started visiting France and Germany and Switzerland just before the war, he had known nothing of Europe. Now he had become a world figure.

One has to keep reminding oneself of his immense reputation in those years when, before the coming of broadcasting and television brought us the doubtful blessing of having great occasions and the figures who are making history brought 'live' before us, an individual commentator could light up the stage and explain the play to us. Wells was one of the earliest visitors to Russia after the Revolution. He went to America at the invitation of the *New York World* to write on the Washington Disarmament Conference. He was paid an immense inclusive fee for the world syndication rights of his articles. The afflictions of a high-pitched squeaky voice and an unfamiliar accent did not distract the readers of his articles. Wells made it all clear with the wonderful gift he had of direct communication. Of course, his account was slanted, but millions read him and quoted him to each other. Geoffrey West reports that the serialization of Wells's Russian articles added 80,000 copies weekly to the sales of the *Sunday Express*, which had the British serial rights. He was a world figure with a world audience. The few hundreds of younger Fabians, his first enraptured audience, had some of them defied parents and left home, fired by the vision of freedom he had conjured up for them. His audience, now numbered in millions, were spectators of the play, not the enthusiastic disciples of yore.

He could not only report what the great ones thought, but argue with them as to whether what they thought was right. They were ready to explain themselves and their philosophy seriously to him, knowing that his report of what they said would be read all over the world. He was invited to address the German Reichstag. He was invited on to the platform of innumerable meetings in London, and he yielded to the temptation and accepted, taking out evenings to rush about delivering his views, while his study remained darkened and his pen lay unused.

That Wells enjoyed all this activity, we cannot doubt. But he was under great strain, his public life led to public quarrels, and in the feverish atmosphere of reconstruction he was spending too much time on public affairs.

How can a man write novels and plan the reconstruction of the world at the same time? It must be admitted that what was happening offered a wonderful opportunity for that Open Conspiracy to step in and clean up the tangle of international rivalries which had brought about the disastrous war. In the years from 1920 to 1924 a Peace Treaty was being hammered out, a League of Nations to enforce peace was under design. Russia and Germany and Central Europe were in collapse, and world revolution threatened unless the repair of the shattered world was skilfully done. It was not the time for a man like Wells, who had had burning ideas of social reconstruction in his mind all these years, to sit in his library weaving fiction.

Towards the end of September 1920, accompanied by his eldest son, he paid a fifteen-day visit to Russia. On this visit he spent most of his time in Petrograd, where his old friend Maxim Gorki acted as his host. To his surprise and pleasure, he found living in Gorki's large apartment the young Marie von Benckendorff whom he had met in St Petersburg when he had been there with Maurice Baring in 1914. Her husband at that time had been attached to the Russian Embassy in Berlin, and they had been home on a visit on that evening when he and Maurice Baring had attended a party at the home of Benckendorff's relatives. With his eye for beauty and intelligence in combination, H.G. had been immediately attracted to this dark-eyed young girl who spoke English fluently and had been at Cambridge for a year before her marriage when Count von Benckendorff had been at the Russian Embassy in London. The Benckendorffs were a family with a long tradition of service in the Russian diplomatic corps.

This girl, Marie Zakrevskaia, was the daughter of a Russian Senator and large landowner in the Ukraine. She had been brought up in aristocratic circles in St Petersburg, spending only the summers on the family estate in the Ukraine, and married Benckendorff, a friend of her brothers in the Petersburg Lycée, in 1911.

Encountered again after the years of war and revolution, she seemed as strikingly beautiful in her drab revolutionary clothes as she had appeared in her fashionable dress in 1914. She had lost everything in the upheaval that followed the Bolshevik seizure of power, and owed her survival to the protection which Maxim Gorki was able to give her. Her husband, an officer in the army at the time of the revolution, had been shot by the Bolsheviks on his own estates in Esthonia. She had been able at the start of the 1917 revolution to smuggle her children through to the Baltic estate, where they were guarded by the English governess who had taught her her first words of English. But a later attempt to escape herself had ended in a prison sentence. Gorki, whose influence at that time was great, had rescued her from the cell in which she had been crowded with more than a score of other women prisoners. Her knowledge of languages – she spoke perfect German and French as well as English – made her an invaluable assistant to him in the work he had undertaken of making the world's classics available in Russian, and this enabled her to have a ration card and an identity.

This beautiful and sparkling girl, whom Wells remembered wearing jewels and an evening gown in the great drawing-room of the Benckendorff St Petersburg home, stood before him now in the single drab dress remaining to her. Not yet thirty, she had lost everything except her beauty and grace, and her courage before the menace which life now offered. She acted as interpreter in the long and earnest conversations H.G. had with Gorki every night during his visit, and she guided him about the city during the day. The populous streets he remembered from 1914 were empty now except for wary figures moving along in the shadows like ghosts. The talks with Gorki were immensely stimulating to him. The two men had come up the same way from humble beginnings to positions of great eminence as literary sages. They had the same interests and the same tastes, and the interpreter who made their long discussions about the future of the world clear to each was this girl brought up in a luxury neither of them had ever known, except from a distance, in their youth.

Wells was a famous man even in this starving, fearful land of revolutionary Russia of 1920 immersed in its own troubles. On 7 October he was invited to address the Petrograd Soviet in the same great chamber where he had seen the Duma meet on his visit in 1914. Through Gorki's introduction, he made the journey to Moscow to see Lenin. Wells was all seriousness, questioning Lenin closely about the present mentality on which he must rebuild this shattered nation. But Lenin discoursed on practical notions about restoring the economy through electrifying industry as province after province of this vast empire came under Bolshevik control, and did not show much interest in theoretical ideas about education. Trotsky, in his life of Lenin, records that Lenin afterwards dismissed Wells as 'What a Bourgeois he is! He is a Philistine! Ah, what a Philistine!'

But Wells thought they parted warmly, and he returned to London convinced that the Bolsheviks were the only party through which Russia could be saved from collapse. This was the view he put forward in *Russia in the Shadows*, the series of newspaper articles he wrote on his return, subsequently published as a book.

Returning, he threw himself into the preparation of a series of lectures he had undertaken to give in the United States in December and January. He intended in these to sound the alarm, to tell his listeners that another European collapse was inevitable unless a just settlement was made, and to press the point that a World State, not a reformed League of Nations, was the only answer. But shortly before he was to leave, he developed congestion of the lungs, and the lectures were cancelled. He went south to recuperate, and to fume over the mess into which the world was blindly drifting.

17

Clissold and the
Open Conspiracy

A COMBINATION of nervous exhaustion through overwork and an overwhelming unhappiness in his private life brought about in 1924 a temporary breakdown. He disappeared from the London scene, settling in Provence, where he established a winter home – somehow an unlikely background for one who had never really shed his cockneyism. But there were sound reasons of health for preferring the sunshine and the pine-scented air of southern France to the smoke of London. His lung trouble still dogged him.

Besides, London agitated him, and this had its effect on his health. Since the war he had been constantly engaged in public controversy. The League of Nations, as finally constituted by the victorious powers, was not a World League. It excluded Germany, Austria, Russia and what remained of the Turkish Empire, and the United States soon excluded itself when in 1919 and 1920, by massive votes, the Senate refused to ratify the Treaty into which the design of the League of Nations, at President Wilson's insistence, had been woven as an integral part. The Peace was being botched. The grand design of an ultimate world sovereignty had become, in a phrase Wells later used, 'homunculus in a bottle, trying to set up the reign of God on earth'.

By 1924 nationalism was already rearing its ugly head in Germany, nourishing itself on the instinct for revenge, betraying itself in incidents like the Munich Putsch in 1923 in which Adolf Hitler first came to prominence, allied with General Ludendorff, and in ominous if petty gestures like the refusal of the German Embassy in Washington to lower its flag on the death of President Wilson in 1924. The war was not over, it only smouldered.

These political developments, all working against the conception of an ultimate World State, agitated him extremely. A world federation of nations was the only answer if the horror of the last war was not to be repeated on a vaster scale. It was a race between education and disaster. Men had to be made aware of their predicament before they would accept the surrender of their native pride. Slow and steady methods had never been to Wells's taste. 'I am extremely obsessed by the thing that might be and impatient with the present. I want to go ahead of Father Time with a scythe of my own.' *

With the break-up in 1922 of Lloyd George's Coalition Government which had ruled Britain since the end of 1916, he thought he saw in the Labour party such a chance. He was not alone in thinking that in it lay the only hope for the future, and he adopted it with the same vehemence he had shown when he joined the Fabians in 1903, even proposing to give up writing fiction and to write in future only about Labour politics. He was the Labour candidate for London University at the General Elections of November 1922 and December 1923, but on each occasion came at the bottom of the poll, although in the first election the Labour party nearly doubled its vote in the country, and in the second came to power for the first time. He had no gift for practical politics. The first Labour Government under Ramsay MacDonald survived only with Liberal support, which effectively ruled out the possibility of introducing a socialist programme, and instead of supporting it H.G. proceeded to attack it on some issues with the same vigour with which he had attacked the Fabians when they rejected him.

He was wearing himself out with these affairs. The newspaper articles in which he defended his views multiplied. On great occasions such as the Washington Disarmament

*Introduction to *The Book of Catherine Wells*.

Conference of 1921–2, he was paid a huge sum by a newspaper syndicate to report the proceedings. Somehow in all this activity he found time to write a novel each year. *The Secret Place of the Heart*, *Men Like Gods* and *The Dream* were written between 1920 and 1923.

But it was as a prophet, not as a novelist, that he was most in demand and his views on what was happening were printed not in one paper but in a hundred, and not in one country but all over the world. That he took himself as seriously in this regard as did his immense public is apparent from the tone of the articles, and from the title – *A Year of Prophesying* – which he gave to the book-form reprint of them. Prophecy had become a vocation with him, a false vocation because he was misusing the creative artist's instinct to shape character and event into some sort of order to propound political solutions which it is beyond the power of the artist to influence. The voice of the novelist telling of life and urging its improvement was gradually being drowned in the shrill tones of the scold. A world-wide audience offered him a respectful hearing, but their lives were not altered one whit by what he wrote, so that there was a dry ashes-in-the-mouth taste to the success so achieved, the brightness of vision thrown away, only the despair retained. Meanwhile his novels were showing a diminishing zest, a poverty of invention as well as a tiredness of phraseology, the more striking if we compare a few pages of one of them with a few drawn at random from any of the novels written before 1910.

As the events of the first years of the Peace mocked the high hopes of his blueprint for the future, a mental depression set in. Was all this work, these millions of words he had poured out, worth it if it left untouched human minds? There were moments when he fancied himself like Roger Bacon, confined to a prison cell for his propositions that then had seemed heretical, scribbling away at long dissertations on a new method of knowledge which in the course of a few centuries were to come to the fullest fruition.

I play at being such a man as he was, a man altogether lonely and immediately futile, a man lit by a vision of a world still some centuries ahead, convinced of its reality and urgency, and yet powerless to bring it nearer. [*Experiment in Autobiography*]

Contributing to his sense of growing despair at this time was almost certainly the depression of spirits caused by the ending of his association with Rebecca West. They were to remain close friends, but the shared life, with all its difficulties and strains, and with all its rapture – the relationship which had been to him the most profoundly satisfying of his life – was ending. Only someone like H. G. could have expected it to continue indefinitely as it had begun. Here was no ignorant girl like Isabel, unable to share his mental excitements, or submissive shadow like Jane, responding tactfully to his every mood, keeping home and family together and providing a stable background to his tempestuous life. Here instead was someone who had her own independent views and her own ambitions and was still only in her twenties when the war ended. She had had to put aside her career and manage a home in a compromised situation which must often have been difficult for someone as proud and sensitive as she was. There were rewards and periods of great happiness – glimpses of them are movingly recalled in William Clissold's remorseful memories of his shared past with Helen – but at the root there was the profound disequilibrium in his character which had been responsible for all the upsets in his stormy life. The dreamer, the visionary, who could plan like an engineer a structure for human life that would bring the greatest happiness and achievement to the race, could not control his own life. Two instincts were at constant war within him: the sexual instinct to dominate, the constructive one to tidy up the disorders that make life so wretched when it promised to be so fine. Pain came of this constant conflict, not only to him but to those who were involved in his life, and in his unhappier moments he knew this, but could not prevent it. He could only offer the defence that the moral jigsaw puzzles which torture so many people were not for them – for him and his mistresses. William Clissold is writing, but it is William Clissold going over a past that is recognizedly that of Wells:

> Neither Helen nor I need to be pitied as those others who are weaker and less coherent are to be pitied; both of us have something in us that sustains us and at last takes us out of all such distresses. At an early limit we grow exasperated, damn the jig-saw puzzle, and sweep it out of the way. The jigsaw puzzle is not a primary thing with us. We are more wilful and more strongly individualized than the common run of people. I have my philosophy of life, my faith, my religion, and she has the compelling impulse of her art.

This disposition to excuse individual disorder where exceptional brains or fine spirits are involved was at the root of all H.G.'s frustration as an artist, and can be read into every important turn in his life, from running away from his first marriage to the sexual adventures he allowed himself outside his second one. Nowhere is it more clearly apparent than in the break-up of this partnership with someone whom he deeply loved and unreservedly admired, and in whose company he had known some of the happiest and most stimulating hours of his life. For it to continue demanded an acceptance on her part of only half his attention, and a submission to him which her pride – the very quality in her which he had most admired – resolutely refused to accept.

She was determined to be a writer and make her own career. Her *Henry James* had shown her probing critical mind at work. In 1920 she published her first novel, *The Return of the Soldier*, which was singled out as among the best novels of the year in the short list of artistic achievements of all kinds in Great Britain offered by the Annual Register. In 1922 she published a much larger work, *The Judge*, which established beyond question the emergence of a new writer in the great tradition of the English novel. Here was someone steadily devoting herself to the art of the novel, who regarded with a less than enthusiastic eye Wells's frenzied public activities in the years following the war, who had been prepared to marry him in the first year or two of their affair, but saw now that this would not happen – at the best she would be fitted into some arrangement that suited his convenience under some high-sounding precept which would sweep aside the moral jigsaw puzzle that kept less gifted people hesitant before a similar adventure.

She had found herself in an unfortunate position, not of the kind that might have been deduced. She felt it unfair that when Jane Wells had long assured her husband that he could have what love-affairs he liked, Jane's friends often treated her as if she had inflicted injury on a wife who had till her advent been enjoying a conventionally happy marriage. The situation seemed to Rebecca of an increasing dishonesty, though – it is important to remark this – her complaint was not against Jane but against Jane's friends. Three of these, a famous novelist, a less famous novelist, and a dramatist, were especially mischievous. She often felt, as she afterwards described it, as 'if I were back at the R.A.D.A.' It happened that one year Rebecca had a bad haemorrhage which meant that she had to be checked for tuberculosis, and though the reports were negative, she was advised to spend the winter abroad. She left her son at school and went out to a southern country, accepting an invitation to stay with a woman with whom she had recently become friendly, the fascinating wife of a charming husband who was obliged to go somewhere else in the world to attend to some business. It was understood she would stay some weeks with this woman friend and then go on to stay in a town where she had a number of friends.

Once she reached the woman's house she found she could not leave it, for the woman became ill. The house was in a lonely spot and the responsibility of looking after a sick person there was grave. Rebecca realized the husband could not come to look after his wife, for a number of reasons; but she wrote to members of the wife's family, explaining she could not go on looking after her hostess. But she never got any reply. Three months passed and she was still there, and her hostess, who had become irritable and exacting through her illness, would not send for help or even employ a professional nurse, and informed Rebecca it was her duty to stay with her. Then Rebecca had one of her haemorrhages, and a very bad one; and saw that the doctor who came to the house suspected her of having lung tuberculosis and she ran some danger of finding herself in a provincial hospital in a foreign country. And this was in the twenties. After she had a disquieting conversation with the doctor, she had an equally disquieting conversation with her hostess, and resolved that the situation must be brought to an end. Greatly distressed, she left the house, went to an English neighbour and told her that from now on the neighbours must take charge, as she must go away and rest.

When she came back to London, she found she was the central figure in a notorious scandal. It was being said by this group of Jane's friends that her hostess had turned her out of the house in the middle of the night because she had found her guest in bed with her husband – her husband who had never been within a thousand miles of the place throughout Rebecca's entire visit. When she complained of this scandal-mongering to Wells, she said, 'It is this sort of thing that is going to break us up', and he answered, 'You make too much of it.' To which she replied, 'I couldn't make too much of it. It is too much.'

There were many other sources of trouble between them: chief among them the physical restlessness which grew on him as the years passed. He became more and more incapable of any calm and economical disposal of his time. He sped like a bullet between Easton Glebe, his flat in Whitehall Court and Rebecca's flat or summer cottage, often arriving on edge from sheer fatigue, insisting on her breaking an engagement or putting down her manuscript if he needed talk or a meal. He also worried her by his fecklessness about money, his wild extravagance, which alternated with ill-judged retrenchments; and her concern was proven as justified by the small size of his estate on his death, long after, following years of heavy earnings. Finally, H.G. committed an indiscretion – it was no more – which gave an eccentric stranger the power to start a scandal which might well have ruined H.G. and done nearly as much damage to Rebecca, who suddenly found herself faced with a situation for which she had no grain of responsibility. She went to a friend of hers who had power in a certain field which enabled him to suppress the story. After a month or two of reflection she decided not to be a prisoner in this lunatic world any longer, and she brought the relationship to an end. But after a few years of alienation the friendship began again and continued until H.G.'s death.

That the rupture of this relationship at this particular time tore at him fiercely, there can be no doubt. Tiredness, ill-health, frustration at the increasing evidence that the New Republic was as far off as ever in a world in which national sovereignty was re-establishing its hold on the ruins of the war added to his mood of despair. But in the past he would have bounced back and fought even more fiercely for his objective. Now for the first time he seemed to throw in the sponge; surrendering to that impulse to flight which had attacked him several times in the past, he left London for a journey round the world which might take a year. He could not resist looking in at the League of Nations at work in Geneva. Then he went to Paris, where he spent several weeks, and it was here that, with the customary tendency to dramatize his own experiences, the figure of William Clissold took shape in his mind. Instead of continuing on his planned journey, he went down to the sunshine of the South of France and, after a little time of wandering about there, took a furnished villa, Lou Bastidon, in Provence. Liking the climate, and finding it a good place to work, he stayed there for three winters, coming home to

Easton Glebe only for the summers. His first attempt to write a major novel again was the first fruits of his life there. *The World of William Clissold* is a lengthy novel – it appeared on publication in 1926 in three volumes – and was intended to be a summing-up of his life's work and ideas. And thereby its fate was foredoomed. That intention meant that the philosophy of William Clissold, who appears as a retired industrialist living in the South of France, would be made perfectly clear, and would unmistakeably be Wells's philosophy, William Clissold himself being simply a mouthpiece, a figure decked out with a few mannerisms and a background with the brusque efficiency with which Wells now tended to attack these fictional formalities before getting down to the real business of the book, that of introducing us to the character's reflections.

He himself felt that he was turning over a new leaf in his life. He was turning to the novel again after experiencing a great personal unhappiness and an equally painful disillusionment in the progress he had hoped for in his absorbing plans for the reconstruction of the world. He meant it not to be a novel in what had become for him the outmoded style of the fictional portrayal of character and incident illustrating some individual problem or parodying some accepted situation. It was to be an attempt to present a thesis upon contemporary life and social development, and it was to take the form of a fictitious autobiography.

Wells has some very interesting things to say in *Experiment in Autobiography* about his approach to the particular narrative form of *The World of William Clissold*. He believed that he was experimenting with a new form, the novel which is an autobiography in which only the names of the characters are fictitious, and the events dealt with and the characters' reactions to them are those that lie in the forefront of everyone's mind – namely, how to clear up the disorder that clutters up life. William Clissold, like Trafford in *Marriage*, like Lewisham – like the picture he must often have entertained of himself as H. G. Wells,

Esq. B. Sc. – is a scientist who has been forced by circumstances to give up pure research for commerce, has made a fortune, and grown bored with life. Trafford went off to Labrador to think things over; Clissold goes to the South of France, and there ruminates on his past life, as he endeavours to find the answer to the puzzle as to what the intelligent man with a strong constructive impulse should do to recondition the world obviously desperately in need of some such attention.

The book is four parts autobiography to one part prescription, with merely a disdainful skein of fiction thrown over it to justify describing it as a novel. Clissold finds his retreat in Provence, as Wells did; Clissold has as his companion there Clementine, who had her original in Odette Keun, who for a few years shared Wells's life there and acted as a stabilizing influence at a time of great unrest for him. Clissold remembers in the tranquility of this retreat the love affairs that had shone earlier in his life, and these have their unmistakable parallels in Wells's life. There was nothing new in this; new only is the intensification into emphatic statement of the idea implicit in his earlier novels, that the relationship between sex and the question 'What shall I do with my life' is not accidental but essential; the brush of two personalities one against the other effects a sensitized meeting-place where may be sorted out the moral jigsaw puzzles in which every individual life is entangled, a necessary prerequisite to a solution of the problem which keeps humanity at war and apart.

Clissold's solution of the larger human problem is the association of modern industry, with its scientific power, and world finance, which controls the arterial supply of credit: the people who have control in these affairs can change the conditions of human life constructively; such men are the actual revolutionaries of the world. It is Clissold's idea that they can cooperate to build up a monetary and economic world republic, openly and before all the world. He calls this the Open Conspiracy, and it represents one more attempt, nearly the last, to establish the New Republic of mankind. As a novel it was a failure. The ideas in it, perfectly sensible as ideas, never caught on; indeed, they suffered the awful fate of the pretentious which fails to impress: they were laughed at. Clissoldism became a term to evoke sniggers, conjuring up a busybody with a blueprint fussing about the necessity for improvement on a familiar design that, while not ideal, was perfectly comfortable.

The sense of failure must have been extreme and painful to Wells. *The World of William Clissold* was published in 1926 with a great fanfare of publicity, the three volumes appearing in consecutive months, and announced by its publishers as a summing-up of Wells's life's work and ideas. The critical comment was almost wholly unfavourable both to its central idea and to the book as a novel. However much he was chagrined by its reception, he was as obstinately determined to press home this attack as he had been to establish the new working arrangement with God after Mr Britling's discovery of Him. Just as *God the Invisible King*, a key to the new scriptures, had followed *Mr Britling*, so *The Open Conspiracy*, a working manual to the general scheme, followed *William Clissold*.

But two years were to pass before it was published. At this point there came a tragic break in his life with Jane's sudden illness and death. She had accompanied him to Paris in March 1927, when he had been invited to lecture at the Sorbonne,* and they had been greatly feted and entertained. They returned to England, unaware that the killing disease had already begun its attack on Jane. He was no longer happy at Easton Glebe and could not work there, and it was not long before he was off to France again. But soon he was recalled by the shocking news that Jane had inoperable cancer and had only a few weeks to live.

He has told the story of their last months together in the preface he wrote to a collection of the few unfinished manuscripts on which she had worked from time to time. None

Democracy Under Revision, Hogarth Press, 1927.

had been published; now he published them under the title *The Book of Catherine Wells*. His preface goes as far as we need to follow in understanding what troubled these two lives and yet held them together for over thirty years. He had always been able to 'explain' things, give self-indulgent courses the look of having been prompted by a higher wisdom. She could not explain things. Instinct told her what was right. His brain moved with the speed of light, a darting, diving thing that soared and swept like the flight of a bird. She fell back on simpler, steadier views while he wove fantastic arabesques of ideas that only afterwards were seen to have taken her assent for granted.

Remorsefully, he sets her steadiness against his erratic tendencies. One thing she seemed to be free of: the mental and physical torment of unassuaged physical desire. H.G. could not have stood it for five days. She stood it for years, hiding what might have been a natural delicacy or a deep reserve behind an air of nervous efficiency which at times maddened him. In his novels she had had to play unsympathetic parts, like Margaret Remington in *The New Machiavelli*, or Mrs Britling. He could not help his conduct, nor she hers. At the heart of their problem was the physical dilemma that plagues so many marriages, where mutual respect and warm but unsexual affection come to cover up the cavernous echo at the basis of the relationship.

Without any question, she had been the most important influence in his life. She had shaped him as no one else had done. He had always been the one who dominated a relationship; but Jane dominated him. Not his mind, but his passions; she was always to be present in spirit even when his behaviour seemed most abandoned. She was the sheet-anchor of his life. She was his conscience and honour, and it is not surprising that both Richard Remington and Mr Britling, erring and driven by something they could not deny, used these same terms when they cried out about their wives.

Her body was cremated at Golders Green. Shaw, an early

advocate of cremation, persuaded Wells that he should watch the actual cremation.

Three years after her death, he sold Easton Glebe – the home which she had made, which was redolent with memories of her – and went to live by Regent's Park, where, nearly twenty years later, death came to him.

The years until then were curious ones. They were not really happy, but they were not unhappy. I got the impression on the occasions on which I met him of a jolly man, still capable of enjoying the good things of life, and very much alive in his mind, certainly not one sunk in melancholy for a vanished past, or morbid with a conviction of the worst hanging suspended in the future. Just a rather round, pink little man with attractive blue eyes, responding sparklingly, if shrilly, to the babel of talk that was nearly always the background to our meetings. I had an intermittent feeling that there was something of the poseur about him, but I suppose all great men who have been long in the public eye adopt attitudes which are expected of them. It takes the eye of a child to see that the Emperor is not wearing clothes. I don't mean by this that he no longer believed in what he was saying. He believed, but I had the fleeting feeling from time to time that he enjoyed the uses of his great authority and reputation, and could no longer have retired to his study to write steadily; he needed contact with the world.

He was oppressed by the thought of the renewal of war, which he saw as inevitable, the more deeply because it might so easily have been avoided if his prescription had been taken. He still wrote with great facility, producing the amazing number of thirty-nine books in the twenty years between Jane's death and his own. He travelled widely, he made speeches, wrote articles, appeared on platforms, interviewed Stalin in Russia and Roosevelt in America, engaged in controversy, dined and laughed with his friends, and made love with the same vigour he had done in all the years so long ago. Some of the novels – *Mr Blettsworthy on*

Rampole Island, The Autocracy of Mr Parham, The Bulpington of Blup, Apropos of Dolores, You Can't Be Too Careful – sparkle with the genuine touch of Wells's genius, lightly ironic but strongly imaginative; not a sign in him of age or weariness yet.

[18]

Stalin and the Shape
of Things to Come

I TOOK it into my head in the Spring of 1934 to see and compare President Franklin Roosevelt and Mr Stalin. I wanted to form an opinion of just how much these two brains were working in my direction of this Socialist World State that I believe to be the only hopeful destiny for mankind.*

It is difficult to think of another writer who could have expressed such a desire and have had it immediately gratified, especially as his declared purpose was to compare Roosevelt's New Deal and Stalin's Five-Year Plan with his own New Republic, and to judge whether these two rulers of opinion were working along the right lines.

He had in mind a more ambitious plan still, not only to estimate the effectiveness of these contrasting programmes of reconstruction, but to persuade these two leaders that both were working for the same end, the emancipation of man from the tyranny of want, and that the process might be expedited if each great nation surrendered a little of its nationalistic character. He was also anxious to press on them his own conviction that a revolution could not succeed in the new technological world unless directed by a trained intelligentsia. Roosevelt's 'Brains Trust' signified the right approach, but its members had no political power, only the status of advisers. The Politburo was not technological enough. What was needed was a Competent Receiver; in the modern world, men who understood science and organization.

The Open Conspiracy of William Clissold was aimed at this ideal. It had made little appeal in the boom year of

*Experiments in Autobiography, p. 870.

1926, but *The Shape of Things to Come* in 1933 had fallen on more receptive ground, and the advocate of the Open Conspiracy had no difficulty in getting these important men to stop in the midst of their terrific labour and explain and defend their programmes to an inquirer backed with the authority of public interest.

President and Mrs Roosevelt entertained him privately to dinner; the interview with Stalin at the Kremlin lasted three hours. The President evidently spoke with frankness but without revealing anything that was not generally known about the New Deal. All Wells could do, and he does it effectively, is to give us a picture of this revolutionary figure, and to do it with that combination of clarity and depth which distinguishes a Karsh photograph of a celebrity from others more superficial. The conclusion Wells comes to is the very opposite of one he had advanced in an article in *Liberty Magazine* six months earlier, in which he had given his reasons for predicting Roosevelt's overthrow. After this exchange of ideas, he sees in Roosevelt's policy something that might eventually lead to the Open Conspiracy, and he records his admiration for Roosevelt's skill in bringing about a revolution in American thought without provoking a revolutionary crisis.

Stalin proved an altogether more difficult customer. Wells had interviewed Lenin and had been greatly impressed with him, although Lenin had not returned that compliment. Lenin had talked about electricity and had been hard to pin down to revolutionary concepts. His successor clearly loved argument, was surprisingly well read, and was prepared to talk indefinitely about the goal of world socialism, and how it should be reached. By the revolutionary seizure of power in the name of the people? Or – Wells's view – by the appointment of a Competent Receiver? And as to a planned economy, which after the war and the world financial collapse everyone now agreed to be essential, how should it be directed? By the state, of course. But acting through the capitalist system – Roosevelt's method; by a

trained intelligentsia with political power – Well's recipe;
or by the abolition of the capitalist system, and with it the
whole principle of private property in the means of production, and the vesting of all property in the state, the
Russian system?

Stalin is an able debater; he has just the right derogatory
inflection, evidently, for what he calls 'Anglo-Saxon
Socialism' as exhibited in Roosevelt's actions on coming to
power. Stalin's simple doctrine is that the capitalist class in
the West owns the means of production, the banks, the
factories, the mines, transport. Opposed to this propertied
class there is only the proletariat, who live by selling their
labour to the capitalists. Even the President is there at the
will of the propertied class.

'I have some experience in fighting for Socialism', says
Stalin modestly, 'and this experience tells me that if Roosevelt makes a real attempt to satisfy the interests of the
proletarian class at the expense of the capitalist class, the
latter will put another President in his place.' As for Wells's
'technical intelligentsia', Stalin has had experience of them
too. Stalin's tone, which has been jocular and ironic so far,
takes on a cutting edge, audible to the imagination of the
reader of this 'Conversation', as he recalls the attempts of
this section of the population after the October Revolution.

We Soviet people have not a little experience of the technical
intelligentsia. After the October Revolution, a certain section of
the technical intelligentsia refused to take part in the work of
constructing the new society; they opposed this work of construction and sabotaged it. ... Not a little time passed before
our trained intelligentsia agreed actively to assist the new
system.

The technical intelligentsia are all very well, he goes on
to say, and they can help, but *political* power is necessary to
transform the world, and to seize political power a great
class, not a minority, is required. 'Big ships go on long
voyages' is his way of putting it.

Wells: Yes, but for long voyages a captain and a navigator are required.

Stalin: That is true, but what is first required for a long voyage is a big ship. What is a navigator without a ship? An idle man.

Wells: The big ship is humanity, not a class.

Stalin: You, Mr Wells, evidently start out with the assumption that all men are good. I, however, do not forget that there are many wicked men. I do not believe in the goodness of the bourgeoisie.

From this they go on to a discussion of the revolutionary method as exemplified by events in history. Wells makes the point ably that communist class-war propaganda is out of date, that the technical intelligentsia is now no more a small class but composed of intellectuals from every class; and he makes a telling point that revolutions are made not by the masses rising in protest, but by a minority seeking power.

Wells: I watch Communist propaganda in the West, and it seems to me that in modern conditions this propaganda sounds very old-fashioned because it is insurrectionary propaganda in favour of the violent overthrow of the social system. This was all very well when it was directed against tyranny. But under modern conditions, when the system is collapsing anyhow, stress should be laid on efficiency, on competence, on productivity, and not on insurrection. It seems to me that the insurrectionary note is obsolete. The Communist propaganda in the West is a nuisance to constructive-minded people.

Stalin replies that the order is indeed breaking down, but violent efforts are being made to preserve it, and he instances fascism, which is trying to preserve the old world with violence. The communists do not want to be caught napping; that is why they say to the working-class: 'Answer violence with violence; do all you can to prevent the old dying order from crushing you, do not permit it to put manacles on your hands, on the hands with which you will overthrow the old system.'

It is then that Stalin shows how well read he is, not only in the history of Russia, but the history of Europe. He quotes Cromwell, the Chartists, the French Revolution to demonstrate that history teaches that never has a single class made way voluntarily for another class, that force is necessary to seize the political power which alone can bring about a revolution.

There is little doubt that Stalin gets the better of the argument. Of course he was in the fortunate position of the practical man who has put his theories to the test and has proved that they will work. He does not disguise the absolute necessity for violence, and beneath the bantering tone one can hear the harsh note of a man who would stop at nothing to achieve his ends, the true revolutionary anarchist. Our Western world, so soon to be involved in a bloody struggle with communism and fascism could not have had a better spokesman than this self-appointed interrogator, Wells. He is just as much of a socialist as Stalin, but he is a theorist, not a man of action; he believes there is a better way for humanity to reach safety than by this bloody, violent upheaval which has placed the Communist party in the Kremlin. He tries hard to put over his idea that education is a revolution and can accomplish the same ends as violent political action. But what he is saying is what people were really hoping for against hope in that breathless interval between the financial crash of 1929 and the outbreak of war ten years later.

The 'Conversation' was reprinted verbatim in a Supplement to the *New Statesman* on Wells's return to England. The full text is a fascinating document, throwing a vitally interesting side-light on the thinking of the man who, with the Communist party as his machine, had seized Russia in the name of humanity, and was ruthlessly running it in the interests of his party. It shed an equally interesting light on the greatest publicist of the age. As was pointed out in the welter of comment that followed, working-class revolutionary leader and New Republican both disregarded humanity except as the ultimate beneficiary of the new order. They were rival engineers with competing sets of blueprints, arguing about which was the best method, and power, not pity, is the continually reverberant word.

Wells had had a journalistic coup, due entirely to the respect in which he was held by the rulers of the world. What Stalin said was not new, but it was implacably said, and it was reasonably argued. Bolshevism was still synonymous with bloody repression in England in 1934, but there was no excuse after this for the public mind to think of him as a peasant butcher revelling in power. His theory that revolution was necessary if the world order was to be changed, that the working class was the social bulwark of revolution, that an auxiliary force was required to steer it and the Communist party was that auxiliary, and that political power had to be seized firmly if the revolution was to maintain order, left no doubt, if there had been any, that any compromise or working arrangement with the capitalist-governed states of the West was out of the question. Wells's idea that the New Deal in the United States was producing a socialized economy, and that some effective partnership might be possible between the two great nations of the East and West, bringing about, in effect, the Open Conspiracy of his dreams, received short shrift from Stalin.

The publication of the 'Conversation' produced two amusing postscripts, interesting not only for what they say but as evidence of what intellectual richness has vanished from our world. In the space of a few weeks one could have a full report of Wells talking to Stalin; Bernard Shaw pulling Wells's leg and offering his own version of what Stalin had meant and what Wells was trying to say; and Maynard Keynes, with wit and intellectual cogency, pointing out that all three – Stalin, Wells and Shaw – were wrong and out of date: 'Time and the Joint Stock Company and the Civil Service have silently brought the salaried class into power. Not yet a Proletariat. But in Salariat surely.'

The sequel to this may be read in Kingsley Martin's autobiography. Shaw loved to tease his old friend, and Wells too often took offence. They replied to each other on this occasion, Shaw enjoying every moment of it and making wilder and more dogmatic assertions as time went on. H.G. sulked and called Shaw a cad. One sympathizes with Wells; he had suffered much from the stings of this gadfly all his life.

With Hitler's succession to the Chancellorship of the German Reich, a year before Wells's conversation with Stalin, the drift towards a second world conflict accelerated. Those who remember the mood of the thirties will recall that it was fatalistic. If the public mind had been impressed with anything, it was with the understanding that the next stage in the struggle would be largely obliterative, and that civilians this time would be slaughtered as fast as soldiers. But there was a curious reluctance to get into a 'flap' about it, and the development of events, which should have helped, did in fact nothing to assist the agitated and inspired founder of the Open Conspiracy to get his ideas accepted. *The Shape of Things to Come*, published in 1933, which vividly forecast the world disaster – dating its beginning to 1940 and offering even more vividly than *Anticipations*, to which it is the logical successor, a horoscope of the future – left the readers of the thirties largely undisturbed. It was a poor time for prophets, since all of them must be Cassandras.

The darkness of despair was beginning to subdue his hopes, but he refused to give in. In the two years following his visit to Moscow, there was more talking than writing. Leaving Moscow, he had gone to Esthonia and spent several weeks beside a quiet lake near Tallin, finishing his autobiography.

His companion there was Marie Budberg, the one whom, as Marie von Benckendorff, Gorki had rescued from prison, and whom Wells had first met when he visited St Petersburg in 1914 in the enlivening company of Maurice Baring. Her history, after he had last seen her in 1920, had been a troubled one. Gorki had helped her to leave Russia in 1921, to join her children in Esthonia. There she had married the young Baron Budberg. That marriage had not been a success, and when Gorki left Russia in 1922 she had joined him in Berlin. They had spent the next years together in Sorrento. Five years later, in 1927, she had come to England on a visit, had again met H.G., and Jane as well, just before Jane's death. Gorki meanwhile was making tentative approaches through Stalin for a return to Russia. While Marie Budberg was visiting London in 1927, he went back for a trial visit. He was given a great reception, and was accorded a triumphal journey down the Volga, the glories of which he had celebrated in his autobiographies. Gorki made several trial visits to Russia before finally settling there in 1933.

When this happened, Marie Budberg had come to England with her children, and it was the following year that I first met her. She was by then closely associated with H.G., and always stood by his side receiving the guests on P.E.N. occasions. She was to remain with him until his death, a very dear, faithful and loving friend whom he remembered with gratitude in his will.

The autobiography faithfully reflects the play of ideas that had passed through his brilliant mind in nearly seventy years, much more faithfully than it reflects the events of his life. Not all that had happened to him could be told because living people were involved, but where frankness did not intrude on any privacy except his own, he was remarkably frank, and the account of his childhood, the struggle to break free from the restrictions of the class into which he was born, and the long, hard climb to the high plateau of achievement and fame is done beautifully, as only a skilled writer could do it.

The autobiography covers closely the first thirty-five years of his life, the story of how he got there, what sort of man he had come to be in this experience, and gives an entertaining and vivid account of the adventures he had had along the way. There is admirable frankness in the dissection of his own character, and he provides brilliant and exact portraits of the personalities, from Henry James to Bernard Shaw, against whom he had stumbled in his advance.

Then we come, halfway through his story, to that division in his life when he became convinced that he had a mission, and that the mission was more important than the pattern of life he was following as a successful creative artist. *Boon* lies like a solid block of granite across the path of his life, and may be taken as an altitude-mark of his advance. But *Boon*, which he barely mentions in his autobiography, was only the culmination of a mood of revolt which had been gathering since he had first demonstrated, soon after he settled into Spade House, that with all his great gifts he was too impatient to settle willingly to the demanding task of weaving a story. *Anticipations*, begun as journalism, was a symptom of the desire to escape this dedication, his taking up with the Fabian Society another. *Kipps* took him three years to write, and *Tono-Bungay* nearly four. The time is surprising, considering how quickly and easily he wrote, but he was well aware that these were important novels, and to get them right, he kept putting out other books, holding these two major works back, determined not to let them go until they were as good as he could make them. *The New Machiavelli* was the last novel he wrote with any great care. He used as an excuse at first that the ideas were important, not the way they were presented; but that this was an excuse rather than a belief is plain from his correspondence with his publisher and with Arnold Bennett, who corrected Wells's proofs and was always admonishing him for stylistic and grammatical laxness.

The autobiography goes to pieces – as an autobiography, not as a book – just at the point at which Wells ceased to be a novelist writing non-fiction books occasionally to air his views and becomes a dedicated, purposive scribe writing anything and everything – novels, non-fiction books, journalism – to establish a viewpoint ... that is too pale a word ... a religious belief in the perfectibility human society might attain to if it ceased to make war, gave up its national consciousness, and joined in the brotherhood of man, making a World Republic of the hundred-odd warring little states. In the autobiography there are nine chapters altogether. The first eight take us up to the building of Spade House in 1900. The ninth and last, entitled 'The Idea of a Planned World', takes us from the writing of *Anticipations* to the account of his visits to Roosevelt and Stalin with the intention of embroiling them and their mighty nations which, however they might describe themselves, were socialistic states, going by different roads towards a common goal. Chronology is no longer followed closely in this last chapter. There is, of course, some tracing of events as they transpired and followed one upon another, but what started as the story of his life ends as an account of his struggle for a Utopia that had come completely to possess his mind. And the autobiography closes on a note of despair that was to sound deeper and deeper in his remaining work until it merged into the last cry of a dying man in *Mind at the End of Its Tether*:

The Truth remains that today nothing stands in the way to the attainment of universal freedom and abundance but mental tangles, egocentric preoccupations, obsessions, misconceived phrases, bad habits of thought, subconscious fears and dreads and plain dishonesty in people's minds – and especially in the minds of those in key positions. That universal freedom and abundance dangles within reach of us and is not achieved, and we who are Citizens of the Future wander about this present scene like passengers on a ship overdue, in plain sight of a port which only some disorder in the chart-room prevents us from entering. Though most of the people in the world in key positions are more or less accessible to me, I lack solvent power to bring them into unison. I can talk to them and even unsettle them, but I cannot compel their brains to see. [*Experiment in Autobiography*]

From 1937 to 1939 he went on writing novels, and that he had lost none of his skill in witty dialogue and sharp observation can be seen in books like *Brynhild, Apropos of Dolores* and *You Can't Be Too Careful*. Plainly these were not books written laboriously by a tired and disillusioned man. They were a relaxation from the intellectual force he was pouring into his work intended to persuade: *World Brain*, which argued the case for an Encyclopedia of World Knowledge, and *The Fate of Homo Sapiens*, which stands as a last warning to mankind:

Adapt or perish, that is and always has been the implacable law of life for all its children. Either the human imagination and the will to live rises to the plain necessity of our case, and a renascent *Homo sapiens* struggles on to a new, a harder and happier world dominion, or he blunders down the slopes of failure through a series of unhappy phases, in the wake of all the monster reptiles and beasts that have flourished and lorded it on the earth before him, to his ultimate extinction. Either life is just beginning for him, or it is drawing rapidly to its close.

When the war came in 1939, it must have seemed the end of all his hopes. He was seventy-three, and was living at 13 Hanover Terrace in a house, adorned with statues of the seven Muses, which faced Regent's Park. From this he refused to move, even when in September 1940 the Germans began their nightly raids on London and the proximity of the house to Broadcasting House, a nightly target, put it very much in the danger zone. His physical strength was ebbing, but the zest and fire of his spirit were as lively as ever, he still wrote and published steadily. *All Aboard for Ararat*, which came out in 1940, is one of the liveliest of his books, a dialogue between Mr Noah Lammock and the Lord God, who calls unexpectedly, and who expresses some sympathy for Mr Lammock in the failure of his mission in life, which turns out to be none other than Wells's. God admits also to having his troublesome adversary, the devil, who casts a shadow over all his good work, the shadow which 'goes about getting hold of physicists and psychologists and mathematicians ... They come along now declaring that space is *finite*. Well, I ask you!'

'Yes,' said the Almighty, not without a touch of malice. 'And man, as he grows clearer and firmer, discovers that he too casts a shadow.'

'There is something in that', said Noah.

'There is everything in that. It is quite possible that Satan and I have played our part in the human drama. I may have become a mere phantom of my former self. That means only that the struggle between benevolence and corrosive resistance, between the light and the shadow it casts, embodies itself anew – in Adam, in man himself, in you and your kind. The old story repeats itself ...'

They decide together to build a new Ark, God begging this time to come along, offering as his pleasurable task to play the harmonium which is to accompany Sunday services on board.

The allegory is beautifully maintained throughout. Particularly marked are the warm affability and humour of the exchanges between God and Noah, showing that in his last years H.G. had lost little of his built-in bounce.

And so they set sail to Ararat, to Shinar again, and so to mankind reunited in one brotherhood, growing in strength and power for ever.

'While the earth remaineth, seed-time and harvest, and cold and heat, and summer and winter, and day and night shall not cease.'

But Noah is determined that God shall be only a passenger: *he* is the captain.

'God has been my inspiration, to a large extent I can still express myself in terms of Him, but the fundamental reality is that He is ceasing to exist in the face of the clearer thinking that dissolves Him. By Him and with Him I shall sail the Ark, but presently He will be at my side no longer, and I, the New Adam, will have to sail it alone.'

Last Days

LITTLE remains that is not sad to tell, and the more quickly told the better. He kept on writing as the bombs fell about his house, and as increasing bodily weakness sapped his strength. His eldest son, Professor G. P. Wells, in a spirited defence of the mood of his father's last books,* lists H.G.'s output of published work in the last five years of his life as evidence that his mental vigour was undiminished. In refutation of the commonly accepted idea that *Mind at the End of Its Tether* represents a final conviction of the hopelessness of the human predicament, and thereby a refutation of all that his life's work had been aimed at, Professor Wells gives evidence to show that this sombre last piece was written at the same time as one of the happiest of H.G.'s books, the autobiographical fragment *The Happy Turning*.

One longs for tidy ends. The leap-up of the flame of his genius with *The Time Machine* had been dramatic; if his life had ended with *All Aboard for Ararat*, how conveniently the circle would have been drawn. *Crux Ansata: An Indictment of the Roman Catholic Church* was a last kick of a rebel against the one persistent authority that had outstayed so many national states, that possessed still so many minds that would not give themselves utterly to his ideal. It was the one central dogma of his mind that the Catholics were wrong. Other religions too, in various degrees. But the Catholics were hatefully, contemptibly wrong, and *Crux Ansata* was a last shot at an old enemy. One is reminded of a story remembered by Sir Richard Gregory.

'Here I am', he said to Rags, who came to see him in the

---

* *The Last Books of H. G. Wells*, edited with an introduction and appendix by G. P. Wells, H. G. Wells Society, London, 1968.

last year of his life when he was lying in bed in this large house, 'with one foot in the grave, and the other kicking out at everything.'

He was desperately ill, but he continued to drag himself to his desk. There was a darkness of mood in these last years that was occasionally lit by a little glow of light as the shadows receded for a moment. *The Happy Turning*, which appeared in 1945, is the work of such a glow. But the power soon failed, and the darkness supervened.

Mind at the End of Its Tether, written as nuclear physics was bringing the war to an end, speaks out of this darkness. It is not Wells as we have known him, but a dying man at the end of a long road who knows that it is time for him to go and he must leave his work unfinished. And he is forced to do so at a time when the power which has brought life into being seems to have turned against it. He plays with a number of terms to find out the one apposite to describe the force that has brought the will to live into existence and now seems intent on destroying it. He settles on the Antagonist as the one best suited to express this power which has endured life so long by our reckoning and has now turned to wipe it out.

Our doomed formicry is helpless as the implacable Antagonist kicks or tramples our world to pieces. Endure it or evade it, the end will be the same, but the evasion systems involve unhelpfulness at the least and in most cases blind obedience to egotistical leaders, fanatical persecutions, panics, hysterical violence and cruelty.

After all, the present writer has no compelling argument to convince the reader that he should not be cruel or mean and cowardly. Such things are also in his own make-up in a large measure, but none the less he hates and fights against them with all his strength. He would rather our species ended its story in dignity, kindliness and generosity, and not like drunken cowards in a daze or poisoned rats in a sack. But this is a matter of personal predilection for everyone to decide for himself.

He lived to see the atomic bomb dropped over Hiroshima, and a new world indeed born in its frightful glare. Asked

to comment on it, he said: 'This can wipe out everything –
good and bad – in this world. It is up to the people to decide
which.'

Nearly a quarter of a century later we still perilously survive. But there have been several narrow squeaks, and,
gloomy though his last message was, it serves to remind us
that life is not secure while human passions dominate the
judgements that control our lives.

Wells died alone, suddenly, quietly, at 4.15 on the afternoon of 13 August 1946. He had been ill for two years, and
knew the diagnosis. That afternoon he had been moving
round his room. Then he went to bed and sent his nurse
away, as he often did. A few minutes later he was dead –
dying, not as he had forecast he would in *Mind at the End
of Its Tether* from the fatty degeneration of the heart that
had affected many of his family, but from cancer of the
liver.

All the world recorded his passing. Even those who were
too young to have read his books were conscious of his name
and fame. But for those who met at the Royal Institution on
30 October 1946 to honour his memory, nearly all of whom
had known him personally and had had their lives to some
degree changed by him, a great character had gone from
the scene, one who had done so much to wake us up and
prepare us for the harsh rigours our century had in store for
us. Of the many tributes paid to his memory on that occasion, Professor G. D. H. Cole's provides the strongest reminder of what Wells tried to do:

For the prophets – of whom H.G. was certainly one – to be
honoured and to be followed are by no means the same thing.
H.G. was not without honour in his own country, which was
the world; nor could he complain of not being loved. His complaint was that he asked so little of mankind: he only wanted
men to behave in their own interest with tolerable common-
sense; and even the reputedly wisest of them would do anything rather than that one simple thing. They would fight, and
die; they would devote endless ingenuity to getting in one

another's way, or to doing one another down. What they would not do was to understand that technical mastery had to go hand in hand with social control, if every fresh victory of science were not to be turned into a fresh defeat for the common man. He could not believe that men, if they but understood, could go on behaving so foolishly; and his life as a writer was one long effort to help them to understand. If, so far, he seems to have failed, that is not because he has taught us little, but because the forces he bade us control have moved unprecedentedly fast. If, even yet, we succeed in catching up with them, no one will deserve more thanks for it than H.G.

Gone. An intense cyclone of activity swirling before our eyes one minute, gone the next. What happened? How is it that a man widely esteemed in the first quarter of this century as the great far-seeing prophet (along with Shaw) of the New Age should be disregarded today? Our immediate ancestors were not so simple as to be taken in by a charlatan. Test him for prophetic accuracy at any point, and he is nearly always right. Read him as a social novelist, and he consistently entertains. His nightmarish fantasies have only slight traces of the Victorian world about them, clinging like wisps of smoke about a fast-circling object. The 'Time Machine' is a sort of bicycle because in 1895 the bicycle had revolutionized life for everybody below the rank of carriage-folk. But the style is modern, direct, swift. It grew lax only when, in his middle period, he started to dream. But when he wanted to be facty, it could still be close-knit, muscular, direct, as *The Outline of History* and *The Shape of Things to Come* show.

He was writing for fifty years, a much longer period of production than most authors know. It would be understandable if he had not been able to keep up with the changing world in the last ten or fifteen years of his life. He not only kept up, he was still in advance of general thought. Why, then, was less attention being paid to him? Why did I, when I first met him, a specimen drop from the ocean of humanity myself, regard him as a great monument of the past, not as someone who could reliably tell me what the future was going to be, or whose new novel it would be fatal to miss?

Our world of the thirties was different. We were much more self-reliant than the Victorians, less hopeful and more fatalistic than the Edwardians. We were of the age of Keynes, as our parents had been of the age of Wells and Shaw. We were neither optimists nor pessimists, but realists. Our parents had been wonderfully caught by the image of being heirs of the scientific revolution, with the last repressions of the silver classical age of Europe ready to be stripped away, and a clean new world waiting to be built with shining new tools. But heaven on earth was not just around the corner. The wave of hopefulness which mounted out of the discoveries of the mechanical revolution had broken in the War and in the Depression that followed it. The future which Wells had painted in such glowing colours for his contemporaries was our present. What had gone out of us was any sense of that eager anticipation of what was to come. If we hoped for anything, it was for a lucky escape out of a threatening doom. No planning could bring that about. What was interesting about Wells was the phenomenon he himself represented. Up from the Victorian world of the lower classes, ignorant, prejudiced, stagnant, dull, had come this bubble which had burst on the surface, and prismatic lights flashed where it had been. A breeze burst it, that wind of scientific knowledge, bringing with it freedom from old restrictions and fears which cleaned away the surface scum and made the water brighter and more restless for a while.

From Atlas House, the formidably named but jerry-built shop-dwelling in the suburbs of industrialized London, this child of the late-nineteenth century had come bursting with brains and energy and feeling, to report in books like *Kipps* and *Mr Polly* the inhumanity of one class to another. But this offence was already being mended, not because he had awoken consciences, but because people like Kipps and Mr Polly were becoming mutinous and thrusting. The old order was passing, and the common man was coming into his own. Wells's greatest books really belong to the Victorian age and its twilight in the first ten years of this century. The nightmare scientific fantasies and the compassionate social comedies demanded no moral attitude from the author, only good reporting.

It was when he turned to contemporary problems that a fundamental defect in his nature became apparent. He was all brains and very little heart. He could see what was wrong with humanity and be passionate about large-scale designs to improve its lot. But man does not need to know only the fate of homo sapiens; he wants to know about himself, and artists are there to interpret the forces that shape his life. To be fair to Wells, he himself rejected the label of artist. He claimed to be only a journalist, and he resolutely resisted all attempts to include him amongst the men of letters. But *Boon* shows that this was only bravado. What he was constantly saying was that art should not be narrowly confined to traditional forms. What he urged in his lecture on the novel was that it was the novelist's business to journalize life, and that any subject, and any way of treating the subject was justified as long as it echoed the authentic sound of life. But to reproduce the echo truly, to reflect without distortion the myriad forces that combine to make life what it is, there must be a very delicate instrument with sensitive reactions to what it is recording. One is reminded of young Bert Wells coming to the Royal College of Science, crammed with knowledge mugged up from the textbooks, but incapable of doing anything in the laboratory until he was shown. Never to have seen a test-tube or looked down a microscope, yet starting out with the vision of becoming a pure scientist. Not to have known life, only to have revolted against the depressing features of a very narrow segment of it, put him in no position to revolutionize its whole structure. Experience of the pain of living was what he lacked. Poverty, hunger, the want of a broad education, the agonizing sense of social inferiority: these are hardships to the intelligent, sensitive mind and the stunted, deprived body of a boy of exceptional vitality and intelligence. But the scars such hardships leave can be envy, spite and an eagerness to dominate any situation – to avoid being dominated. Such experiences do not enrich one's knowledge of humanity; they sharpen resentment but do not enlarge understanding and sympathy.

Remembering his beginnings, one can understand why he should not care much about individual man, whom he had to thank only for bullying him and for trying to keep him in chains. But Wells had great charm and a warm personality. Once he had burst free of the hateful world of shops and was experiencing the happiness of life at the Royal College, one would have expected him to submerge himself gratefully in the great sea of humanity in London and become involved in its colourful life. He did not. He attended only one political meeting; his time was spent within the narrow circle of his student friends, discussing the future with great energy, but disregarding the painful present. Man's failure to be happy was due to ignorance and inertia. Given the right conditions, all would be well, and he set himself strenuously to work out those conditions.

For a little while these visions made a great appeal. The world was passing through a phase when any goal seemed within reach of mankind. But myths dissolve in the face of harsh experience, and the world woke up to reality, leaving the mythmaker frustrated and angry, forced to turn to fresh sources for inspiration. The whole history of man as he saw it had been a series of false starts. Perhaps it was possible for God and man to make a fresh beginning that would not end again in frustration and catastrophe. But the religious myth had failed him, as the scientific and sexual ones had done, and he was left unhappy at the end.

What one sees in his life is the almost complete absence of any moral values. I do not mean only his own sexual behaviour. I mean that he seems to have had no idea of the moral resources of humanity, that essence which makes men endure the accidents and threats of existence and still keep upright. It was a limitation in an artist. He did not write about these things because he attached no value to them, and that was because he did not possess them himself. Yet no great endurable artist but has them, and looks for them in the characters he creates. It was what Henry James was tactfully suggesting in his affectionate criticisms of Wells's novels. In the best of them we have the perfect reporter; in the others we have novels about ideas. Yet no writer since Dickens had so much influence and stirred so many readers as Wells did. In a revolutionary phase, ideas are at a premium. But in the permanent world of art, individual man is the study – not what he shall do with his life, but what makes him a man, what makes him both the creature and a worthy adversary of his God.

The service of Public Homage to his memory at the Royal Institution on 31 October 1946 was held in the same room where forty-five years earlier the young and eager Wells had leant over the lectern, reading to the assembled notabilities of the scientific world his paper on *The Discovery of the Future.* So great on this occasion was the press of famous men and women who came to pay their respects that the meeting overflowed into an adjoining room to which the speeches were relayed. Speeches were made by Professor G. D. H. Cole, J. B. Priestley and David Low, and messages from Sir Richard Gregory and Desmond MacCarthy were read. Lord Beveridge was in the chair. Tributes were paid by the Prime Minister, Clement Attlee, and the former Prime Minister, Winston Churchill. To Clement Attlee, Wells had been 'a great awakener of men'. Churchill, with deeper penetration, observed: 'Few first-class men of letters have more consistently crabbed and girded at the national society and the social system in which they have had their being. Fewer still have owed so much to its ample tolerations and its magnificent complications.'

At the end we are left with a puzzle. The times so often make the man, not the men the times. Over a long and productive life Wells exerted through his work a tremendous influence. It could not have been because he had no stiff competition. Not only Conrad, Galsworthy, Shaw, but Henry James, Barrie and Stevenson. He competed with or triumphed over or at least came equal with the late Victorians, led easily among the Edwardians, held his own while the post-war generation was changing the direction and pace of literature, and even to within a few years of his death was continually surprising and stimulating. If Wells is nearly forgotten now, and we remember Galsworthy and Conrad and Shaw, is it that our times prefer the romantic prints of a forgotten time to the uncomfortable realization of our present?

Wells's message, plugged home insistently in nearly every book from *Anticipations* on, was that scientific and industrial progress had made a world state inevitable, and that attempts to postpone the sweeping away of outdated national boundaries and ancient privileges could only be made at the expense of the common man. The world wars of the twentieth century were witness of this. Social planning on a planetary scale had become essential. The alternatives were plain: unite or perish.

Through unimaginable risks we have survived so far the crisis that he foresaw. Its warnings no longer ring in our ears. It is possible that what we are enjoying is another armistice and the risk may well grow large and threatening again. Then this shrill voice, pouring out brilliant stimulating ideas and warnings, may be remembered. One day when there is planetary peace, men may turn again to the voluminous work of a writer who, prodding at his generation and stirring them from the blind lethargy, lifted them imaginatively over the bridge they had to cross from the days before Darwin to the days after Hiroshima.

One is reminded in this last glimpse of this little figure of an exchange of notes between H.G. and G. K. Chesterton in 1933, arising out of what I do not know. H.G. wrote to Chesterton:

If after all my Atheology turns out wrong and your Theology right, I feel I shall always be able to pass into Heaven (if I want to) as a friend of G.K.C.'s. Bless you.

Temporarily laid out in bed, unable to acknowledge at length but able to appreciate H.G.'s letter, Chesterton replied:

As to the fine point of theology you mention. If I turn out to be right, you will triumph, not by being a friend of mine but a friend of Man, for having done a thousand things for men like me in every way, from imagination to criticism. The thought of the vast variety of that work, and how it ranges from towering visions to tiny pricks of humour, overwhelmed me suddenly ...

For that service to mankind and for his bubbling humour, his outpouring of vitality, his stimulation of our insensate blindness, he surely deserves our thanks and our remembrance.

Bibliography

Bergonzi, Bernard: *The Early H. G. Wells* (1961)
Brown, Ivor: *H. G. Wells* (1923)
          Shaw in His Time (1965)
Chesterton, G. K.: *Heretics* (1905)
Cole, Margaret: *Makers of the Labour Movement* (1948)
Edel, Leon, and Gordon N. Ray, eds.: *Henry James and H. G. Wells* (1958)
Ellmann, Richard, ed.: *Edwardians and Late Victorians* (1960)
Flower, Newman, ed.: *The Journals of Arnold Bennett* (1932–3)
Fremantle, Anne: *This Little Band of Prophets* (1960)
Kagarlitski, J.: *The Life and Thought of H. G. Wells* (1966)
Levin, Dan: *Stormy Petrel: The Life and Work of Maxim Gorky* (1965)
Martin, Kingsley: *Father Figures* (1966)
Morgan, Charles: *The House of Macmillan* (1943)
Pease, E. R.: *History of the Fabian Society* (1916)
Raknem, Ingvald: *H. G. Wells and His Critics* (1964)
Routh, H. V.: *English Literature and Ideas in the Twentieth Century* (1948)
Swinnerton, Frank: *The Georgian Scene* (1934)
          Swinnerton: An Autobiography (1948)
Ward, Maisie: *G. K. Chesterton* (1944)
Webb, Beatrice: *Our Partnership* (1948)
Wells, G. P., ed.: *The Last Books of H. G. Wells* (1968)
West, Anthony: *Principles and Persuasions* (1957)
West, Geoffrey: *H. G. Wells: Sketch for a Portrait* (1930)

A complete bibliography of H. G. Wells's work is published by The H. G. Wells Society, 21 Fawe Park Road, London S.W.15, England. This includes, as well as Wells's books, his many pamphlets, lectures and film-scripts. The extensive character of the bibliography in Ingvald Raknem's *H. G. Wells and His Critics* has already been mentioned. Raknem includes a list with dates of all the reviews of Well's books, many of which amount to lengthy essays on his work.

With all that readily available, the casual reader may find it more helpful to be reminded of the kind of books Wells was writing at different stages in his long career. The following arbitrary selection has been made with that object in view.

THE SCIENTIFIC ROMANCER AND SHORT STORY WRITER 1895–1901

NOVELS

The Time Machine 1895
The Wonderful Visit 1895
The Island of Dr Moreau 1896
The Wheels of Chance 1896
The Invisible Man 1897
The War of the Worlds 1898
When the Sleeper Wakes 1899
The First Men in the Moon 1901

STORIES AND SKETCHES

Select Conversations with an Uncle 1895
The Stolen Bacillus and Other Incidents 1895
The Plattner Story and Others 1897
Certain Personal Matters 1897

THE SERIOUS NOVELIST, PROPHET AND PLANNER 1901–10

THE NOVELIST

Love and Mr Lewisham 1900
The Sea Lady 1902
The Food of the Gods 1904
Kipps 1905
In the Days of the Comet 1906
The War in the Air 1908
Tono-Bungay 1909
Ann Veronica 1909
The History of Mr Polly 1910

THE PROPHET AND PLANNER

Anticipations 1901
The Discovery of the Future 1902
Mankind in the Making 1903
A Modern Utopia 1905
First and Last Things 1908

THE 'DIVIDE' – FOUR YEARS OF STRESS
1911–15

The New Machiavelli 1911
Marriage 1912
The Passionate Friends 1913
The World Set Free 1914
The Wife of Sir Isaac Harman
  1914

Bealby 1915
Boon 1915
The Research Magnificent
  1915

THE 'THEOLOGICAL' PHASE
1915–19

Mr Britling Sees it Through
  1916

God the Invisible King 1917
The Undying Fire 1919

THE RECONSTRUCTOR
1918–30

NOVELS
Joan and Peter 1918
Men Like Gods 1923
The Dream 1924
Christina Alberta's Father
  1925
The World of William Clissold
  1926
Meanwhile 1927
*Mr Blettsworthy on Rampole
  Island* 1928
The Autocracy of Mr Parham
  1930

EXPOSITORY AND
DIDACTIC
The Outline of History 1920
Russia in the Shadows 1920
The Salvaging of Civilization
  1921
A Year of Prophesying 1924
Democracy Under Revision
  1927
The Open Conspiracy 1928
The Way to World Peace
  1930

WORLD FIGURE
1930–40

The Bulpington of Blup 1933
The Shape of Things to Come
  1933
Brynhild 1937
Apropos of Dolores 1938
Babes in the Darkling Wood
  1940
All Aboard for Ararat 1940

The Science of Life 1931
*The Work, Wealth and Happi-
  ness of Mankind* 1932
The Stalin–Wells Talk 1934
Experiment in Autobiography
  1934
The Anatomy of Frustration
  1936
World Brain 1938
The Fate of Homo Sapiens
  1939
The New World Order 1940
The Rights of Man 1940

LAST YEARS
1941–5

The Happy Turning 1945
You Can't Be Too Careful
  1941

Guide to the New World 1941
*The Outlook for Homo
  Sapiens* 1942
Mind at the End of Its Tether
  1945

Index

MORE ABOUT PENGUINS
AND PELICANS

Penguinews, which appears every month, contains details of all the new books issued by Penguins as they are published. From time to time it is supplemented by *Penguins in Print*, which is a complete list of all available books published by Penguins. (There are well over three thousand of these.)

A specimen copy of *Penguinews* will be sent to you free on request, and you can become a subscriber for the price of the postage. For a year's issues (including the complete lists) please send 30p if you live in the United Kingdom, or 60p if you live elsewhere. Just write to Dept EP, Penguin Books Ltd, Harmondsworth, Middlesex, enclosing a cheque or postal order, and your name will be added to the mailing list.

Note: *Penguinews* and *Penguins in Print* are not available in the U.S.A. or Canada

H. G. WELLS IN PENGUINS
AND PELICANS

THE ISLAND OF DOCTOR MOREAU (1896)

Doctor Moreau carved grotesque beast-men from living animal tissue; but his creations pass out of his control.

THE WAR OF THE WORLDS (1897)

In one of the first and greatest works of Science Fiction, written before Man had learned to fly, H. G. Wells conceived the horrifying idea of a Martian attack on England.

THE WAR IN THE AIR (1908)

Bert Smallways gets involved, quite accidentally, in Prince Karl Albert's massive airship raid on New York ... first step in a war which soon flares into world-wide catastrophe.

ANN VERONICA (1909)

Ann Veronica is beautiful, twenty-two, a successful biology student ... and an Edwardian rebel with a cause.

THE NEW MACHIAVELLI (1911)

H. G. Wells's masterly novel is still an illuminating exploration of the 'corridors of power' ... a study of a man's progress towards the leadership of the nation ... and his love for a woman who was not his wife.

also available

SELECTED SHORT STORIES

Twenty-one of Wells's best stories, including *The Time Machine, The Country of the Blind*, and *Under the Knife*.

ABOVE BOOKS NOT FOR SALE IN THE U.S.A.

A SHORT HISTORY OF THE WORLD (*A Pelican Book*)

Wells's brilliant general view of history and the great adventure of mankind, now revised and brought completely up to date by his son, Professor G. P. Wells, and Raymond Postgate.